BLUESPRINT

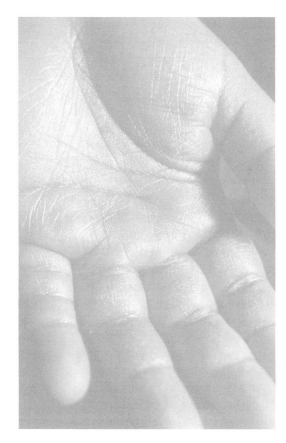

Black
British
Columbian
Literature
and
Orature

Bluesprint

edited by Wayde Compton

Arsenal Pulp Press
Vancouver

ARSENAL PULP PRESS
103-1014 HOMER STREET
VANCOUVER, B.C.
CANADA V6B 2W9
arsenalpulp.com

The publisher gratefully acknowledges the support of the Canada Council for the Arts and the British Columbia Arts Council for its publishing program, and the Government of Canada through the Book Publishing Industry Development Program for its publishing activities.

Book and cover design by Solo
Front cover photograph by Rosalee Hiebert
Back cover photograph by Melinda Mollineaux
Printed and bound in Canada

Efforts have been made to locate copyright holders of source material where available. The publisher and editor welcome hearing from any copyright holders of any material who have not been contacted.

NATIONAL LIBRARY OF CANADA CATALOGUING IN PUBLICATION DATA:
Main entry under title:
    Bluesprint

ISBN 1-55152-118-0

    1. Canadian literature (English) – Black-Canadian authors.*
    2. Black Canadians – Literary collections.*
    3. Canadian literature (English) – British Columbia.*
    4. Canadian literature – 20th century.* I. Compton, Wayde, 1972-
        PS8235.B53B58 2002   C810.8'08960711   C2001-911701-9
        PR9194.5.B55B58 2002

Acknowledgments

Dedicated to the writers – past, present and future.

A great many people were helpful at both the formative stages of this anthology and throughout the research and editing processes. I would like to thank the following for their interest and encouragement, and in many cases for their generous help in locating and accessing authors and texts:

Ryan Knighton, Brad Cran, Brian Lam, Blaine Kyllo, Robert Ballantyne, Linda Field, Adam Rudder, Michael Turner, Karina Vernon, Anne Stone, Renee Rodin, Nadine King Chambers, Michelle La Flamme, Beverly Yhap, Chris Turnbull, George Bowering, George Stanley, Kathie Knighton, Truman Green, Phyllis Greenwood, Michelle Lee Williams, Janisse Browning, Reg Johanson, Carole Itter, Sol Guy, David Best, Ellen Best, Roger Farr, Steven Collis, Roy Miki, Daphne Marlatt, Craig McLuckie, Jane Rule, Shelagh Day, david-george morgan, Nadine Sims, and the editors of all the anthologies, periodicals, and special issues who published the writers and orators herein. Thanks to my mother and father who remembered many of the people, places, and circumstances of the Hogan's Alley period, and did a lot of phoning around and useful reminiscing. Thanks also to David Stouck for editorial advice throughout the course of this project.

There are four scholars whose work preceded me in this area, making such an anthology possible. Very special thanks are due to:

James W. Pilton, who wrote the first serious study of black B.C. history, *Negro Settlement in British Columbia, 1858-1871* (UBC MA thesis, 1951); Crawford Kilian, for *Go Do Some Great Thing: The Black Pioneers of British Columbia* (Douglas and McIntyre, 1978); Peter Hudson, for his diverse work as editor, writer, and critic of black B.C. arts; and George Elliott Clarke, whose "Africana Canadiana: A Primary Bibliography of Literature by African-Canadian Authors, 1785-1996/97, in English, French and Translation" (*Canadian Ethnic Studies* 28.3 [1996]) was an invaluable research tool.

Contents

Foreword

Wayde Compton

The original idea for this anthology came about during a conversation with my friends, the Vancouver poets Brad Cran and Ryan Knighton, at Havana on Commercial Drive in the summer of 1999. Ryan had recently become the editor of *The Capilano Review* and suggested I guest edit an issue. I considered taking him up on his offer by producing a special issue focusing on black writers from British Columbia. However, I knew that Peter Hudson had edited an issue of *West Coast Line* on African-Canadian writing in 1997, and I was worried that another similar project so close on its heels was too soon. For my book *49th Parallel Psalm* I had researched the black pioneer history of B.C., and I mulled over the idea of including some of the pioneers' writing in this special issue – to put the newer writers in context – but the mandate of *The Capilano Review* is to publish new material. Still, the idea of new black B.C. writing alongside the writing of our pioneer ancestors seemed a good one. Brad casually suggested, "Do it as an anthology."

I began the research almost immediately, still not quite certain if there was enough material to produce such a book. I had known about the writing of the pioneers, but had thus far only looked at it as historical material rather than for its literary value. I knew of several younger, contemporary black writers, most of whom had been publishing in literary journals and anthologies during the 1990s, and a few of them publishing first books. What I was initially uncertain of, however, was the vast period in-between – the first half of the twentieth century, and the second half up to the nineties. The prospect of blindly researching this gap, one in which there had been almost no historical or literary study, was daunting, but also exciting. I scoured bibliographies, anthologies, videos and journals, archives, libraries, and the Internet; I asked the writers I knew to refer me to other writers; I asked those writers in turn to refer me to others; I scanned biographical notes of journals and anthologies looking for references to B.C. residence. In order to concentrate fully on this work, I proposed the editing of the anthology as my MA thesis at Simon Fraser University – an unconventional type of thesis, but one that David Stouck supportively considered just the sort of work English departments should encourage when he agreed to be my supervisor.

During the editorial process I tried to keep my intervention to a minimum, preferring to maintain the integrity of the original texts – perceived errors and all – but in a few of the earlier texts some license was necessary. In Sir James Douglas's journal entries and Marie Stark Wallace's transcription, for example, I have regularized punctuation and spelling, except in the case of place names which had not been conventionalized at the time of the writing. With Douglas's journal and with Isaac Dickson's letters, I created extensive footnotes because the nature of these texts requires some local context for purposes of clarity and readability.

As a person of mixed black and white ancestry who grew up in B.C., I, like many others, grew up knowing more about black culture from elsewhere than I did about the black cultural legacy of my own province. The powerful and widely disseminated black cultural products of the United States, the Caribbean, and Africa are imports that every Canadian is at least passingly familiar with, and black Canadians like myself often first draw inspiration from these cultures, which are also sometimes the source cultures of our immigrant families. In high school, I knew about Public Enemy and Bob Marley long before I'd heard a single word about Sylvia Stark or Mifflin Gibbs. But eventually the realization that my experience and the experiences of my friends and family were not exactly represented by the images imported from afar began to take hold. I began to pay close attention to African-Canadian history and literature, first discovering writers such as George Elliott Clarke from Nova Scotia and Dionne Brand from Ontario. Spiraling still closer to the local, I desired to know about how other writers like myself had responded to this place specifically – these cities, mountains, islands, and streets.

I hope the gathering of these writers, and the tracing of a sort of phantom lineage – a succession of black B.C. writers who did not necessarily know they had ancestors or would have descendants, but which I regard as a lineage nonetheless – will create a long overdue conference of sorts; that the pioneer writers, the orators of Hogan's Alley, and the writers of the seventies and later will all sit side-by-side within these pages, meeting and speaking to each other at last. Another reason for this project is to "rescue," so to speak, some of the texts herein, meaning, at the very least, to bring them into the public consciousness, and into the Canadian and African-Canadian literary canons. Much of the work of the past that appears in this anthology is unknown to contemporary black writers, and having access to this writing which has heretofore been scattered across libraries and archives has the potential of edifying and raising the self-awareness of black B.C. writers and critics. For those who continue to write, and those who are yet to come, I hope this book and the sounding line it extends backwards into history will provide a foundation of sorts, one for which I have often felt an aching need; that those who write afterward will see that the subjects and subjectivities which appear in their writing are not isolated features, but rather parts of an experience that is over 150 years in the making.

Cadboro Bay, Victoria, where, from the time of their 1858 arrival from California,
Canada's West Coast black settlers held Emancipation Day picnics every
August 1st in remembrance of the West Indian abolition of slavery.
PHOTO BY MELINDA MOLLINEAUX.

Introduction

Wayde Compton

1

The Barbadian poet and theorist Kamau Brathwaite coined the term *tidalectics* to describe an Africanist model for thinking about history. In contrast to Hegel's *dialectics*, which Brathwaite calls "another gun: a missile" (Torres-Saillant 704) – that is, expansionism – *tidalectics* describes a way of seeing history as a palimpsest, where generations overlap generations, and eras wash over eras like a tide on a stretch of beach. There is change, but the changes arise out of slight misduplications of the pattern rather than from essential antagonisms. Repetition, whether in the form of ancestor worship or the poem-histories of the *griot*, informs black ontologies more than does the Europeanist drive for perpetual innovation, with its concomitant disavowals of the past. In a European framework, the past is something to be gotten over, something to be improved upon; in tidalectics, we do not *improve upon* the past, but are ourselves *versions* of the past. Brathwaite's term is useful for describing British Columbia's fluctuating black population.

In his history *Go Do Some Great Thing: The Black Pioneers of British Columbia* (1978), Crawford Kilian narrates the mass migration that brought the first black population to the colonies that would eventually become B.C. Six hundred blacks moved here en masse from San Francisco during the spring and summer of 1858. The move was spurred by gold findings in the interior, but it was also an exodus from racial persecution in California. In the 1850s, the California legislature had passed a series of increasingly repressive racial laws, culminating in the proposal of a bill that would ban outright any further immigration of blacks to California. Feeling that they had no future in the state of California, roughly half the black population of San Francisco decided together to find a new place to emigrate to outside the United States. While they were considering Mexico and Panama as possible destinations, the gold rush in B.C. was beginning. An invitation penned by the governor of the British colonies, James Douglas, clinched their decision to move to the colonies.

Born in British Guyana, Governor Douglas was the son of a Scottish planter and a "free coloured woman," but his appearance was such that he could "pass" for white. Douglas's motivation for inviting the blacks to settle in B.C. may have been double: he needed an industrious, loyal population to act as a buffer between the British colonial regime and the influx of Americans that the gold rush would bring, and, perhaps, in some unvoiced way, he was also sympathetic to the blacks' plight in California. The promises he made to lure them to the colony included citizenship and suffrage, which were not to be granted as easily as he had originally led them to believe.

Following the original 600 blacks who made the journey in 1858, enough arrived over the next few years to increase the black population of the colonies to an estimated height of 1,000 (Kilian 147). In a population of roughly 10,000 settlers, blacks were a large and visible presence. The black pioneers had come to Canada not only for economic relief, but to fulfill their dreams of full citizenship and equality under British law, which was – on paper, at least – non-discriminatory.

The black pioneers were organized, eloquent, and loyal to their adopted homeland. As much as they were allowed, they participated in commercial and political life, and even established the colony's first militia, formed to counter the threat of American annexation. Both their writing and their civic actions make it clear that the pioneers, centred mainly in Victoria, were willing to lend all their support to any government that would grant them nothing less than basic human rights. However, while racism against blacks was not "on the books" in B.C., it was often enough in the hearts of their white neighbours, including those who held political power. There are numerous accounts in early B.C. of segregation in churches, theatres, and public houses, as well as political corruption that accounted for such things as the spurious cancellation of black ballots in an election.

Victoria Pioneer Rifle Corps. BCA C-06124.

After the victory of the North in the American Civil War – or, more correctly, after the defeat of the South, and of slavery – more than half the blacks in B.C. returned to the United States. Suffrage had not been granted as easily as was promised them, and their efforts to prove themselves loyal had been routinely rebuffed; these facts, together with the hope that the abolition of slavery in the U.S. would signal an age of greater racial equality, made repatriation attractive. The desire to reunite with extended families, and the solace of life in larger and more established black communities, also motivated their return. So, the first black population of B.C. had dwindled to fewer than 500 people according to the 1871 census, just six years after the end of the American Civil War (Kilian 147).

In the late nineteenth century and on into the twentieth, blacks continued to come to B.C. from the United States, Britain, the Caribbean, Africa, and other parts of Canada. The blacks who came here in the early- to mid-twentieth century seem to have arrived as individuals from their respective homelands rather than as part of larger exoduses, but have at least formed a community here at one historical point. For a time, the East Vancouver neighbourhood of Strathcona – east of Main Street, and between Hastings Street and Terminal Avenue – contained "Hogan's Alley," an inner city black neighbourhood which lasted from the 1910s until the 1960s. The origins of the community might be explained by the location of the train station at Main and Terminal, many of the black arrivants to Vancouver being porters who worked the railways across Canada; when stopping over in Vancouver, they found themselves in Strathcona, and a number of them made it their home. Civic rezoning together with a gradual defrosting of Vancouver's unofficial but notoriously *de facto* segregation resulted in many blacks who had lived in Strathcona moving to various neighbourhoods of the Lower Mainland by the mid-1960s. Since the decline of the community in Strathcona, Vancouver has never had another centralized black community – a wholly unusual thing for a North American city of its size. Perhaps it can be said that the disbanding of Hogan's Alley as a black locus in Vancouver mimicked the dissolution of the pioneer community of the nineteenth century, except that these blacks drifted to other neighbourhoods within the Lower Mainland, and continue to come together for cultural and familial events, but live with neither a commercial nor residential centre.

While a comprehensive history of blacks in twentieth century B.C. remains to be written, oral histories are recorded in both transcribed and video forms. Interviews with black residents of Hogan's Alley, included in this anthology, are found in *Opening Doors: Vancouver's East End* (1979). Part four of the *Hymn to Freedom* video series, *B.C. the West: On this Rock* (1994), documents the stories of black migration to B.C. and Alberta through interviews with the Collins and Alexander families. Andrea Fatona and Cornelia Wyngaarden's wonderful video documentary *Hogan's Alley* (1995) preserves oral histories of Leah Curtis, Pearl Brown, and Thelma Towns, all former Strathcona residents. And on the black

Canadian porters, some of them Vancouverites, there is Selwyn Jacob's fascinating documentary *The Road Taken* (1996).

From the time of the first arrivals in the nineteenth century, B.C.'s black history has been one of continued exodus, immigration, settlement, exploration, desertion, miscegenation, communitarianism, integration, segregation, agitation, uprooting and re-rooting and re-routing. In other words, it has been a population and history always in flux. Much of the first black population of the nineteenth century left after being here for seven years; the children of the black immigrants who came here in the 1950s and 1960s often emigrate to Toronto, the United States, Britain, or the Caribbean, craving the succour of life in a large black community; and, conversely, blacks arrive here from the U.S., Caribbean, Africa, and other parts of Canada daily. Black B.C. has never been a single monolithic population. It does not locate its roots in an easily discernable common origin, nor has it ceased to shift and transform today. It is a population that has never truly reified, and, as such, has remained less fiercely demarcated than others. If there is a unifying characteristic of black identity in this province, it is surely the talent for reinvention and for pioneering new versions of traditional identities that such conditions demand.

Hogan's Alley. CVA BU.P.508-53, N.623-53.

2

With such an indeterminate history, perhaps it is fitting that black writing in B.C. begins with Sir James Douglas, a figure whose blackness was for years the subject of rumour and speculation. While it is a matter of historical record that both Douglas's mother and maternal grandmother were racially designated as "free coloureds" – a term used at that time to describe a person with any mixture of black and white ancestry – he "passed" for white his entire adult life (Adams 1). He was, however, often "accused" of being black by his contemporary political enemies – Mathew Macfie, a Congregationalist clergyman in Victoria, called Douglas a "gentleman of large property, reported to be of Mulatto origin" (Kilian 59), meaning to discredit him. Since Douglas "passed," and remained always silent about his mother's ancestry, it is impossible to know whether or not *he* ever considered himself black. The writing Douglas produced – letters, both private and administrative, as well as journals of his voyages and tours of service in the fur trade – is generally business-like and non-personal. The *Journal of James Douglas, 1843. Including Voyage to Sitka and Voyage to the North-West Coast* is an in-the-field document of the founding of Victoria, and, as such, it is utilitarian, though Douglas's writing is competent and at times evocative. (Upon the founding of a city, the appearance of a comet in

Sir James Douglas. VPL 901-A.

the sky does not motivate him to speculate on it as an omen or sign of any sort; this is a measure of the literalness of his outlook.)

The black pioneers produced a plethora of writing in various styles and on various subjects. Upon the eve of their flight from San Francisco, the city's *Daily Evening Bulletin*, describing the mass emigration, makes the first speculative reference to a body of literature that would follow:

> All this puts one in mind of the Pilgrims . . . when those adventurers embarked for their new homes across the sea. When the colored people get their "poet," he will no doubt sing of these scenes which are passing around us almost unheeded, and the day when colored people fled persecution in California may yet be celebrated in story. . . . The sixty-five yesterday went off in the Commodore and are pushing up towards the north, bearing their *lares* and *penates* to found new homes. . . . Whatever may be their destiny, we hope the colored people may do well. (quoted in Pilton 12)

In fact, the blacks migrants already had their poet among them, and *she* was named Priscilla Stewart. Her poem "A Voice from the Oppressed to the Friends of Humanity" was composed on the occasion of their departure. Though written while she was still in San Francisco, in topic and teleos it should be considered the first black British Columbian poem. The poem expresses the sincerity of the community's intent in becoming citizens of the colonies to the north, making it clear that they were not merely transient opportunists, but people who were fully prepared to reconstruct their identities as British subjects if it would afford them the basic human right of citizenship. The poem suggests they will do better seeking prosperity in Canada, but in the last three stanzas the speaker says "Farewell" to those who presumably helped their cause in the U.S., admonishing them to "Never desert your principles / Until you've redeemed your land" (Pilton 37). It is both a forward- and backward-looking poem, addressed partly to those left behind. Stewart evinces an ambivalence that will recur in black B.C. writing to come.

Rebecca Gibbs is the second black B.C. poet, a woman who lived in Barkerville, the gold mining boomtown of B.C.'s interior, in the 1860s. Like Stewart, Gibbs also wrote primarily occasional poems. She mainly published her work in the town's newspaper *The Cariboo Sentinel*. The Scottish balladeer James Anderson included some of her work, along with various other regional songs and poems, in a kind of appendix to the second edition of his *Sawney's Letters and Cariboo Rhymes* (1869), which was published in Barkerville where it enjoyed popular success. Gibbs's poem "The Old Red Shirt" shows us something of the poverty of the Cariboo's transient population during that time. The speaker, a washerwoman hired to clean a miner's shirt, admonishes us to "Have pity on the men who earn your wealth" and "Grudge not the poor miner his food" (Anderson 64). In "A Vital Presence: Women in the Cariboo Gold Rush, 1862-1875," Sylvia Van Kirk points out that Gibbs, herself a washerwoman by trade, ostensibly addresses this poem to the exploitation of the miners, but in doing so indirectly documents her own experience as a labourer (26-27).

The earliest controversies around black speech and "authenticity" are evident in the reception of the prose of both Isaac Dickson and Mifflin Wistar Gibbs.[1]

Like both Priscilla Stewart and Rebecca Gibbs, Mifflin Gibbs wrote in a kind of elevated, standard English (the use of the word "testify" in Rebecca Gibbs's "Lines Written After the Great Fire at Barkerville, 16th September, 1868" seems to be the only lexically black cue in the entire poem [1]). As a successful businessman, politician, and community activist, Mifflin Gibbs wrote many letters to both *The British Colonist* in Victoria and the black newspaper *The Elevator* in San Francisco, often on behalf of the black community during their political struggles against racism and segregation. Later in life, Gibbs wrote *Shadow and Light: An Autobiography with Reminiscences of the Last and Present Century* (1902), which contains a substantial section about his time in B.C. Gibbs's language is often lofty, as was the style of his era. His description of Vancouver Island is an example of the ostentatiousness of his prose:

Mifflin Wistar Gibbs. BCA B-01601.

Many afterward sighed for former times, when Vancouver Island, proud beauty of the North, sat laving her feet in the genial waters of the Pacific, her lap verdant with beautiful foliage and delicious fruits; her head raised with peerless majesty to brilliant skies, while sunbeams playing upon a brow encircled by eternal snows reflected a sheen of glorious splendor; when, conscious of her immense wealth in coal, minerals, and fisheries, her delightful climate and geographical supremacy. (94)

Whites in Victoria responded negatively to this sort of speech and manner affected by blacks. Lt R.C. Mayne of the Royal Navy at Esquimalt patronizingly described the blacks of Victoria, writing, "As a rule these free negroes are a very quiet people, a little given perhaps to over familiarity when any opening for it is afforded, very fond of dignity, always styling each other Mr, and addicted to an imposing costume, in the way of black coats, gold studs and watch-chains, &c." (351). Similarly, when travelling through Victoria, Sophia Cracroft (the niece of Sir John Franklin) described the blacks in a letter as "a most orderly and useful and loyal section of the community . . . they certainly do speak with a propriety & degree of refinement which is peculiar to their race, & certainly superior to the same rank among Englishmen." Of Wellington Moses and his wife, black residents of Victoria, Cracroft writes, "Mr Moses calls himself an Englishman, which of course he is politically & therefore justly. She is a queer being, wears a long sweeping gown without crinoline – moves slowly & has a sort of stately way (in intention at least) which is quite amusing. . . . The language of both is very good" (quoted in Killian 79). The scrutiny these whites applied to the speech of the blacks shows a clear expectation of "inferior" speech.

Isaac Dickson's letters to *The Cariboo Sentinel* derail these interpretations drastically. Dickson writes in a dialected English that the two historians of black B.C., James W. Pilton and Crawford Kilian, disagree about in terms of its "authenticity." While Pilton describes Dickson's language as "the usual phonetic spelling of the almost illiterate negro" (163), Kilian argues that Dickson "used dialect to poke fun at life in the gold fields," and that his use of dialect is a "means of mixing humour and social criticism" despite what sounds to contemporary ears like the "unpleasant overtones of Stepin Fetchit" (93). Kilian rightly recognizes Dickson's letters as *performances* of language, rather than some sort of essential effluent. It is significant that in his letters Dickson re-writes or "translates" Robert Burns into black English, Burns being a dialect poet a white audience – many of whom in the Cariboo were Scottish – would have recognized as legitimate. It is possible to look at Dickson's letters as inside humour made public, the overplaying of a black stereotype for a white audience in such a way that only black readers can see that the joke is actually on the gullibility of the whites[2] – or as significations upon the "darky" stories B.C. newspapers commonly reprinted from American papers at that time. What is clear from the responses to both Gibbs's style of speech and Dickson's text is that black language in B.C. has always been scrutinized and held to standards of authenticity to which white writers rarely find themselves held. Like all writers, Dickson and Gibbs employed language strategically, whether for satire, serious employment of dialect, or class ascendency. Their textual performances were consciously created, and their modes of speech carefully chosen. The notion of black speech and writing as something that should be artless and natural in order to be authentic is racist, and denies the agency and individuality of these writers.

William H.H. Johnson's *The Life of Wm. H.H. Johnson, from 1839-1900, and the New Race* (1904) and Marie Albertina Stark Wallace's *Notes made by Marie Albertina Stark (afterwards Mrs Wallace) from the recollections of her mother, Sylvia Stark* (1966) are both classical slave narratives, tracing very different routes of passage, each ending in B.C. Much like Mifflin Gibbs, Johnson can be too public about the telling of his life, writing about politics for pages, but concentrating on his personal feelings only in flashes. In contrast, Wallace's rendering of the life of Sylvia Stark is rich in detail and emotion, and doubtless preserves much of the oral phrasing of Stark as she told these episodes. Both texts assume a mythic quality at points. Johnson's story of pursuing bloodhounds who fall miraculously and inexplicably asleep at a runaway slave's feet is a racialized version of Daniel in the lion's den. Wallace's recounting of her mother's family's journey from Missouri to California and on to Saltspring Island is similarly mythic, akin to "Exodus" in its desperation, drama, and redemption.

While the oratory of Sylvia Stark lives on in her daughter's textualization, much orature of black B.C. has been lost. The speeches and sermons of the nineteenth century blacks will remain to us forever apocryphal, though we do have some hints. Willis Bond, a self-styled orator from Victoria's black community, took his public speaking so seriously that he built a lecture room as an addition to the pub he owned, calling it his "Athenaeum Room." He spoke to whomever would listen, on a variety of subjects political and cultural, and he occasionally

Marie Stark Wallace (standing) and Sylvia Stark.
COURTESY NADINE SIMS.

held debates with well-known local figures (Pilton 62). In 1886, Victoria's *Daily Colonist* published a story about an anti-Chinese rally held at city hall at which Bond was one of only two who spoke out in defence of the Chinese. Bond was shouted down, but his sympathies were at least recorded there in partial quotation (2). Ultimately, a smattering of quotations in Victoria newspapers like the *Daily Chronicle* and the *Daily Colonist* are all that survive of his oratory, as well as a few descriptions of his lectures, which included debates over Free Trade with the United States (which Bond argued against) and others with titles such as "The word negro and its application" (Pilton 62-63).

Given the Bond example, Daphne Marlatt and Carole Itter's book *Opening Doors: Vancouver's East End* (1979), which preserves orature that would have otherwise gone unrecorded, is a blessing. In the late 1970s, Marlatt and Itter recorded and transcribed the words of Nora Hendrix, Rosa Pryor, Leona Risby, Austin Phillips, and Dorothy Nealy. In these oral memoirs we hear the art of story-telling and history-telling performed by the community's elders, and their accounts are savvy, insightful, and entertaining. What makes these interviews particularly important is that there seems to exist no written account by a black person composed during the Hogan's Alley period. However, another account of the period, written later, can be found in Rosemary Brown's autobiography *Being Brown: A Very Public Life* (1989). In it she describes her and her husband's first impressions of coming to Vancouver in the mid-1950s. Comparing Brown's narrative with that of the *Opening Doors* interviewees, we see two different views of Vancouver: one of a black immigrant's arrival, and one from a member of an "indigenous" black community; one of a middle-class, West Side writer, and one rooted in the working-class East End. Brown also introduces a common theme for black writers in B.C. – isolation:

> Although we occasionally saw other Black people in the city and would always smile and say hello, it was not until Bill's third year in medicine that we actually became acquainted with any members of the British Columbia Black community. During a hospital rotation at the Vancouver General Hospital, Bill met a patient named Dolores Collins. He was so excited that he phoned me on his lunch break that day to tell me of this first meeting with a real live Black Canadian in Vancouver. Mrs Collins seemed genuinely pleased to know him, and they chatted every day that she remained in the hospital. On her discharge we were invited to her home for dinner and there we met Frank, her husband, and their children, and learnt about the B.C. Association for the Advancement of Coloured People, which was just in its formative year – Frank was the president. (52-53)

Once Brown finds the black community in Vancouver, she embraces it and is embraced by it. But while she writes, "There was no highly visible Black ghetto as in Montreal and in many American cities" (53), Dorothy Nealy's description of the situation just ten years earlier contradicts her. Nealy's Strathcona is a conspicuously black neighbourhood. She says, "When I came here, this district was Negroes, from Main Street to Campbell Avenue, like you see the Chinese here now. Whole apartment blocks that were all full of Blacks. In '44 it was a ghetto" (169).

l-r: Nora Hendrix, Rosa Pryor, Austin Phillips, Dorothy Nealy.

Whether the community had transformed in the space of ten years or whether Brown simply did not see this part of the city is unclear. However, both narratives mention the influence of the BCAACP, which seems to have transcended class and neighbourhood in uniting members of the black community from all over the city.

From 1904, when William H.H. Johnson published his slave narrative with Bolam and Hornett, until 1969, when Christopher James published his first poetry chapbook *Rhapsody of the Satanic Dancer*, it appears that no book-length work was published by a black person in B.C. – sixty-five years of publishing silence out of a 144-year history of presence in the province. However, the exiled South African poet Arthur Nortje lived and taught high school English classes in Hope, B.C. from 1967 to 1969, where he wrote many of the poems that were eventually collected in his posthumously published book *Dead Roots* (1973).[3] Most of the writers who broke the twentieth-century publishing silence in the 1970s – Christopher James, Truman Green, and Fred Booker – were self-publishing, suggesting that the dearth of books in this interim may not have been due to a lack of writing, but rather unwillingness or disinterest on the part of professional presses to take on black writers.[4] With the case of Truman Green's novel *A Credit to Your Race* (1973) – the first black B.C. novel – when the manuscript was turned down for publication by Anansi Press, Green published it himself in a limited-run of 300 copies. It has not been reprinted since, being presently available in only two libraries in all of Canada.

A Credit to Your Race is an important document of an "indigenous" black experience. It is set in Surrey, B.C. circa 1960 where the protagonist Billy Robinson, a fifteen-year-old porter's son, falls in love with the white girl next door. If isolation is a key theme of black B.C. writing, Billy Robinson is perhaps its most fully-drawn expression. Green describes in detail the Canadian brand of racism of which Rosemary Brown speaks – the kind consisting of polite denials, back-handed compliments (hence the title), and a disingenuous tolerance motivated more often than not by one-upmanship with the United States. When Billy's girlfriend becomes pregnant, the young interracial couple feel the full weight of Canadian racism brought down upon them. One of the interesting things about *A Credit to Your Race* is that its narrative voice is the simple speech of Billy Robinson, which together with

the age of the characters gives the novel the feel of a young adult book, but the range of content – including interracial sex, abortion, and racist vigilantism – makes it a study in controversies that are still powder kegs of controversy.

Christopher James's spate of poetry chapbooks published in the early 1970s – three plus some mimeographed folios, all in the space of two years – suggests the beginning of a promising career, which unfortunately appears to have ceased after 1971. James's chapbooks feel young, both in the era's youth culture that they reflect, and in their looseness of style. In "out of order / talk'n about them folks jimi – a tale of black male of black mail," set at a Jimi Hendrix concert at the Pacific National Exhibition Forum, the LSD-spiked lines meander towards a final critical pronouncement on the black experience here:

> [. . .] the speakers address
> themselves to the complacent, sitting hands folded
> and grinning, shocked out of their minds at the language
> that has changed them through the years. they have seen
> some things, and the only expectation is the burst of
> games to their hysterics, as the jubilance carries
> everyone to a high of defiance. between the teeth
> lies the sneer that leads in a funny way to war.
> oh what a freak i must be amongst you! (n.p.)

James's work is free-wheeling, and his *Two Sides* (1971) carries the inscription:

> A TRIBUTE TO ALL THOSE WHO DRINK MUSCATEL
> IN ALLEYS. FOR THE SPIRITS, WHO WELL MAY KNOW
> THE VIRTUES OF THIS CHANGE, TO THE HO BO. (n.p.)

James's interest in the figure of the transient shows up in many of his poems, including "talk'n about ho bo'n it jimmy," a bluesy song, and his only extended foray into dialect writing.

Fred Booker published several poems in literary journals across Canada during this period and self-produced, with help from his friend the novelist Jane Rule, three musical LPs, whose lyrical contents show his gift as a poet. In the liner notes to *Book One: Songs, Voice & Guitar of Fred Booker* (1974), the first of his trilogy of folk-blues albums, Booker places his interest in both text-based poetry and song lyricism within the context of a culture that does not emphasize a division of textuality and orality, but thrives on generic cross-fertilization:

> I was Baptist reared. That means that I was exposed to a
> great American tradition of spoken poetry as well as its
> great tradition of gospel singing. Baptist preaching is a most

phenomenal kind of oratory; literary in the sense that it is poetic, miraculous in the sense that the eloquence is so often spontaneous. Many a preacher under whose influence I grew up had been a student of James Weldon Johnson and Paul Lawrence Dunbar, black American poets who captured so well the world of the black American's faith and sense of mystery.

Booker goes on to comment that for him these African-American tropes have blended with Canadian themes: "In Canada one of the strongest elements present in the new songs being written by the person on the street was the element of travel. Travel is as indigenous to Canada as apple pie is to our American neighbor and as war seems to be to the Middle East." Indeed, the two lyrics from his trilogy included here – "Powell Street Conspiracy" and "One Road to the Sea" – both, like James's poetry, feature images of restlessness and motion, and the latter, dedicated in part to Sylvia Stark, blurs the narrative of her family's journey out of slavery with his own travels from the United States into and across Canada. Included also are poems from Booker's unpublished manuscript titled "Blue Notes of a White Girl." In one section of this verse-novel, the black male author

BOOK ONE

SONGS, VOICE & GUITAR
OF
FRED BOOKER

writes through the persona of a white female artist, who is mysteriously compelled to place a black man in a landscape she is painting, and then finds herself placing *herself* in the painting as "a series of identical blonde figurines" around the man's neck. The black man, who is also the mythical first man Adam, asserts his African-Canadianness by calling down ancestors, challenging the white artist's traditionally all-possessing eye which has set out to "capture" this landscape but has inadvertantly produced him. The white female persona voices the paradoxical ground upon which the two meet: "I catch his eye / our interests connecting." The sequence spirals into a *mise-en-abyme* of power relations leaving one to wonder which character is the object and which the objectifier, or if the oscillation itself is the necessary space of negotiation between the two marginalized agencies.

While the pioneer writers were aware of each other's work (which often appeared in local newspapers), and the writers of the 1990s to the present similarly are known to each other, the writers of this "middle period" – specifically, Green, James, and Booker – all appear to have produced their work in isolation, neither knowing one another nor involved in an ongoing community of writers. The poet Hope Anderson, who had moved to Vancouver by way of Jamaica and Montreal, co-edited the anthology *The Body* in 1979 with David Phillips, featuring writing by Sharon Thesen, Brian Fawcett, Barry McKinnon, and George Stanley; for this, Anderson as a black B.C. writer represents something of a turning point, being the first writer traceably connected to the larger avant-garde scene in B.C. His *Slips from Grace* (1987) is a rich and accomplished book of

poems that weaves Caribbeanist imagery and aurality with the formal influences of the contemporary west coast literary scene. For younger black B.C. writers, Anderson can be seen as a kind of signpost or precedent, one who announces that the age of precarious publication and writing in isolation is over. With him, a convergence with the Canadian literary mainstream has, for better or for worse, arrived. In fact, Anderson's *détournement* in his poem "1980" of a racist sign spotted outside a small town – "niggers who can read beware / niggers who can't read better beware" (14) – can be seen as a message to younger black writers and critics: your ability to *read* this place and its dangers is wrapped up with your possibilities for *articulating* your experience; your survival is bound up with a literacy of the local. Later in the same poem, the speaker's pronouns shift, indicating "slips" of identity – racial, communitarian, and individual:

> I'm another domino falling
> & cannot tell how we feel
> until that moment, i become
> the speech of the other
> the one to which i speak (15)

Whichever problems of speaker and audience Anderson is evoking here can be reconstituted in this anthology as a new issue facing the writers of the "nineties-to-now" generation: now that there is an incipient concept of a "black B.C.," with roots at least somewhat recovered by black cultural work of the 1990s, to whom do black writers speak, and what contexts of dissemination and reception can we now create?

3

Blacks in B.C. have always recognized the need for distinct cultural spaces. Even though it can be said that the population has generally been integrationist in tendency, cultural contexts in which our writing and orating can be disseminated and understood on its own terms have been sought since the pioneer era. When the mainstream has shown itself to be either hostile, disinterested, or unable to put its support behind relevant and complicated black cultural products, black journals, theatre companies, and anthologies have existed as self-initiated responses to the unacceptable alternative – silence.

While the nineteenth-century black B.C. writers published their work in the popular print media – *The British Colonist* and *The Cariboo Sentinel,* for example – they also read and contributed to the black-owned and -edited newspaper from San Francisco *The Elevator,* for which Mifflin Gibbs sometimes wrote, and which, for a time, had a Barkerville correspondent (Kilian 90). Through *The Elevator,* blacks in B.C. kept apprised of political and social issues pertaining to black communities up and down the west coast of North America. In the twentieth century, the aforementioned BCAACP published the BCAACP *Quarterly* which ran from 1966 to 1972, providing a space for black community dialogue. Later serials such as Michelle Lee Williams's *The Afro News: The Voice of the Black Community* and *The Talking Drum: Official Newsletter of the African Canadian Association of B.C.*, both founded in 1986, have served to create a sense of community and provide a locus for black journalism in the province. In the mid-1990s, Peter Hudson edited and published the astonishingly good but short-lived *diaspora: a magazine of black consciousness and culture,* which showcased new writing, criticism, and artist's pages, the first and only journal of its kind in B.C.

In her essay "The 'Whole' Truth: Nothing But 'Images,'" Siobhan Barker profiles B.C.'s two black-run theatre companies, Sepia Players and Black Theatre West. Similarly, playwright Lorena Gale, in her essay "Into the Margins," also describes this dramatic tradition which has continued on the west coast, sporadically at times, since the 1970s. In the 1980s, Ralph Taylor and Jay Burns founded the Free Black Creative Arts Theatre (or "Free Black C.A.T."), which taught black culture to youth through drama (Elliott 37). Theatrical endeavours such as these, which have survived with little financial support and often only through sheer force of will, have played a vital role in nurturing and sustaining black dramatic literary production in the province.

Black writers and orators from B.C. have also published their work in the various national anthologies. Two in particular feature a large amount of writing from B.C.: *Miscegenation Blues: Voices of Mixed Race Women* (1994) and *North: New African Canadian Writing* (1997).[5] Also, the aptly titled audiocassette *Void to Voice: Musical/Vocal Xperiment of Afro-Canadian and First Nation RESISTANCE* (1993) features dub poetry by Mercedes Baines, Michelle La Flamme, David Odhiambo, Michelle Thrush, and the Millionaire Liquidators, and is the only B.C. project of its kind.

The black B.C. writers of the nineties-to-now are a unique group in that they all seem, in one way or another, in communication with each other; or, at the very least, they are aware of each other's published work. There now exists something of a community of black writers in the province in a way that has not previously been seen. Organizations like the Black Writers Network, founded by Roger Blenman, sponsored readings and workshops in

Michelle La Flamme (l) and Mercedes Baines
at Light Raye Studio, February 1993.
PHOTO BY DAVID-GEORGE.

the mid-1990s, and kept black writers in the city apprised of each other's doings through a newsletter and contact list. And the exponential increase of black writing in B.C. after 1990 has as its corollary a diversification of genres and interests. It has been said that tradition is a double-edged sword – that being born into a repertoire can either inspire or stifle, depending on how one views it; but black writers in B.C. have often had to deal with a sense of traditionlessness, apart from whatever memories of "back home" they may retain. While it is unsatisfying to merely transplant Afrocentrism, or sentimental longings for homeland, or easy-access African-Americana to B.C., it is equally self-defeating to try to "fit ourselves into" the white scripts of nation-building or the spice rack vapidness of liberal multiculturalism. It is also too easy to say that rootlessness gives one the leisure of self-definition, because there is nothing luxurious about fighting against erasure or elision. But through the process of speaking and listening to each other, a black B.C. aesthetic may now be in discernable formation.

Contemporary writers such as C.S. Giscombe, Peter Hudson, and myself begin with black history in B.C. as itself the point of departure in their work, and seek self-awareness through an examination of the ancestors and the black author's relationship to them. Hudson's essay "Natural Histories of Southwestern

British Columbia" could almost stand as an alternative introduction to this anthology, seeking as it does the *raison d'être* of blackness in B.C., with equal parts skepticism and sincere desire for roots. Similarly, in my book of poems *49th Parallel Psalm* (1999) I try simultaneously to write a history of black B.C., place myself within it, and yet keep the myth-making process transparent enough that the arbitrariness of identity and place is shown. Giscombe's two books, *Giscome Road* (1998) and *Into and Out of Dislocation* (2000), both trace a black history of B.C. in a similarly fluid way. Giscombe is an African-American, but my claim on him as a "B.C." writer is fair in the sense that these two books follow the trail of a nineteenth-century black explorer of B.C. – John R. Giscome – who may have been his blood ancestor; Giscombe, an African-American re-enacting John R.'s exploration, in writing, produces books very much *of* B.C., meditations on the way this particular landscape and political economy refracts blackness.

Women have been writing and orating at every stage of black B.C.'s history, but it is in the work of the black feminist writers of the nineties-to-now that we see a consciousness of gender, race, and place aestheticized in a way previously unseen. Lily Spence, whose evocative poems arrive by way of St. Lucia, describes the sexism of the artistic scene in which she grew up in the 1950s:

> [A]t one time, [Derek Walcott] came to my home in St. Lucia when he was not famous at all, to compare my art work with St. Omer's, an artist (a friend of his and mine) who exhibited paintings in Expo '86; it was for him that Walcott entitled one of his books, *Omer*. It had been a slew of friends, intellectuals, lovers of the arts, among them Garth St. Omer (novelist), Walcott, etc. who met at Dunstan's, a stone's throw from my house, for debates, discussions and to listen to classical music. In those days a woman, even if she wanted to, could not participate in such intellectual past-times; this meeting had been for men only; society then just did not sanction such minglings of the sexes.[6]

Though patriarchy, in both the black community and the larger community, has similarly operated in B.C., black women writers like Spence have always resisted attempts to marginalize them. Writers like Nikola Marin, Nadine King Chambers, and Michelle La Flamme are producing feminist and queer work that makes fresh the empowerment rhetoric of the "identitarian nineties." The result is a kind of roots-genderfuck, an examination of gender roles that seizes its myths (both time-less and contemporary) from the coloured side of the returned gaze. Mercedes Baines, Karina Vernon, and Sara Singh Parker-Toulson similarly seek to make space for new subjectivities by exposing, disrupting, and ultimately dispelling the supremacy of male discourses. Andrea Thompson's poem "Black Mary," in which a black mannequin is used as decoration in a man's basement suite, examines the rote representation of black women as ambiance. Black Mary is placed at the centre of the apartment – the chimney is likened to her "spine" – and the male inhabitant is "(not

Nadine King Chambers at the Pitt Gallery, May 1993.
PHOTO BY DAVID-GEORGE.

alone)" (66) because of her presence, bound to the Other in an illusion of normativity. Thompson gives us this fragment of the black Madonna / black mother (mammy, nanny, or the exoticized "Hottentot"), as both "hollow" and "holy" (63) – absent and present, the contradiction upon which male and white subjectivities have both traditionally been structured.

Many of the writers in this anthology identify themselves as mixed-race, and exhibit a variety of strategies to represent or discuss the issues arising from this. Janisse Browning and Michelle La Flamme, both writers of black and First Nations ancestry, stand as a kind of counterpose to the colonial positions taken by James Douglas and Mifflin Gibbs towards First Nations people in their writing. In La Flamme's screenplay *Threads* (2001), she presents a racially diverse *dramatis personae*, and is thus, as a mixed-race author, able to speak through their various subject positions, which are sometimes in contention, and at other times critically allied. David Odhiambo's novel *diss/ed banded nation* (1998) offers a rare portrayal of an interracial relationship between a black man and a native woman living in B.C., through the characters Benedict Ochieng and Anna:

> "think about the match we make. both beautiful. both
> native."
> "native?"
> "yeah. i mean . . . what they were staring at . . . two
> native people."
> ". . . i guess."
> "i mean, you said you're luwow."
> "luo. right."
> "right."
> "and being gitskan."
> "kitskun."
> "gitskan, man. gitskan."
> "being kitshun . . ."

"well, we're like one of the oldest cultures in the americas. like i'm assuming the lowow are in africa."

"old? i don't really know. they originated up in the nile basin. migrated down near this beautiful lake . . . lake victoria. named like victoria b.c. to commemorate that whole imperial waltz around the globe."

"maaan, you have to come up to prince rupert with me one day. i mean the guy it's renamed after was an english sadist . . . but, the water's turquoise up there . . . we could swim. sweat. get in touch with our ancestors." (110)

Odhiambo's is a study of a kind of interracial relationship that in North America has been historically common, but has infrequently been represented in fiction.

With the contributions of Kathy-Ann March, Karina Vernon, and Sara Singh Parker-Toulson, this anthology, in a sense, comes full circle. These writers can be contrasted with James Douglas, a person who went to great pains to hide his black ancestry, whereas these contemporary writers are interested in developing a sustained, complicated consciousness about mixed-race. While we have something of a language to talk about mixed-race, it is a language rooted in segregation and responses to segregation, but in March's "Like Koya," Vernon's "Aunt Ermine's Recipe for Brown Sugar Fudge," and Parker-Toulson's "On Being a Black Woman in Canada (and Indian and

David Odhiambo at the Pitt Gallery, May 1993.
PHOTO BY DAVID-GEORGE.

English Too)" we see entirely new social configurations of the topic of miscegenation. Avoiding the autoexoticist "tragic mulatto" narratives, these writers seek to dismantle binary and standardizing racialized epistemologies. Vernon and Parker-Toulson occupy and claim the gap between media representations of blackness or Eurocentric rationalism (both seen as external but determining discourses) and their lives as people whose racial experiences are socially unrecognized. By composing their texts from spaces of unsatsifactory discourses, and intentionally blocking or corrupting those discourses, Vernon and Parker-Toulson take power over and detour hegemonic notions of "authenticity" that are, ultimately, the very roots of racism. It's a long way from Douglas's silence to here.

While Lily Spence, E. Centime Zeleke, Lorena Gale, and Tanya Evanson all write poems set outside a notion of "homeland," each does so for very different reasons, though all three are similarly symptomatic of a new black relationship to diaspora and travel. Spence's "Koopab . . ." hinges, in both its narrative and aesthetic style, on dispersal and return. It is written in St. Lucian "nation language."[7] Most of the poem is in the voice of a mother desperately urging her son Koopab not to leave home: "Pa fe sa, ish mwen, pa fe sa. / Ish mwen, la pa ni l'or en chemen d'aut peyi-on! / Ish mwen, en-kondwi, d'aut peyi ky vale-u tut-a-fet / mwen di u tut-a-fet kon u mete go zotyi-u en lawi-li" (60).[8] The last stanza of the poem, however, reverts to a less-dialected English, demonstrating Koopab's deculturation and his inability to comprehend the island as he once did. Zeleke's poem "Tizita" can be seen as an answer to Spence's. The *tizita* is a genre of Ethiopian poetry in which the speaker recalls lost loved ones; Zeleke's poetry, including her audio recording of the same name in which she interviews women relatives in Ethiopia,[9] is concerned with the maintenance of connection to her country and culture of origin, and the bridging of the cultural divides created by contemporary patterns of immigration. Part of a "domestic diaspora," both Gale and Evanson are black-Québecois, and each writes of that very particular subject space, taken abroad: Gale to B.C., and Evanson to Asia and Latin America, each charting the ways race and national identity morph in the course of their travels. Added to this is the poetry of Joy Russell and Vanessa Richards, two writers from B.C. who migrated to and developed their skills in Britain, publishing there in the important anthologies *The Fire People: A Collection of Contemporary Black British Poets* (1998) and *IC3: The Penguin Book of New Black Writing in Britain* (2000), the former having returned, the latter maintaining ties to B.C. through the organization of events such as Transmetaphoria, a cabaret-style showcase of black spoken word held in Vancouver in 2001.

The genre diversification of contemporary black B.C. writing is widening along with an increase in the quantity of work being produced. Shane Book is one of the few black B.C. poets committed to the long poem, his craft having extended from an earlier precise lyricism towards an avant-garde seriality. Tanya Evanson, Vanessa Richards, Roger Blenman, and Seth-Adrian Harris have arisen out of the "spoken word" literary scene, which, for black writers, is less a new phenomenon as it is a tradition traceable to oral cultural genres such as rap, dub, and the sermon. Included here also is a transcription of Yvonne Brown's speech at a Black History Month event, which both describes and demonstrates the importance of orature in the diaspora. The most popular form of black orature today is hip hop, and the internationally-acclaimed Rascalz's "Dreaded Fist" provides an example of the "bending" of the

English language which Brown describes in her speech. In prose, the "new narrative" work of Lawrence Ytzhak Braithwaite is yet another example of black hybridizing, reworking, and re-encoding of received languages. In his novels *Wigger* (1995) and *Ratz Are Nice (PSP)* (2000), Braithwaite creates an idiosyncratic patois out of the social debris of rudeboyism, gangster rap, and lumpenproletarian gay culture. In "Trunk Music" Braithwaite queers the gangster pose and gun talk of hip hop. His work continues to evolve as a foil to black upliftment

narratives similar to the way Chester Himes's work refused to follow the "program" of the Black Arts Movement. Terence Anthony's graphic serial *Shadowtown* (1992-1994) represents yet another type of narrative strategy. The illustrated story of an alternative black nationalist future, *Shadowtown* is an intelligent and original re-examination of the formative ideologies of the 1960s, and can be considered the first black science fiction to come out of B.C.

In *Into and Out of Dislocation*, C.S. Giscombe retells an old African-American joke: "no matter where you go, no matter how far, no matter to what unlikely extreme, no matter what country, continent, ice floe, or island you land on, you will find someone else black already there" (10). I believe it is a cautionary aphorism, phrased in that particularly African-American way of dryly expecting the worst: *There will be no remove to individuality*, it tells us, *there will already be the images and tensions of your race wherever you get yourself stranded, so don't get any ideas about getting away from it*. But in this existential parable, the writers of this anthology *are* the "someone black already there" – the lost tribe of the lost tribe. The population continues to be unstable, and continues to be difficult to figure. Some of these "B.C." writers no longer live here. Some are included in this book on the strength of a few years spent stopping over, and the work they produced in that window of time. Some are here to stay.

This anthology is a first collection and, as such, only a blueprint – a sketch that suggests future possibilities. It is not complete. Nor is it the last word. Nor does it necessarily indicate that "black B.C." is something that needs to be brought to a sum. Much of the uniqueness of the work in this anthology is exactly the result of the shifting patterns of migration and the absence of a sharply defined regional tradition. If an aesthetic is in development, it may be best to view it – from the ground floor – as provisional rather than as a progression towards an essence.

NOTES

1. While there is no clear mention of the relationship between Rebecca Gibbs and Mifflin Gibbs, Kilian deduces that Rebecca was possibly married to an "I.P. Gibbs," Mifflin Gibbs's brother, who lived in Barkerville for some time. Unfortunately, Mifflin Gibbs writes very little about his family – much of which moved to B.C. after him – in his autobiography. See Kilian, pp. 94-95.

2. See Henry Louis Gates, "The Blackness of Blackness: A Critique of the Sign and the Signifying Monkey," *Black Literature and Literary Theory*, Henry Louis Gates, ed. (New York: Routledge, 1984), 285-321.

3. Arthur Nortje lived in Canada for three years, moving afterwards to Oxford, England to attend university. He died there of a barbiturate overdose in 1970. The collection *Dead Roots* was gathered together from his private papers by friends and published in 1973. Both *Dead Roots* and the recent *Anatomy of Dark: Collected Poems of Arthur Nortje* (Unisa Press, 2000) include poems he wrote while living in B.C. For an excellent account of the three years Nortje spent in Canada, including interviews with his former students and co-workers in Hope, see "'The Raw and the Cooked': Arthur Kenneth Nortje, Canada, and a Comprehensive Bibliography" by Craig W. McLuckie and Ross Tyner in *English in Africa* 26.2 (October 1999), and for a study of coloured South African identity and the Canadian experience in Nortje's work, see "Arthur Kenneth Nortje (1942-1970)" by Craig W. McLuckie and Ross Tyner in *Major African Writers of theTwentieth Century*, Ernest Emenyonu, ed. (Africa World Press, 2001).

4. There is the near exception of E. Curmie Price, whose collection of poems *State of the Union* was published by the B.C. small press Sono Nis in 1970. Price, an African-American writer who lived in Bellingham, Washington at the time, never actually resided in B.C., though he was actively involved in the literary scene on both sides of the border in the 1960s.

5. *North* is a special issue of *West Coast Line* 31.1, No. 22 (spring/summer 1997).

6. From correspondence with editor.

7. See Kamau Brathwaite, *History of the Voice: The Development of Nation Language in Anglophone Caribbean Poetry* (London: New Beacon, 1984).

8. Spence's translation, from editor's correspondence: "Don't do this, my child, don't do this! / My child there is no gold in the other country! / My child, on the contrary, the other country will swallow you altogether . . . completely . . . I tell you . . . as soon as you put your toe near it."

9. E. Centime Zeleke, "Tizita: Conversations with My Mother's Sisters," *Ecgo/Location: Artist in Residence Projects at Vancouver's Co-operative Radio Vol 1* (Vancouver: Co-op Radio, 2000).

Works Cited

Adams, John. *Old Square-Toes and His Lady: The Life of James and Amelia Douglas.* Victoria: Horsdal and Schubart, 2001.

Anderson, Hope. *Slips from Grace.* Toronto: Coach House Press, 1987.

Anonymous. "Public Meeting." *The Daily Colonist* 56.43 (31 January 1886): 2.

Barker, Siobhan R.K. "The 'Whole' Truth: Nothing But 'Images.'" *diaspora* 1.2 (fall 1994): 14-16.

Booker, Fred. Liner notes. *Book One: Songs, Voice & Guitar of Fred Booker.* North Vancouver: Rulebook Records, 1974.

Brown, Rosemary. *Being Brown: A Very Public Life.* Toronto: Random House, 1989.

Clarke, George Elliott. "Africana Canadiana: A Primary Bibliography of Literature by African-Canadian Authors, 1785-1996/97, in English, French and Translation." *Canadian Ethnic Studies* 28.3 (1996): 107-209.

Elliott, Lorris. *Literary Writing by Blacks in Canada: A Preliminary Survey.* Ottawa: Department of the Secretary of State, 1988.

Gale, Lorena. "Into the Margins." *Canadian Theatre Review* 83 (Summer 1995): 16-19.

Gates, Henry Louis. "The Blackness of Blackness: A Critique of the Sign and the Signifying Monkey." *Black Literature and Literary Theory.* Ed. Henry Louis Gates. New York: Routledge, 1984. 285-321.

Gibbs, Mifflin Wistar. *Shadow and Light: An Autobiography with Reminiscences of the Last and Present Century.* New York: Arno Press, 1968.

Gibbs, Rebecca. "The Old Red Shirt." *Sawney's Letters and Cariboo Rhymes.* Barkerville, B.C.: Barkerville Restoration Advisory Committee of the Province of British Columbia, 1962. 64.

_____. "Lines Written After the Great Fire at Barkerville, 16th September, 1868." *The Cariboo Sentinel* 6.7 (19 December 1868): 1.

Giscombe, C.S. *Into and Out of Dislocation.* New York: North Point Press, 2000.

James, Christopher. *Two Sides.* N.p.: 1971.

Kilian, Crawford. *Go Do Some Great Thing: The Black Pioneers of British Columbia.* Vancouver: Douglas and McIntyre, 1978.

Mayne, R.C. *Four Years in British Columbia and Vancouver Island.* London: John Murray, 1862.

Nealy, Dorothy. [Untitled.] *Opening Doors: Vancouver's East End.* Victoria: Aural History Program, 1979. 169-174.

Odhiambo, David Nandi. *diss/ed banded nation.* Vancouver: Polestar, 1998.

Pilton, James W. *Negro Settlement in British Columbia, 1858-1871.* Vancouver: University of British Columbia MA thesis, 1951.

Spence, Lily. "Koopab . . ." *North: New African Canadian Writing.* Ed. Peter Hudson. Special issue of *West Coast Line* 31.1, No. 22 (spring/summer 1997).

Thompson, Andrea. *Eating the Seed.* Victoria: Ekstasis Editions, 1999.

Torres-Saillant, Silvio. "The Trials of Authenticity in Kamau Brathwaite." *World Literature Today* 68.4 (Autumn 1994): 697-707.

Van Kirk, Sylvia. "A Vital Presence: Women in the Cariboo Gold Rush, 1862-1875." *British Columbia Reconsidered: Essays on Women.* Eds. Gillian Creese and Veronica Strong-Boag. Vancouver: Press Gang, 1992. 21-37.

Sir James Douglas [1803-1877]

from Journal of James Douglas, 1843. Including Voyage to Sitka and Voyage to the North-West Coast

The prevalent wind during that period has been south east, adverse to us, and adding greatly to the duration tedium and discomforts of the voyage. It was therefore doubly pleasant to see the bright sun rising in his majesty, diffusing a glorious light over the clear blue sky, tingeing the masses of vapour that still are seen hanging heavily about the mountain sides, and throwing a certain cheerful light even over the dark gloomy forests that overhang the Straits.[1] The wind is from the eastward and still adverse, but it fortunately fell after a few hours rain, and we had a dead calm during the rest of the day. In consequence of the anchor breaking loose after it was weighed and the vessel had swung into deep water, it ran out 60 fms[2] of chain, before the windlass could be checked. This accident caused a detention of nearly an hour, and it was past 6 o'clock before we were on the move. The tide being in our favour, the vessel flew along at the rate of 11 miles [an] hour and brought us to Point Mudge[3] nearly in the afternoon. A dense fog, which obscured every object from view, brought us to a stand at the entrance of the Gulf of Georgia. There being no prospect of the fog clearing after lying to for [a] short time, we ran in for the shore of Vancouver's Island and anchored in 35 fms water. We soon discovered that the anchor would not hold, as an impetuous current acting on the vessel was dragging the vessel rapidly to the northward; a second and heavier anchor was let go with 60 fms of chain in order to bring the vessel up but without success; she drifted as fast as ever in the direction of the tide. Night soon came upon us, and a more unpleasant sight I never witnessed, all hands kept the deck, and nobody seemed disposed to sleep. The jerking of the anchors, dragged over an uneven rocky bottom, made every timber shake, while the harsh grating sound they made was dismal beyond description. The night was so thick and dark that we could not venture to get under way, and it was almost as dangerous to remain in our perilous position. At ten, the current having abated, the vessel brought up and the smallest anchor was weighed, we found the stock split and forced down upon the flukes, so as to be of no further service until repaired. At midnight the vessel began to drive again in the opposite direction towards the southward. We were soon after alarmed by a frightful jerk which announced that the chain or anchor had parted, and we spent the remainder of the night in a state of the most painful suspense and indescribable anxiety. The longest night must however have an end, and so had this memorable one; day at length dawned upon us and, the fog having cleared, we got a glimpse of the land and found that we were in no immediate danger. The chain was weighed and, as we suspected, the anchor was gone, having parted at the ring which was still fast to the chain.

THURSDAY 14TH. [FEBRUARY]
We now made for the south end of the Island of Texada but the wind was against us and we were obliged to give up the attempt, and run for Bewan Harbour. We made it at 2 o'clock and dropped our disabled anchor in 10 fms. It is a most fortunate circumstance that this anchor did not break last night or we should now be in a rather dangerous position. The wood cutters all at work.

FRIDAY 15TH.
Passed the day in Bewan Harbour, taking in wood. The weather cloudy and dry until the evening, when it rained heavily for a few hours. A large canoe came to our anchorage yesterday with twelve men on board; one of these a decent looking man, with a high forehead and mild expression of countenance informed us, in reply to our inquiries, that his name was Nickayaze and that he was chief of one of the strongest gangs of the Lay cul tah tribe,[4] and that the people of his canoe are his followers, in part freemen and others slaves. They were all more or less dressed in English woollens or stuffs made by themselves from the wool of the mountain goat, or the white woolly dog found among the Cowegins,[5] or from the inner rind of the cedar bark. They carried no weapons of any description, either firearms or the weapon of [the] native, the bow and arrow. The hair of the temples is combed towards the crown of the head from infancy leaving their features fully exposed. The chief had the forehead, as far down the face as the line of the eyebrows, painted with red ochre; the eyes are black and of moderate size, nose straight, and small mouth and chin, well formed cheekbones slightly prominent. They [have] generally strong bushy beards and appear to take some pains in trimming a good looking moustache which they wear on the upper lip. The Laycultah are considered the most restless and warlike tribe on this part of the Coast and have rendered themselves so formidable to the other tribes that they are not now without reason the terror and scourge of the Sound.[6]

SATURDAY 16TH.
Continued our journey this morning. Wet as usual. Wind right ahead from the South East. Anchored opposite the mouth of Fraser's River on Vancouver Island.

SUNDAY 17TH.
A strong tide last night again caused us some degree of uneasiness, no accident

however occurred. Started early in the morning, with the wind fair and pleasant weather. Anchored in the evening in a bay a few miles south of Widbey's Island.[7] Sent the woodcutters ashore & cut four cords of drift wood.

MONDAY 18TH.
Started at midnight with the flood and anchored off Nisqually[8] at five o'clock this morning. Immediately sent horses off to the Chutes[9] to which we also proceded in the steam vessel at half past eleven. Found the horses in readiness, started and encamped in the first plain from the Sound.[10]

TUESDAY 19TH.
Left our encampment at the dawn of day, and reached the Cowlitz[11] at 3:20 PM 10½ hours from the Chutes.

WEDNESDAY 20TH.
Our men and baggage came up this morning and we left the Cowlitz at 10:40 AM. The Cowlitz River very low, our boat, though nearly light, drags at every shallow.

We arrived after dark near the mouth of the River and encamped with the people at the cattle plain.

THURSDAY 21ST.
Left our encampment this morning at 2 AM. Arrived in the afternoon at Fort Vancouver.[12]

WEDNESDAY 1ST MARCH, 1843.
Left Vancouver, encamped at the entrance of Cowlitz River.

2D.
Slept below the Forks.

3D.
Above forks.

FRIDAY, 3RD, 4 & 5.
Cowlitz Farm[13]

MONDAY 6.
Cowlitz Farm

7TH.
Mountain Plain.

8
North end Grand Prairie, began to snow this evening.

THURSDAY 9TH.
Fort Nisqually – Snowed all day to the depth of 18 inches.

FRIDAY 10, SATURDAY 11, SUNDAY 12.
Fort Nisqually snow melting fast so that patches of the plains are bare.

MONDAY 13TH MARCH, 1843.
Left Nisqually at 10 AM and anchored at dusk a few miles south of Port Townsend.

TUESDAY 14TH.
Got under way in the morning, ran into Dungeness,[14] landed and saw the plain which is there. It contains probably 200 acres of land, the surface is rocky; large boulders of granite are seen piercing the surface here and there. It is on a high bank on the sea shore, at the foot of which runs a fresh water river. There is a large village of Clallamshere, and great quantities of salmon are taken in the autumn here. Skid or Ink fish. Skate – Buckis. The Indians have small gardens on the plains and grow very fine potatoes. Bought a few fish from the Indians, one kind are very like the herring or Pilchard. A little rain in the afternoon. Found ice upon the small lake behind the Fort, but no snow on the ground, which is not frozen. The grass is also shooting, being in one place nearly 4 inches long. The Indians say that there was at one time 18 inches of snow on the ground last winter, but it did not lie long having soon melted away. And there was more snow than usual, as some winters there [is] little or none.

WEDNESDAY 15TH MARCH.
Went out this morning with a boat and examined the wood of the north shore of the harbour;[15] it is not good, being generally short, crooked and almost unserviceable. On the south shore the wood is of a better quality and I think we will have no difficulty in getting enough for our purpose. Small wood for picketing is scarce, particularly cedar which answers better than any other kind for that purpose from its lightness and greater durability under ground. We will probably have to bring such as we require from a distance.

The Indians say that the Pilchard or herring arrives in April and are taken in great abundance along the coast and in this harbour.

The salmon ascends the straits[16] in August and are caught in great quantities. They continue to yield well until September when the great pass is over. They however take the bad salmon until November and an excellent salmon by trailing until the middle of Feb[ruar]y.

I am at a loss where to place the Fort, as there are two positions possessing advantages of nearly equal importance, though of different kinds. No 1. has a good view of the harbour, is upon clear ground, and only 50 yds from the beach; on the other hand, vessels drawing 14 feet cannot come within 130 feet of the shore. We will therefore either have to boat cargo off and on at a great destruction of boats, and considerable loss of time or be put to the expense of forming a jettie at a great amount of labour. No 2., on the other hand, will allow of vessels lying with their sides grazing the rocks, which form a natural wharf, whereon cargo may be conveniently landed from the ships yard, and in that respect would be exceedingly advantageous, but on the other hand, an intervening point intercepts the view so that the mouth of the Port cannot be seen from it, an objection of much weight in the case of vessels entering and leaving the Port. Another disadvantage is that the shore is there covered by thick woods to the breadth of 200 yards so that we must either place the Fort at that distance from the landing place, or clear away the thickets which would detain us very much in our building operations. I will think more on this subject before determining the point. The weather rather cloudy, but dry, and beautifully clear in the afternoon.

THURSDAY 16.
The weather clear and warm. The gooseberry bushes growing in the woods beginning to bud.

Put 6 men to dig a well and 6 others to square building timber. Spoke to the Samose[17] today and informed them of our intention of building in this place, which appeared to please them very much, and they immediately offered their services in procuring pickets for the establishment, an offer which I gladly accepted and promised to pay them a Blanket. (2½) for every forty pickets of 22 feet by 36 inches which they bring. I also lent them 3 large axes, 1 half sqre head Do[zen] and 10 half round head axes, to be returned hereafter, when they have finished the job.

Bought a few salmon today at 2 charges of ammunition each. At Cape Flattery they are bought for 2 leaves of tobacco each. Whole length of this fish 2 feet 7 inches including head & tail. Round the shoulders 1 ft. 6 in. Weight 12¾ lbs. Back dark, Belly white silvery, Teeth 18 lower jaw, 32 upper jaw. Indian name Quayt chin. 5 Men squared 1½ pce of 40 feet, & 1 pce of 32 feet today. 6 men digging the well.

Salmon	all winter	Quayt chin enter Camosack.
	June	Suk küy do not enter "
	"	Hun nún " " " "
	"	CKud-jucks enter Camosack in greatest numbers.
	"	Quaal ough enter " in greatest numbers.
Trout	"	Ta-unus Camosack River with weir and basket.
Pilchard	April	Fil-a-ong-at Enter Camosack[18]

FRIDAY 17TH.

Clear warm weather. Frost last night. The five squares finished ½ pcs of 40 feet and 1 of 32 feet. Saw a luminous streak in the heavens this evening, which lasted from dusk until 9 o'clock, when the moon rose and obscured it. Its highest altitude was at Betelguix[19] in Orion, due south from the position we occupied at the time of its appearance & extended from thence, in a continuous line to the south west point of the horizon forming an arc of about 90 degrees. At Betteguix its breadth was --- arcs ------ and it diminished gradually towards the south west horizon. We cannot account for this phenomenon, unless we may suppose that it is produced by the reflexion of the waters in the Straits of De Fuca, although it is difficult to account for its existence even on any such principle. It was also seen last night.

Six men digging the well.

SATURDAY 18TH.

Men employed as yesterday. The well is now about 11 feet deep. The luminous appearance still visible in the same position it occupied last night. It faded away about 11 o'clock.

Saturday 18	)	Fine weather. Luminous column still visible in
Sunday 19	)	its former position.[20]
Monday 20	)	
Tuesday 21	)	

[1843]

Notes

1. The Strait of Georgia.

2. Fathoms.

3. Cape Mudge on Quadra Island.

4. The Lekwiltok of the Kwakwaka'wakw Nation.

5. The Cowichans of the Hul'qumi'num Nation.

6. The Gulf of Georgia.

7. Whidbey Island.

8. Fort Nisqually, founded in 1833 by the Hudson's Bay Company, at the present-day site of DuPont, Washington.

9. A waterfall.

10. Puget Sound.

11. The Cowlitz River in south-western Washington state, a tributary of the Columbia River.

12. Before Victoria was established, Fort Vancouver was the Hudson's Bay Company's main depot in the region; it was on the Columbia River at the present-day site of Vancouver, Washington.

13. A Hudson's Bay Company trading post on the Cowlitz River, near present-day Vader, Washington.

14. On the Olympic Peninsula.

15. That is, the south-easternmost tip of Vancouver Island. Douglas has landed at the future site of Victoria.

16. The Strait of Juan de Fuca.

17. The Songhees Nation.

18. Douglas is creating an annual chart of the patterns of local salmon migration, phoneticizing the Straits Salish names of the fish. The Camosack River's name is derived from the word meaning "a rush of water."

19. Betelgeuse, a star in the constellation Orion.

20. This was "the Great Comet of 1843," visible throughout the Pacific Northwest.

Priscilla Stewart [dates unknown]

A Voice From the Oppressed to the Friends of Humanity

Composed by one of the suffering class.

Look and behold our sad despair
Our hopes and prospects fled,
The tyrant slavery entered here,
And laid us all for dead.

Sweet home! When shall we find a home?
If the tyrant says that we must go
The love of gain the reason,
And if humanity dare say "no"
Then they are tried for treason.

God bless the Queen's majesty,
Her sceptre and her throne,
She looked on us with sympathy,
And offered us a home.

Far better breathe Canadian air,
Where all are free and well,
Than live in slavery's atmosphere
And wear the chains of hell.

Farewell to our native land,
We must wave the parting hand,
Never to see thee any more,
But seek a foreign land.

Farewell to our true friends,
Who've suffered dungeon and death.
Who have a claim upon our gratitude
Whilst God shall lend us breath.

May God inspire your hearts,
A Marion raise your hands;
Never desert your principles
Until you've redeemed your land.

[1858]

Rebecca Gibbs [1808-1873]

Lines Written After the Great Fire at Barkerville, 16th September, 1868

Come ye many sufferers, and testify with me
How this village flourished, in the year of '63:
Although it did lack nothing, in the year of '64,
It then sustained a thousand, aye a thousand men or more.

Still years roll on until, it reaches sixty-eight,
And we are still together, and with you I share my fate;
We hear distressed mothers, and children in the street –
Inhabitants of Cariboo, why should we then not weep.

The Almighty architect, though wicked we have been,
Looked down and smiled upon us, when we commenced again;
We viewed this waste-laid village, with all her wealth and pride
As Sodom and Gomorrah, this cannot be denied.

Then we for the future, should choose the better part,
Our riches soon fly from us, though much it grieves the heart;
Far beyond there is a region, although we cannot see,
Where everlasting riches, are prepared for you and me.

[1868]

The Old Red Shirt

A miner came to my cabin door,
 His clothes they were covered with dirt;
He held out a piece he desired me to wash,
 Which I found was an old red shirt.

His cheeks were thin, and furrow'd his brow,
 His eyes they were sunk in his head;
He said that he had got work to do,
 And be able to earn his bread.

He said that the "old red shirt" was torn,
 And asked me to give it a stitch;
But it was threadbare, and sorely worn,
 Which show'd he was far from rich.

O! miners with good paying claims,
 O! traders who wish to do good,
Have pity on men who earn your wealth,
 Grudge not the poor miner his food.

Far from these mountains a poor mother mourns
 The darling that hung by her skirt,
When contentment and plenty surrounded the home
 Of the miner that brought me the shirt.

[1869]

Mifflin Wistar Gibbs [1823-1915]

from Shadow and Light: An Autobiography with Reminiscences of
the Last and Present Century

CHAPTER VIII

Early in the year 1858 gold was discovered on Fraser River, in the Hudson Bay
Company's territory in the Northwest. This territory a few months later was
organized as the Colony of British Columbia and absorbed; is now the western
outlook of the Dominion of Canada. The discovery caused an immense rush of
gold seekers, traders, and speculators from all parts of the world. In June of that
year, with a large invoice of miners' outfits, consisting of flour, bacon, blankets,
pick, shovels, etc., I took passage on steamship Republic for Victoria. The social
atmosphere on steamers whose patrons are chiefly gold seekers is unlike that on
its fellow, where many have jollity moderated by business cares, others reserved
in lofty consciousness that they are on foreign pleasure bent. With the gold seek-
er, especially the "tenderfoot," there is an incessant social hilarity, a communion
of feeling, an ardent anticipation that cannot be dormant, continually bubbling
over. We had on board upward of seven hundred, comprising a variety of tongues
and nations. The bustle and turmoil incident to getting off and being properly
domiciled; the confusion of tongues and peculiarity of temperament resembled
the Babel of old. Here the mercurial Son of France in search of a case of red wine,
hot and impulsive, belching forth "sacres" with a velocity well sustained. The
phlegmatic German stirred to excitability in quest of a "small cask of lager and
large box of cheese;" John Chinaman "Hi ya'd" for one "bag lice all samee hab one
Melican man," while a chivalric but seedy-looking Southerner, who seemed to
have "seen better days," wished he "might be – if he didn't lay a pe-yor of boots
thar whar that blanket whar." Not to be lost in the shuffle was a tall canting spec-
imen of Yankeedom perched on a water cask that "reckoned ther is right smart
chance of folks on this 'ere ship," and "kalkerlate that that boat swinging thar war
a good place to stow my fixin's in." The next day thorough system and efficiency
was brought out of chaos and good humor prevailed.

Victoria, then the capital of British Columbia, is situated on the southern
point of Vancouver's Island. On account of the salubrity of its climate and proximity to the spacious land-locked harbor of Esquimalt it is delightful as a place of

residence and well adapted to great mercantile and industrial possibilities. It was the headquarters of the Hudson Bay Company, a very old, wealthy, and influential English trading company. Outside the company's fort, enclosing immense storehouses, there were but few houses. The nucleus of a town in the shape of a few blocks laid out, and chiefly on paper maps, was most that gave promise of the populous city of Victoria of the present. On my arrival my goods were sold at great advance on cost, an order for more sent by returning steamer. I had learned prior to starting that city lots could be bought for one hundred dollars each, and had come prepared to buy two or three at that price. A few days before my arrival what the authorities had designated as the "land office" had been subjected to a "Yankee rush," which had not only taken, and paid for all the lots mapped out, but came near appropriating books, benches, and window sashes; hence the office had to close down and haul off for repairs, and surveyed lots, and would not be open for business for ten days. Meanwhile those that were in at the first sale were still in, having real estate matters their own way. Steamers and sailing craft were constantly arriving, discharging their human freight, that needed food, houses, and outfits for the mines, giving an impetus to property of all kinds that was amazing for its rapidity. The next afternoon after the day of my arrival I had signed an agreement and paid one hundred dollars on account for a lot and one-story house for $3,000 − $1,400 more in fifteen days, and the balance in six months. Upon the arrival of my goods ten days later I paid the second installment and took possession. Well, how came I to take a responsibility so far beyond my first intended investment? Just here I rise to remark: For effective purposes one must not be unduly sensitive or overmodest in writing autobiography – for, being the events and memoirs of his life, written by himself, the ever-present pronoun "I" dances in such lively attendance and in such profusion on the pages that whatever pride he may have in the events they chronicle is somewhat abashed at its repetition.

Addison truly says: "There is no passion which steals into the heart more imperceptible and covers itself under more disguises than pride." Still, if in such memoirs there be found landmarks or precept or example that will smooth the ruggedness of Youth's pathway, the success of its mission should disarm invidious criticism. For the merit of history or biography is not alone the events they chronicle, but the value of the thought they inspire. Previous to purchasing the property I had calculated the costs of alteration and estimated the income. In twenty days, after an expenditure of $200 for improvements, I found myself receiving a rental of $500 per month from the property, besides a store for the firm. Anyone without mechanical knowledge with time and opportunity to seek information from others may have done the same, but in this case there was neither time nor opportunity; it required quick perception and prompt action. The trade my mother insisted I should learn enabled me to do this. Get a trade, boys, if you have to live on bread and apples while attaining it. It is a good foundation to build higher. Don't crowd the waiters. If they are content, give them a chance. We received a warm welcome from the Governor[1] and other officials of the colony, which was cheering. We had no complaint as to business patronage in the State of California, but there was ever present that spectre of oath denial and disenfranchisement; the disheartening consciousness that while our existence was tolerated, we were powerless to appeal to law for the protection of life or property when assailed. British Columbia offered and gave protection to both, and equality of political privileges. I cannot describe with what joy we hailed the opportunity to enjoy that liberty under the "British Lion" denied us beneath the pinions of the American Eagle. Three or four hundred colored men from California and other States, with their families, settled in Victoria, drawn thither by the two-fold inducement – gold discovery and the assurance of enjoying impartially the benefits of constitutional liberty. They built or bought homes and other property, and by industry and character vastly improved their condition and were the recipients of respect and esteem from the community.

An important step in a man's life is his marriage. It being the merging of dual lives, it is only by mutual self-abnegation that it can be made a source of contentment and happiness. In 1859, in consummation of promise and purpose, I returned to the United States and was married to Miss Maria A. Alexander, of Kentucky, educated at Oberlin College, Ohio. After visits to friends in Buffalo and my friend Frederick Douglass at Rochester, N.Y., thence to Philadelphia and New York City, where we took steamship for our long journey of 4,000 miles to our intended home at Victoria, Vancouver Island. I have had a model wife in all that the term implies, and she has had a husband migratory and uncertain. We have been blessed with five children, four of whom are living – Donald F., Horace E., Ida A., and Hattie Gibbs; Donald a machinist, Horace a printer by trade. Ida graduated as an A.B. from Oberlin College and is now a teacher of English in the High School at Washington, D.C.; Hattie a graduate from the Conservatory of Music at Oberlin, Ohio, and was professor of music at the Eckstein-Norton University at Cave Springs, Ky., and now musical director of public schools of Washington, D.C. [. . .]

CHAPTER IX

Among the estimable friendships I made on the Pacific Coast forty years ago was Philip A. Bell, formerly of New York City, one of nature's noblemen, broad in his humanity and intellectually great as a journalist. As editor of The Elevator, a weekly newspaper still published in San Francisco, he made its pages brilliant with scintillations of elegance, wealth of learning, and vigor of advocacy. To his request for a correspondent I responded in a series of letters. I forbear to insert them here, as they describe the material and political status of British Columbia thirty-five years ago – being well aware that ancient history is not the most entertaining. But, as I read them I cannot but note, in the jollity of their introduction, the immature criticism, consciousness of human fallibility, broadening of conclusions, mellowed by hope for the future that seemed typical of a life career. Like the horse in "Sheridan's Ride,"[2] their beginning "was gay, with Sheridan fifty miles away;" but if they were helpful with a truth-axiom or a moiety of inspiration – as a view of colonial conduct of a nation, with which we were then and are now growing in affinity – the purpose was attained.

At first the affairs of British Columbia and Vancouver were administered by one Governor, the connection was but nominal; Vancouver Island had control by a representative Parliament of its own; the future seemed auspicious. Later they, feeling it "in fra dig" to divide the prestige of government, severed the connection. But Vancouver finding it a rather expensive luxury, and that the separation engendered strife and rivalry, terminating in hostile legislation, determined to permanently unite with British Columbia.

But alas, for political happiness. Many afterward sighed for former times, when Vancouver Island, proud beauty of the North, sat laving her feet in the genial waters of the Pacific, her lap verdant with beautiful foliage and delicious fruits; her head raised with peerless majesty to brilliant skies, while sunbeams playing upon a brow encircled by eternal snows reflected a sheen of glorious splendor; when, conscious of her immense wealth in coal, minerals, and fisheries, her delightful climate and geographical supremacy. It is said of States, as of women, they are "fickle, coy and hard to please." For, changed and governed from England's Downing Street, "with all its red tape and circumlocution," "Tile [Barnacle]," incapacity, and "how-not-to-do-it" ability that attached to that venerable institution, its people were sorely perplexed.

During the discussion which the nature and inefficiency of the Government evoked several modes of relief from these embarrassments were warmly espoused, among them none more prominent than annexation to the United States. It was urged with much force that the great want of the country, immigration and responsible government, would find their fulfillment in such an alliance. All that seemed wanted was the "hour and the man." The man was considered present in Leonard McClure, editor of a local, and afterward on the editorial staff of the San Francisco Times. He was a man of rare ability, a terse writer, and with a force of logic labored assiduously to promote annexation. But the "hour" was "non est." For while it was quite popular and freely discussed upon the forum and street, influential classes declined to commit themselves to the scheme, the primary step necessary before presentation to the respective Governments. Among the opposition to annexation, naturally, were the official classes. These gentry being in no way responsible to the people, an element ever of influence, and believing that by such an alliance they would find their "occupation gone," gave it no quarter. Added to these was another possessed of the prestige and power that wealth confers – very conservative, timid, cautious, self-satisfied, and dreading innovations of popular rule, but especially republicanism. Amid these two classes, and sprinkled among the rank and file, was found a sentiment extremely patriotic, with those who saw nothing worth living for outside of the purview of the "tight little island."[3]

There seems a destiny in the propriety of territory changing dominion. God seems to have given this beautiful earth, with its lands, to be utilized and a source of blessing, not to be locked by the promptings of avarice nor the clog of incapacity; that it should be occupied by those who, either by the accident of locality or superior ability, can make it the most efficient in development. There should be, and usually is, regard for acquired rights, save in the case of Africans, Indians, or other weak peoples, when cupidity and power hold sweet converse. Nor should we slightly estimate the feeling of loyalty to the land of birth and the hearths of our fathers, the impulse that nerves the arm to strike, and the soul to dare; that brings to our country's altar all that we have of life to repel the invader of our homes or the usurper of our liberties. That has given to the world a Washington, a Toussaint, a Bozzaris – a loyalty that will ever stand with cloven helmet and crimson battle-ax in the van of civilization and progress. But, like other ennobling sentiments, it can be perverted, allowing it to permeate every view of government, finding its ultimatum in the conclusion that, if government is despotic or inefficient, it is to be endured and not removed. Such patriots are impressed with the conviction that the people were made for governments, and not governments for the people. A celebrated poet has said –

> "Our country's claim is fealty,
> I grant you so; but then
> Before man made us citizens
> Great Nature made us men."[4]

Men with essential wonts and laudable aspirations, the attainment of which can be accelerated by the fostering love and enlightened zeal of a progressive government.

In 1859 at Esquimalt, the naval station for British Columbia, I had a pleasant meeting with Lady Franklin, widow of Sir John Franklin, the Arctic explorer, who sailed in 1845 and was supposed to have perished in 1847. With a woman's devotion, after many years of absence, she was still in quest, hoping, from ship officer or seaman of her Majesty's service, some ray of light would yet penetrate the gloom which surrounded his "taking off" in that terra incognito of the North pole, whose attraction for the adventurer in search of scientific and geographical data in the mental world is akin to its magnetic attraction in the physical. To her no tidings came, but still lingered "hope, the balm and life-blood of the soul."

In 1868 the union of British Columbia with the Dominion of Canada was the political issue, absorbing all others. But the allurements of its grandeur and the magnitude of promised results were insufficient to allay opposition, ever encountered on proposal to change a constitutional polity by those at the time enjoying official honors or those who benefit through contracts or trade, and are emphatic in their protest; these, however, constitute an element that is unwittingly the safety valve of constitutional government. Wherever the people rule the public welfare is ever endangered whenever radical changes are to be introduced, unaccompanied with a vigorous opposition. A healthy opposition is the winnowing fan that separates the politician's chaff from the patriot's wheat, presenting the most desirable of the substantial element needed. At the convention in 1868 at Fort Yale, called by A. Decosmos,[5] editor of The British Colonist, and others, for the purpose of getting an expression of the people of British Columbia regarding union with the Dominion of Canada (and of which the writer was a delegate), the reduction of liabilities, the lessening of taxation, increase of revenue, restriction of expenditure, and the enlargement of the people's liberties were the goal, all of which have been attained since entrance to the Dominion, which has become a bright jewel in his Majesty's Crown, reflecting a civilization, liberal and progressive, of a loyal, happy people.

The "British America Act," which created the Dominion of Canada, differs from the Constitution of the United States in important particulars. It grants to the Dominional, as well as the provincial Legislatures the "want of confidence principle," by which an objectionable ministry can be immediately removed; at the same time centralizing the national authority as a guard against the heresy of "State rights" superiority. Among the terms stipulated, the Dominion was to assume the colonial debt of British Columbia, amounting to over two million dollars; the building of a road from the Atlantic to the Pacific within a stipulated time. The alliance, however, contained more advantage than the ephemeral assistance of making a road or the assumption of a debt, for with confederation came the abolition of the "one-man system of government" and in its place a responsible one, with freedom of action for enterprise, legislation to encourage development, and assist budding industries; the permanent establishment of schools, and the disbursement of revenue in accordance with popular will.

It is ever and ever true that "right is of no sex, and truth of no color."[6] The liberal ideas, ever struggling for utterance and ascendancy under every form of government, are not the exclusive property of any community or nation, but the heritage of mankind, and their victories are ever inspiring. For, as the traveler sometimes ascends the hill to determine his bearings, refresh his vision, and invigorate himself for greater endeavors, so we, by sometimes looking beyond the sphere of our own local activities, obtain higher views of the breadth and magnitude of the principles we cherish, and perceive that freedom's battle is identical wherever waged, whether her sons fight to abolish the relics of feudalism or to possess the ballot, the reflex influence of their example is mutually beneficial.

But of the Dominion of Canada, who shall write its "rise, decline, and fall"? Springing into existence in a day, with a population of 4,000,000 people – a number larger than that possessed by the United States when they commenced their great career – its promise is pregnant with benign probabilities. May it be the fruition of hope that the banner of the Dominion and the flag of our Republic, locked and interlocked, may go forward in generous rivalry to bless mankind.

The most rapid instrumentalities in the development of a new country are the finding and prospecting for mineral deposits. The discovery of large deposits of gold in the quartz and alluvial area of British Columbia in 1858 was the incipiency of the growth and prosperity it now enjoys. But although the search for the precious is alluring, the mining of the grosser metals and minerals, such as iron, lead, coal, and others, are much more reliable for substantial results.

The only mine of importance in British Columbia previous to 1867 was at Nanaimo, where there was a large output of bituminous coal. In that year anthracite was discovered by Indians building fire on a broken vein that ran from Mt Seymour, on Queen Charlotte Island, in the North Pacific. It was a high grade of coal, and on account of its density and burning without flame, was the most valuable for smelting and domestic purposes. A company had been formed at Victoria which had spent $60,000 prospecting for an enduring and paying vein, and thereafter prepared for development by advertising for tenders to build railroad and wharfs for shipping. Being a large shareholder in the company, I resigned as a director and bid. It was not the lowest, but I was awarded the contract. The Hudson Bay Co. steamship Otter, having been chartered January, 1869, with fifty men, comprising surveyor, carpenters, blacksmiths, and laborers, with timber, rails, provisions, and other necessaries for the work I embarked at Victoria. Queen Charlotte Island was at that time almost a "terra incognito," sparsely inhabited solely by scattered tribes of Indians on the coast lines, which were only occasionally visited by her Majesty's ships for discovery and capture of small craft engaged in the whiskey trade.

Passing through the Straits of Georgia, stopping at Fort Simpson, and then to Queen Charlotte Island, entering the mouth of Skidegate River, a few miles up, we reached the company's quarters, consisting of several wooden buildings for residence, stores, shops, etc. At the mouth and along the river were several Indian settlements, comprising huts, the sides of which were of rough riven planks, with roof of leaves of a tough, fibrous nature. At the crest was an opening for the escape of smoke from fires built on the ground in the center of the enclosure. As the ship passed slowly up the river we were hailed by the shouting of the Indians, who ran to the river side, got into their canoes and followed in great numbers until we anchored. They then swarmed around and over the ship, saluting the ship's company as "King George's men," for such the English are known and called by them. They were peaceful and docile, lending ready hands to our landing and afterward to the cargo. I was surprised, while standing on the ship, to hear my name called by an Indian in a canoe at the side, coupled with encomiums of the native variety, quite flattering. It proved to be one who had been a domestic in my family at Victoria. He gave me kind welcome, not to be ignored, remembering that I was in "the enemy's country," so to speak. Besides, such a reception was so much more desirable, as I was depending upon native labor for excavating and transportation of heavy material along the line of the road. While their work was not despatched with celerity of trained labor, still, as is general with labor, they earned all they got. "One touch of nature makes the whole world kin."[7] I found many apt, some stupid; honesty and dishonesty in usual quantities, with craft peculiar to savage life.

Their mode of stealing by stages was peculiar. The thing coveted was first hid nearby; if no inquiry was made for a period deemed sufficiently long the change of ownership became complete and its removal to their own hut followed, to be disposed of when opportunity offered. If you had a particle of evidence and made a positive accusation, with the threat of "King George's man-of-war," it was likely to be forthcoming by being placed secretly nearby its proper place. But through it we see the oneness of human frailty, whether in the watered stock of the corporation or that of its humble servitor the milkman, there is kinship. To get something for nothing is the "ignis fatuus" ever in the lead. My experience during a year's stay on the island, and constant intercourse with the natives, impressed me more and more with the conviction that we are all mainly the creatures of environments; yet through all the strata and fiber of human nature there is a chord that beats responsive to kindness – a "language that the dumb can speak, and that the deaf can understand."

The English mode of dealing with semi-civilized dependents is vastly different from ours. While vigorously administering the law for proper government, protection of life, and suppression of debauchery by unscrupulous traders, they inspired respect for the laws and the love of their patrons. Uprisings and massacres among Indians in her Majesty's dominions are seldom, if ever, to be chronicled. Many of our Indian wars will remain a blot on the page of impartial history, superinduced, as they were, by wanton murder or the covet of lands held by them by sacred treaties, which should have been as sacredly inviolate. Followed by decimation of tribes by toleration of the whiskey trade and the conveyance of loathsome disease. The climate of the island was much more pleasant than expected. The warm ocean currents on the Pacific temper the atmosphere, rendering it more genial than the same degree of latitude on the Atlantic. A few inches of snow, a thin coat of ice on the river, were the usual attendants of winter. But more frequently our camp was overhung by heavy clouds, broken by Mt Seymour, precipitating much rain.

After being domiciled we proceeded with the resident superintendent to view the company's property, comprising several thousand acres. Rising in altitude, and on different levels, as we approached Mt Seymour, croppings of coal were quite frequent, the broken and scattered veins evidencing volcanic disturbance. The vein most promising was several hundred feet above the level of the sea, and our intended wharf survey was made, which showed heavy cuttings and blasting to obtain grade for the road. The work was pushed with all the vigor the isolated locality and climatic conditions allowed. Rain almost incessant was a great impediment, as well as were the occasional strikes of the Indian labor, which was never for more wages, but for more time. The coal from the croppings which had been at first obtained for testing, had been carried by them in bags, giving them in the "coin of the realm" so many pieces of tobacco for each bag delivered on the ship. There was plenty of time lying around on those trips, and they took it. On the advent of the new era they complained that "King George men" took all the time and gave them none, so they frequently quit to go in quest. The nativity of my skilled labor was a piece of national patchwork – a composite of the canny Scotch, the persistent and witty Irish, the conservative but indomitable English, the effervescent French, the phlegmatic German, and the irascible Italian. I found this variety beneficial, for the usual national and race bias was sufficiently in evidence to preclude a combination to retard the work. I had three Americans, that were neither white nor colored; they were born black; one of them – Tambry, the cook – will ever have my grateful remembrance for his fatherly kindness and attention during an illness.

The conditions there were such that threw many of my men off their feet. Women and liquor had much the "right of way." I was more than ever impressed with the belief that there was nothing so conclusive to a worthy manhood as self-restraint, both morally and physically, and the more vicious and unrestraining the environment the greater the achievement. Miners had been at work placing many tons of coal at the mouth of the mine during the making of the road, the grade of which was of two elevations, one from the mine a third of the distance, terminating at a chute, from which the coal fell to cars on the lower level, and from thence to the wharf. After the completion of the road and its acceptance by the superintendent and the storage of a cargo of coal on the wharf, the steamer Otter arrived, was loaded, and despatched to San Francisco, being the first cargo of anthracite coal ever unearthed on the Pacific seaboard. The superintendent, having notified the directors at Victoria of his intention to return they had appointed me to assume the office. I was so engaged, preparing for the next shipment on the steamer.

Chapter x

My sojourn on the island was not without its vicissitudes and dangers, and one of the latter I shall ever remember – one mingled, as it was, with antics of Neptune, that capricious god of the ocean, and resignation to what seemed to promise my end with all sublime things. The stock of oil brought for lubricating cars and machinery having been exhausted, I started a beautiful morning in a canoe with three Indians for their settlement at the mouth of Skidegate River for a temporary supply. After a few hours' paddling, gliding down the river serenely, the wind suddenly arose, increasing in force as we approached the mouth in the gulf. The high walls of the river sides afforded no opportunity to land. The storm continued to increase in violence, bringing billows of rough sea from the ocean, our canoe dancing like a feather, one moment on a high crest by its skyward leap, and in the next to an abyss deep, with walls of sea on either side, shutting out a view of the horizon, while I, breathless with anxious hope, waited for the succeeding wave to again lift the frail bark. The better to preserve the equilibrium of the canoe – a conveyance treacherous at the best – wrapped in a blanket in the bottom of the canoe I laid, looking into the faces of the Indians, contorted by fright, and listened to their peculiar and mournful death wail, "while the gale whistled aloft his tempest tune." [8]

I afterward learned that they had a superstition based upon the loss of many of their tribe under like conditions, that escape was impossible. The alarm and distrust in men, aquatic from birth, in their own waters was to me appalling. I seemed to have "looked death in the face" – and what a rush of recollections that had been long forgotten, of actions good and bad, the latter seeming the most, hurried, serried, but distinct through my excited brain; then a thought, bringing a calm content, that "To every man upon this earth death cometh soon or late;" [9] and with a fervent resignation of myself to God and to what I believed to be inevitable; then a lull in the wind, and, after many attempts, we were able to cross the mouth of the river to the other side – the place of destination.

In 1869 I left Queen Charlotte Island and returned to Victoria; settled my business preparatory to joining my family, then at Oberlin, Ohio. It was not without a measure of regret that I anticipated my departure. There I had lived more than a decade; where the geniality of the climate was excelled only by the graciousness of the people; there unreservedly the fraternal grasp of brotherhood; there I had received social and political recognition; there my domestic ties had been intensified by the birth of my children, a warp and woof of consciousness that time cannot obliterate. Then regret modified, as love of home and country asserted itself.

> "Breathes there a man with soul so dead
> Who never to himself hath said:
>   'This is my native land' –
> Whose heart has not within him burned
> As homeward footsteps he has turned
> From wandering on a foreign strand?" [10]

En route my feelings were peculiar. A decade had passed, fraught with momentous results in the history of the nation. I had left California disfranchised and my oath denied in a "court of justice" (?); left my country to all appearances enveloped in a moral gloom so dense as to shut out the light of promise for a better civil and political status. The star of hope glimmered but feebly above the horizon of contumely and oppression, prophetic of the destruction of slavery and the enfranchisement of the freedman. I was returning, and on touch of my country's soil to have a new baptism through the all-pervading genius of universal liberty. I had left politically ignoble; I was returning panoplied with the nobility of an American citizen. Hitherto regarded as a pariah, I had neither rejoiced at its achievement nor sorrowed for its adversity; now every patriotic pulse beat quicker and heart throb warmer, on realization that my country gave constitutional guarantee for the common enjoyment of political and civil liberty, equality before the law – inspiring a dignity of manhood, of self-reliance and opportunity for elevation hitherto unknown.

Then doubt, alternating, would present the immense problems awaiting popular solution. Born in the seething cauldron of civil war, they had been met in the arena of fervid Congressional debate and political conflict. The amendments to the Constitution had been passed, but was their inscription a record of the crystallization of public sentiment? Subsequent events have fully shown that only to the magnanimity and justice of the American people and the fruition of time can they be commended. Not to believe that these problems will be rightfully solved is to doubt not only the efficacy of the basic principles of our Government, but the divinity of truth and justice. To these rounds of hope's ladder, while eager in obtaining wisdom, the Negro should cling with tenacity, with faith "a higher faculty than reason" unconquerable.

[1902]

NOTES

1. James Douglas.

2. A poem by Thomas Buchanan Read.

3. Britain.

4. James Russell Lowell, "On the Capture of Fugitive Slaves near Washington."

5. Amor De Cosmos, the second premier of British Columbia.

6. Frederick Douglass.

7. Shakespeare, *Troilus and Cressida* 3.3.

8. A paraphrase of a line from Barry Cornwall's poem "The Sea."

9. Thomas B. Macaulay, "Lays of Ancient Rome."

10. A nearly accurate quotation from Sir Walter Scott's "My Native Land."

Isaac Dickson [dates unknown]

letters to The Cariboo Sentinel

SHAMPOOIN 'STABLISHMEN,[1]
BARKERVILLE, JUNE 10TH '65.

TO DE EDITER OF DE 'CARIBOO SENTAL.'

It gibs me much pleasure indee to see genelman ob your cloth on Wiliams Crek[2] dis air season, an' hope, sar, de indefatable entarprice an' de talen I sees 'splayed in de columbs ob yer valable jernal will meet wid its juss rewad, dat is, dat de paper will pay big; for 'low me to tell yer, mister editer, its de dimes we's all arter in dis counry, de boys dey says "its every man for hisself an' de debil for us all" in dis air counry, but I hope, sar, de debil wont get you or de paper eider; but take de culed fren's adwice 'bout looking arter No. 1.

I bleave, sar, I wont be disapointed in hopin yer a goin to stick up for wats rite an' on de squarr, an' gib eberything an' eberybody a rap on de knuckles dats wrong an' not on de squarr; dont be scared, mister editer, to talk up to de boys, dey like it all de better for dat, juss like wat I sees in de 'Spatch' bout a young genelman dat walops him wife till she sing 'murder' an' runs 'way, nex day write him lobing 'pistle, 'claring she neber will be happy agin till 'longside ob her own dear Charley.

I dont dout, sar, de paper will 'tain heap dat's headifying and instructin to de miners ob dis country but dont flatter yerself, mister editer, dat de teaching will be all on your side ob de kitchin, an 'emneting from yer own valable resaucers 'tirely, coss if yer does yer slip up on dat air 'rangment you got darn sight to larn from de poplation ob dis garden of 'Lestials,[3] Injuns, white men and culed genelmen an darn sight to see dat'll sprise an' muse yer. Dere's de breed ob dogs dat habits dese regons, dey's a curosity dey is demselves; nobody in dis worl eber seed sich a lot ob carnines togeder, or eber heerd sich a noise as dey makes; dey's de bery 'centrated ensense ob bliss dey is 'specially when dere's a muss 'mong 'dem, dey seems to lib on musses, yet dey propgates offal fas. Arter de dogs dere's de udder animal dat puzzles me 'markable, de genelman dat goes round all de day wid de hans in de pocket an' puts on de frills, dont know how him lib on BOOKS, on DECK,[4] if dats de case him awful vegtarian, an' grate charity of Capin Cox[5] to change him diet, an' sen him below. Dere's de style of pugilistickism in dis counry, bery heady-fyin an' 'musin; if eber you get in a muss, mister editer, neber tink to get out ob it on de squarr, if yer do yer gon in shure, pick up trifle like de axe, crowbar, or anyt-ing ob dat sort dat's not too hard, dat's de style, if dere's noting ob dat kine round de boot berry good substute, or shub de tum into de corner ob his eye, and be sure de eye cums out 'fore de tum, den when its out kick it in 'gain wid de boot, dat de style Maris. Dere's de new 'scobery in de surgical 'fession dat oughter gain worl wide 'nown for de 'scoberer an' also de leder medal ob de inhumane sciety, de genelman dat vented de "gum boot gout," sar is wastin de valable time in Cariboo, 'fessin what he oughter be larnin in some counery more 'dapted for de study ob de biz; de 'spectable youth oughter "trow fisick to de dogs,"[6] or quit for sum place where he cud larn someting ob de 'fession. Dere's de Dush[7] gals, dey's purty smart gals, mister editer, to hold dere own in dis counry, poor gals, I hope dey may continy to do so; de stokeepers is offul down on 'em, coss dey krell all de dimes, bully for de gals, dey's on it, you bet, on de make I means, sar; de sloon keepers, dere offul down on de gals too, coss dey draw de boys, and draw de dol-lars; but de sloon keepers oughter know dat de dance galls aluss took better dan anyting else in Californey, de meenus man will spen a dollar for a dance, coss "him dearly lubs de lasses, O."[8] I hear de boys say dere's to be a 'lection at de Mouth[9] soon, I hope, sar, yer goin to put de bes man in, de culed genelmen de best, but as de 'jority ob de boys is not culed genelmen, best for de country's good to put in de white man, assiss de subjecs, mister editer, ob dis loyel counry to get good resprentives. Hopin dese few 'marks will fine yer well, an' rum for 'sertion in yer valable columbs,

I am yours in bruderly 'fliciton,

DIXIE

P.S. I'd most forgot to add, on behaf ob de 'tilligent culed population on dis crek, days 'pointed me de litary cracker to sen 'butions to yer valable jernel.

[1865]

Barkerville, June 24th, 1865.

TO DE EDITER OB DE CARIBOO SENTAL.

I's bery sorry indee, sar, dat any ob de contens ob my last 'pistle shud hab hurt de feelings ob any genelmen whatsever, or gib him 'noyance, an' humly ax pardon for de 'fence; but yer knows yerself, sar, its impossable for publick carack- ers like us to keep rite an' up wid eberybody, in fac we doesn't 'temp anyting ob de kine, we says wat we tink good for de boys an' if dey gets dere back up at wat we gibs for adbice we's bery sorry, dey oughter know dat de 'Sental' is alus 'spect- ed to do him dooty, dat is keep his weder eye open, and let dem know dat wishes to shirk his obseration dat him got weder eye, an' dat it is alus open; shud de 'Sental' make mistake him alus willin' to 'polergise an' if I bluner in my las an' genelman's 'feshnal stanin' is raily exaled 'bove any adbice I offer, why ob cuss I 'polergises for my inserlance.

I don't tink Mr Editer, dere is a more motly kermoonity in de worl dan dat ob Cariboo, war so mush ob de genwine dust and black san' is 'malgamated an' passes at de same rate ob curncy, yet in dis same little kermoonity war equality is alus sposed to lay on de same rok, an' war no uppa streek effises, deres some foo bright specimens dat tinks deys from de uppa streek, an' dat de sack in which deys 'posited 'tains noting but black san', ob coss alus exceptin' derselves, dey knows eberyting an' is smarter dan de balance. It's to some ob dese bright specimens I's 'bout to say a foo words, an' if de cap I's 'bout to 'facter fits any ob de boys, de bes ting dey can do is to ware it widout saying a word, and den praps nobody but der- selves an' dere culed fren' will be any de wiser; at de same time I kermends to dere notis de follerin' words:

> "O, wad sum power de gify gib us,
> To see us-selbes as udders see us."[10]

De fus ob dese wiseakers is in de spirtooal line, and oughter be "patching up his owl soul for heben," I mean he 'tend to de spirtooal wants ob dose dat 'dulges in tan- gle-leg and rot-gut at two bits de drink, an' neber open him out widout saying someting bery wity – wat him tinks wity, but eberybody else bery dirty. I hab herd ob genelmen being kermended to war a mustash for de durty words to wipe dere feat on, but neber herd one dat 'quired one more dan him I's speakin on, an' tho' it's in my line ob bis – its rader a delercat order to slisit – but I wud cerenly like to sply de gent wid a gud stout article ob de kine. But dis genelman, like eberybody else, hab him good qualtys, an' deserbes de tanks ob de leddies for his volunery an' gratutus saveses as night watchman durin pas winter; no 'voted luber eber suffed more from cowl wile singeing undar winer ob his gal's chamer dan dis venable owl cuss las winter wile watchin like a teef for de hoptunity to pilfa de fair name ob 'specable women.

De nex foo 'marks I 'tends to 'dress to a son ob old Mars, but weder a 'gitimate son or not is for dem to juge dats herd him yarn ob "akshun in de tented fiel." I hab red shakspuses yarn ob de culed genelman ob Veners dat was tried for 'lopeing wid de owl genelman's darter, an' when 'fore his noble massas towl a 'fecting story 'bout 'listing for de army when him only seben year owl,[11] but de hero ob my yarn licks dat ob Shakspuses all to fits for he mus hab undegon a pile ob grief from triles by coatmashal, wonce for useuping de comman' of a 'tashment ob de army 'fore 'Bastapool[12] an' puscribing doses to de Rooshans dat 'listed materily in de fall ob dat fortess an' for which owl Nick, de late Emprer,[13] has long 'count gin him shud day eber meet on de uder side ob Jordan; as a fren' I adbise my hero not to ware his medals when he croses de stream for fear de owl genelman shud spot him.

I had considable more to say, Mr Editer, but on secon' toat will not trude more on yer valable spas at presen, an' specfully begs to 'scribe myself, yoars,

DIXIE

P.S. Exkuse me, sar, but I want to ax you solbe a problem for me. If de tax ob only two hundred dollas de month is lebied on de hard-gudies, as perposed by a loyal member ob de Gran' Jury, what shud be de tax on some uder institootions.

[1865]

Notes

1. Dickson was a barber.

2. After the discovery of gold there in 1861, a string of mining towns, including Barkerville, were established along Williams Creek.

3. Celestials: archaic term for Chinese, deriving from "Celestial Dynasty" or an empire ruled by a heaven-appointed dynasty.

4. Dickson is referring to the professional gamblers of Barkerville.

5. Judge Cox, one of a few judges located in the Cariboo at the time.

6. Shakespeare, *Macbeth* 5.3.

7. See Sylvia Van Kirk, "A Vital Presence: Women in the Cariboo Gold Rush, 1862-1875," in G. Creese and V. Strong-Boag, eds., *British Columbia Reconsidered: Essays on Women* (Vancouver: Press Gang, 1992). Van Kirk points out that the women of the Cariboo dance halls – called "hurdy-gurdy girls" or "hurdies" – had first come to San Francisco for the 1849 gold rush, and had moved on to Barkerville when gold was found there in the 1861. Van Kirk writes, "Originally of German origin, these women were imported into California under a kind of indenture to provide dancing partners for the miners who thronged the saloons" (29). When Dickson calls them "Dush gals" he probably means "Deutsch."

8. From "Green Grow the Rashes, O" by Robert Burns: "The wisest man the world e'er saw, / He dearly lo'ed the lasses, O!"

9. The mouth of the Fraser River.

10. Compare to Robert Burns' poem "To a Louse" (1786): "O wad some Pow'r the giftie gie us / To see oursels as others see us!"

11. Shakespeare's *Othello*; the paraphrase of "action in the tented field" is from 1.3.

12. The siege of Sebastopol, the main battle of the Crimean War (1854-1856).

13. Czar Nicholas I of Russia (1796-1855).

William H. H. Johnson [1839-1905]

from The Life of Wm. H.H. Johnson, from 1839-1900,
and the New Race

CHAPTER XI

The Northern Light, which was the fastest boat running on the upper lakes at that time, called at only two points on the way down and as usual with the Lake Superior boats, did not delay very long at these, having a full cargo before she sailed. At Cleveland the crew had the usual three days rest while the cargo was being discharged, and during that time it was a source of great pleasure to me to go about the beautiful city and gaze at the magnificent buildings and beautiful drives and splendid parks. But the greatest pleasure of all was to be on those beautiful lakes when the weather was calm. There was something very fascinating and indescribable about it all which never failed to hold an influence over me and a charm that never seemed to fade. In my leisure moments I would go up on the hurricane deck to view the beautiful panorama as we passed: the little emerald islands, the hundreds of little pleasure boats dashing to and fro, the mighty hills covered with their mantle of sombre forest and all that wonderful picture which makes the Great Lakes country a place to be cherished and loved. On this natural beauty spot I would gaze with great pleasure, because I knew that it was God's handiwork, but I did not transmit my thoughts to my companions because I knew that their minds were wandering far from the beauties of sublime nature to something far different. Their leisure hours were spent for the most part in card playing, which seemed to be the main ambition in life with them.

So it happened one beautiful evening as I was sitting on the deck in the moonlight one of the passengers of the Northern Light came up the companion-way and sat down by my side. He was silent, with but a slight bow for me, which I politely recognized by touching my hat. I could see at a glance that he was a gentleman and a white one, and I thought it strange that he should choose to come up there and sit beside me with the ship full of passengers who at least affected greater culture and intelligence. So I sat silent waiting for him to commence any conversation. Finally he spoke, asking me how long I had been on the Northern Light, and when I told him he said he had often wanted to speak to me but had not had any opportunity to do so before. In answer to his next question, I told him that my permanent home was at Windsor, Ontario. He then asked me what I followed at Windsor, and I told him that I had no particular calling, that I was just a common laborer. Then the gentleman asked me was I ever a slave, and I told him not in fealty, although I was born a slave in a so-called free state, and continuing, gave him a brief sketch of my life and earlier experiences. The gentleman seemed very much interested, and was thoroughly conversant with the Fugitive Slave Law, by which this seeming paradox was possible.[1] We had a long and animated conversation, in which I told him that my grandfather had been a king in Africa. He asked me how I knew this, and I told him that it was really only by tradition, having heard my father tell how his father had been kidnapped and sold into slavery in the state of Virginia. He asked: "Did you remember your grandfather then?" I told him that I had only an indefinite recollection, as I was only four years old at the time that he died. "But," I said, "I will relate an incident, [indecipherable] of [indecipherable], and told the gentleman that in order to understand my story right it was necessary to take into account the fact that in those days the relations existing between father and children were very different to the present day. I then related how on one occasion many years ago we had all gone to church together, and when we were returning my father made some remark to my grand-father which the latter did not like, and regardless of time and place the old man took my father to task and punished him on the spot for his incivility, and this notwithstanding that my father had an infant sister of mine in his arms at the time.

Some of the people asked my grand-father why he had whipped my father. Grand-father said because my father had sauced him. I also informed the gentleman that, although so young, I could remember the incident well to this day. He was very much amused at the incident and laughed heartily. Then he asked me, did I know my royal parents' names, that [is], their native names, and I answered that I did not, but I thought that I had heard the names but could not remember them. The gentleman remarked that if I could remember the name it might be a benefit to me. He said that it was too bad that I should be deprived of what I should have by right, and if I could in any way find out what my grand-father's name was he thought that he could put me in a way to be benefited by it. I told the gentleman there was no doubt in my mind but that my grand-father was an African king, as I had heard my father speak of it a number of times, but I was very young in those days and did not take the interest I should have done or I would very likely have gained some information that would have been of service to me.

CHAPTER XII

I had a very agreeable conversation with this gentleman while the marine palace, the Northern Light, was making her way through the waters of Lake Superior. He thought I was not at the right business, that I would be better working as a waiter or some such lighter task, but I told him that I did not mind the hard work at all, although at times it was a trifle trying. I was then asked whether my grandfather could speak his native tongue, to which I replied that I thought he could, as we always had considerable difficulty in understanding him in English.

"So," says my interviewer, "your [grand]father was a king in the island of Madagascar, and he was captured and brought to America and sold as a slave into the state of Virginia?" To which I said, "Yes, sir: and he was in slavery for many years, during which time he took part in the Revolutionary war and the war of 1812. He was with General Harrison,[2] fought at Bunker Hill and Brandywine. Later he was with the American army that invaded Canada, and was with Colonel Richard Johnston of Kentucky at the battle of the Thames, when Tecumseh was killed. I have heard my father's brother say that when the Indian chief was killed that the American soldiers flayed him and divided his skin in strips among themselves as trophies. If this be true it was a most barbarous treatment of a brave enemy."

"So," asked the gentleman, "was your grand-father given his liberty at the close of the war?"

"No, sir. After his faithful service to the nation he was taken back into slavery and made to serve many years, until some years later, when his owners discovered his royal birth, when he was released."

"Did your grand-father ever receive a pension for his services during the war?" the gentleman asked.

I replied that he had not, after which he asked where my father was living now, and when I told him that he was at Drummondsville,[3] he said that he would very much like to meet him. It would have pleased me very much too, to have had this gentleman meet my father, but when our conversation closed he went down the companion-way again and I never saw him after. [. . .]

CHAPTER XIX

I stayed at Brantford until the latter part of 1887, when I removed to Dundas, Ont., to set up a business for myself, but in this venture I failed. About the time of my failure I received an offer from the owners of a furniture factory at Woodstock who wanted me to enter their employ. On condition that they would take the remnants of my little stock off my hands I consented to go to Woodstock and there I stayed until 1890. About this time I heard a good deal of British

Columbia, and although I did not give the matter very much attention at first, after hearing so much that was of good report about the western province, I one day asked my wife how she would like to go out there to live. I found that she was quite agreeable, and we decided to go. I informed my employers of my intention and they expressed the most serious regret that I should make such a move. I must say that during the time that I worked for Messrs Hay & Co., that no grievance of any kind ever existed between us and that our relations were in every way satisfactory. But I had firmly made up my mind to go west. It was the 13th day of September when we left and we reached Toronto on the same evening. Here we took the train for the west, which we did not leave until we got to Vancouver on the 19th. Two days after starting we arrived at Port Arthur, the principal Canadian port on the shores of Lake Superior.

Touching at several minor stations we at last came to the beautiful city of Winnipeg, the capital of the Province of Manitoba, situated at the junction of the Red and Assiniboine rivers. The train remaining here for some time, we were enabled to see a great portion of the city, where a few years ago all that marked the spot was the chief post of the Hudson's Bay Company. I was much surprised to see such a city, with its stately buildings and wide paved streets, where so recently had been only a solitary fort. We again started for our destination and soon arrived at Portage la Prairie, situated on the Assiniboine river, the centre of the greatest wheat growing district of the prairies. Brandon was the next stop of any importance, this town being the principal wheat market of the Province of Manitoba, having no less than eight grain elevators. After touching at some twenty stations we arrived at Qu'Appelle, some four miles from Fort Qu'Appelle. The next town was Regina, the capital of the Northwest Territories:[4] a short stay here and then on to Moosejaw, which is a market town of some importance, and derives its name from an accident which a white man experienced here in the pioneer days. His cart breaking down he repaired it with the jaw bone of a moose, or moosejaw. The next stop was at Swift Current, situated near a great sheep run. Medicine Hat was the next place of any importance, and here we stopped thirty minutes. This is a mounted police station, and near it also an Indian reserve. Indians are in evidence in numbers at the station, where they may be seen all the time selling bead work, buffalo horns, bear, deer skins and other furs. Passing several stations we arrived at Calgary, another police station and Hudson's Bay post, and a very fine town. On leaving Calgary, we now see the snow capped tops of the Rocky Mountains, which we soon enter through what is called the Gap. The Kicking Horse river is grand and the whole scenery most impressive and interesting. At Banff the railway company have a splendid hotel. Here are also hot springs, so that the place is a great health and pleasure resort. Castle Mountain station is at the base of the mountain, and a grand view is obtainable here. Field and Glacier stations are the next in importance, the last named from the great glacier near which it is situated. Passing several mountain stations, the next stopping place of importance is Revelstoke, situated on the Columbia river, which is spanned by a very long bridge, over which the train goes. Travelling over many dangerous places (as I thought having many narrow escapes) we stopped at the beautiful town of Kamloops, on the Thompson river, near Kamloops lake. This is also a Hudson's Bay post. On leaving this place we skirt the shores of the beautiful lake. At Savonnas the lake ends; then we enter the Thompson river canyon, which at last joins the Fraser river canyon below Lytton. The train did not go very fast over this portion of the road, so that we had every opportunity to see the eternal hills of God and the magnificent works of nature generally. Below Thompson Siding we crossed the Nicola river just before stopping at Spence's Bridge station; then on through the Black Canyon to Lytton. Crossing the Fraser at Cisco, passing through several tunnels and over many trestles, we came to north Bend, then on to Yale and Hope, where we saw many Indian huts. On the opposite side of the river is Hope, at the foot of the Hope mountains. Passing Ruby Creek, Agassiz, Harrison Lake, Nicomen, and stopping a short time at each station, we arrived at Mission Junction, and after a short stay there, we proceeded on our journey. Crossing Stave river we get a magnificent view of Mount Baker. We saw several stumps of large trees at different times which gave me an idea of the huge growth here. We arrived at Westminster Junction, which is situated on the banks of the Fraser river, and the provincial penitentiary and insane asylum are situated here, and many other handsome buildings, and the headquarters of the salmon canning industry. The next stopping place was Port Moody, situated at the head of Burrard Inlet, and after passing Hastings we soon arrived at Vancouver. We knew that we were at our destination after a long ride across the continent. I was informed on my arrival that the city had been destroyed by fire, all except one house, in the year 1886, just four years before my arrival, but it did not look possible that such had been the case, and it was verified by a great many people that were here at the time. Vancouver is a beautiful city with a grand location. I think that in the matter of natural drainage and a natural harbor, that this city excels any that I have seen anywhere.

Shortly after my arrival in this city I secured a location on which to build a house, on Fourteenth avenue, Mount Pleasant, which was then comparatively a wilderness, though in every other way a charming location. My wife was well pleased with the change, especially as regards the climate, the winters here being much milder than in Ontario. We found the people in Vancouver very friendly, and in fact I cannot say that I have ever lived among a more sociable set than in this city. In a general way I have got along very well since coming to Vancouver. After clearing a couple of lots I erected a shop and started the manufacture of varnish, but not having sufficient capital to compete, I was forced to give it up.

The white people in a general way were very kind to my wife and myself. My own people were very kind, excepting two or three, who seemed to try to be very indifferent for some cause, and I do not think today they can give any reason for being so. The worst treatment I ever received during my life, I am very sorry to say, was from two of the new race[5] since my residence in Vancouver. After the death of my good wife, in the year of 1897, I admitted two people of my own race into my house, thinking that as I was alone, they would be great comfort in my bereavement, but I had cause to regret this step, as it appeared to me a short time after. They thought that I was a mere plaything or some inferior animal from the way they acted, and I was very much surprised at their rude actions. I will not mention their names, as I do not wish to hurt even my worst enemy's feelings, but these insulting actions emanated from a source which I was not thinking of. I did not think when giving any person shelter that there would be any so base as to turn my kindness into ridicule, and that in the face of the fact that that shelter was all that they had. Yet such happened in my case, and I say it with pride that I did not rebuke these people, as I would have done fifty years ago, for that would have been entirely wrong and un-Christian like. [...]

I have often heard men remark that they were slaves through the difficulties which they had overcome in their labor to make a living. That is a great mistake. What they think to be slavery is not even a prelude to the horrors of slavery that the African was subject to. The former have their individual liberty to get an education and to educate their children. They have the rights of the franchise and are protected by law when they labor. They receive wages and are not compelled by law to labor all their lives for no reward. Their families and themselves are protected by law. The wife is not taken from the husband and sold to go north, and the husband sold to other parties to go south, and some of the children sold to go east and the remainder to go west, never to meet again during this life. Neither is the husband prohibited from protecting his wife and daughters from insult, nor from furnishing his children with books and teaching them at home. They can own land, horses, wagons, buggies, or anything they are able to buy, and be protected by law in their rights. Yet, with all these God-given rights, many men are not satisfied and say they are slaves. The African slaves were victims to everything just now enumerated, because the laws then existing in a Christian land did not allow my people the rights of man. There were many exceptions, but in general the slaves in the United States were treated as brutes. If white people, with all the favorable circumstances they enjoy, say they are slaves, what would they say if they were under the yoke of African slavery as practised in the United States? Man, with few exceptions, is dissatisfied even under favorable circumstances. I have often noticed men who were said to be "born with a golden spoon in their hand," that is they were supplied with everything that heart could wish for – heirs to great fortunes and never had to labor – and who could and did enjoy themselves, yet with such golden privileges, they destroyed themselves to meet a worse lot after death.

Many people know of the ferocity of Spanish bloodhounds: those ferocious beasts were imported into the United States during the time of slavery and trained to hunt my afflicted people in case they should run away. Many times have I heard sad stories from fugitive slaves, who were chased by the hounds. One case I will relate here. This black man was making his escape from Missouri, and after travelling several days and crossing the Ohio River into Indiana, he was shocked one night by hearing the bloodhounds near. Fortunately, at this critical juncture, he was near the base of the mountains, to which he bent his way through the woods as fast as possible. He had ascended quite a distance before the hounds came up to him; he was well armed, his armory consisting of a large bowie knife, a six-shooter, and a sword made from a scythe blade. Yet he was terror stricken at the idea of being attacked by several ferocious bloodhounds, so he could only trust in God, which he did. At that horrible moment his supplications were not in vain, for God was with him as he was with Daniel in the lion's den in Babylon. The High and Holy One delivered this black man from his awful enemies. While resting from his tiresome journey, the hounds came up with him, and instead of taking hold of him, simply looked at him and walked around. He sat on a log and snapped his fingers and the hounds came to him, looked at him and laid down at his feet. They did him no harm and were soon sound asleep. This may seem strange to my readers, but we must remember that our God will never change, for He is the same now as in the days of Daniel and the other Hebrew children we read of in Holy Writ. Bloodhounds were trained to obey the sound of the horn. When at a great distance, the owner would blow his horn and the hounds would habitually return to their master at once. This black man heard the horns several times while the hounds lay at his feet snoring. The hounds did not move and the black man, after getting a rest, proceeded on his journey towards Canada, the land of freedom; the dogs never attempted to follow him. The north star was the only guide of this man, and the best of all is the very man that acted this part is now a resident of Vancouver. The circumstances were related to me by himself, therefore I do not hesitate to insert this and many other thrilling events I know to be true.

[1904]

NOTES

1. Johnson was born after his mother had escaped slavery in Kentucky. According to the Fugitive Slave Act, even though he was born in Indiana, a free state, he was still legally the property of his mothers' owner.

2. William Henry Harrison: American general who later became the ninth president of the United States; Johnson's namesake.

3. Drummondsville, Ontario.

4. When Johnson visited Regina in 1890, it was the capital of the Northwest Territories. Saskatchewan became a province in 1905.

5. Throughout his narrative, Johnson refers to blacks in the Americas as "the new race."

Marie Stark Wallace [1867-1966]

from Notes made by Marie Albertina Stark (afterwards Mrs Wallace) from the recollections of her mother, Sylvia Stark, who was born a slave in Clay County, Missouri, and settled on Salt Spring Island with her husband, Louis Stark, and family in the year 1860, as homesteaders

> I heard the tread of pioneers
> Of cities yet to be
> The first low wash of waves
> That soon shall roll a human sea.

> Anon.

There was nothing unusual in taking a trip to Saltspring Island. I had passed through the pretty Islands that dot the Gulf of Georgia many times, and mused under the spell of their enchantment.

But strange to say the peaceful hills and dreamy coves had never appealed to me as they did now. I was on a visit to my aged mother and brother of the Stark family. Perhaps it was the beauty and Grandeur of scenery that awakened me to the realization of the value of things.

How true is the scripture, there is no speech or language where the voice of nature is not heard. (Psalm 19, 3rd verse.)

Over the shimmering waters I viewed as through the mist of years, the pantomime of yesteryears; I saw again the race of the big canims (Indian canoes), heard the dip, dip of their ghostly paddles, and the wild chant of the happy potlatch song as the natives raced to their yearly potlatch feast. And I thought of our Pioneer fathers who crossed these troubled waters many years ago, seeking a home in the land of the free; troubled waters for the natives of this country as well as those brave pioneers. For the dark clouds of conquest hung heavily over the land, and the triumph of the conquerors was deeply resented by the natives; they retaliated by slaying the settlers. So the pioneers lived in constant fear of their lives.

That was a time when men were willing to go into the wilderness with axe and gun only, at their own risk. They are the forgotten men whose courage and constancy blazed the trail and laid the foundation of our western civilization.

They are the uncrowned kings of pioneer days.

The shadows were growing long on the grass when brother Willis and I, in his one horse wagon, came to the home he shared with our mother. Sylvia Stark and her son, Willis, were the last of those colored pioneers who came to Saltspring with their families in the early 60s.

Willis was about 4 years old when he landed with his parents and a sister on Saltspring in 1860, and he was the last of the Stark family to stand by his mother through some of the most trying days of her life.

His home was the fourth ranch in B.C. on which mother and son had worked and cleared the land. Much of the clearing had grown all over again, as each season's new growth mingled with age and decay marked the changes of time on the old place. But the rock heaps and boulders were still standing where he had put them nearly fifty years ago; they stood as monuments of the courage and strength of Willis Stark when he was young.

And in his prime now, he was old and crippled from hard work and the rough road he had pioneered; he had to engage the help of a neighbor, John Whims, to do his plowing. He could still bring in wood. He would sit up late when the winters were cold, to keep the house warm for his aged mother.

The first cabin Willis had built was torn down to make room for a new house. The two oldest boys had planned it that way between them. Willis would stay with their mother and John would parcel support or cash when necessary.

So the two brothers with the help of a carpenter and a neighbor, built a new house for their mother, and she was very proud of her new house.

But the first cabin Willis had built, and which had been torn down to make room for the new house, held many pleasant memories for me. It had been the home not only for our mother, but our grandfather, and invalid brother and myself. Now the toilsome years were telling on the health of Sylvia and her son, Willis. The old spinning wheel stood idly by gathering dust, but she was always busy with her knitting.

As I watched those toilworn hands, I saw a lifetime of service in every line and wrinkle. Near seventy years had passed since she had faced the uncultivated soil of B.C., yet her memory was still good. She loved to talk about the fine gardens she made after they had cleared the land. She had vegetables to give away. Willis raised his own grain for his chickens and did his thrashing with an old-fashioned flail. He did all of his mowing by hand; sometimes he cradled his grain by moonlight as when he cradled for other people. He was pressed for time.

Their chickens ran wild over the farm, but Sylvia took delight in hunting the hens' nests, even to belling a hen with a dinner bell. She found the nests all right.

She filled two crates a week with eggs. It more than paid for their groceries. They traded with the Brodwell store, at central Saltspring. Those days farming was profitable for beginners even in the primitive way. The claims were paying for the toil of clearing them. But with World War I, followed by the grading system and the high cost of farm necessities, it was very difficult for the small farmer. Fruit was left on the ground to spoil. The cost of boxes prohibited profit. Howbeit, those hardy farmers survived.

> Through many spans of lean benighted years,
> Through generations born to doubts and fears,
> We've trodden the wilds of life's abandoned ways,
>
> But low today we stand amidst the throng,
> Possessing more than just a native song,
> Dark pilgrims up from Antebellum days.
>
> Ode to Booker T. Washington,
> by L. Lynch.

It is said that Memory is the heritage of old age.

It was to Sylvia Stark a diary richly filled with the strange and unusual happenings of her past life. It was on those occasions when she seemed to be living in the past, she would tell some of her early experiences, and I kept silent for fear of breaking the spell. Although at that time, I had no thought of preserving those memories, I was simply interested in listening to her tales.

Some of those tales were very sad, relating to the condition of the slaves. The blood of those poor tortured souls cry to God from the ground, but the Great Creator has a time set for judgment of the oppressor and a new life for the oppressed.

Sylvia Stark's maiden name was Sylvia Estes. She was born in Clay County, Missouri in 1839; was the youngest of three children, who with their mother, Hannah Estes, worked for a German baker, named Charles Leopold.

Their father, Howard Estes, worked for a Scotsman named Tom Estes. The slaves bore the name of their masters. Sylvia's father considered himself lucky to be privileged to visit his family over the week-ends.

The abolitionist movement sponsored by William Lloyd Garrison had been in operation since 1831; it was a menace to the slave owners. They tried to suppress it, to no avail. Mr Leopold was very much impressed with the movement. He said he was against slavery, and would quit the traffic eventually, but he could not return to Germany. He said all Germans going to the U. S. were under oath; if they ever held slaves, the penalty would be death. He said, "If I went back now, they would cut off my head."

Mrs Leopold was not in accord with her husband; she thought they should conform to the southern rules for handling slaves. It was one Xmas morning when little Sylvia had her first awakening. The children were very agreeable; they were allowed to play together at this special season. While waiting for their tree to be arranged in another room, they challenged who would be the first to see the tree. "I will," cried little Sylvia, and being small she crept in close to the door. When the door was opened she was the first one in. Suddenly she felt herself jerked roughly back and Mrs Leopold scolding loudly cried, "Ni – –, let the white children come first." "Never do that again," said Mr Leopold. He had put a nice doll on the tree for Sylvia, but the joy of Christmas was lost to Sylvia. That incident had served its purpose and never had to be repeated again. From that time on, Sylvia was thinking with the mind of a slave. When her mother became ill she was anxious and wondered what will happen to me if Ma dies, where will I go.

Sylvia's first recollection of her childhood days were associated with work. She said she must have been very small. She remembered that her mother used to tie her big apron around her neck and stand her up on a chair to dry dishes for the white folks, and there were so many dishes to wipe.

She seldom took part in play with other children outside. Sometimes she would fight if other children were abusive but most of her time was spent learning to sew or knit. Her first knitting was done on broom straws. "When you learn to knit," her mother said, "I will get you some knitting needles."

She practically taught herself to read. The little Leopold child she used to nurse taught her the alphabet and when the white children did their homework, she would listen. When they went out to play and left their books, she would look at them and rehearse them to herself. Mrs Leopold would have been very angry if she had known this was going on, as it was against the law to teach a slave. With these small beginnings Sylvia learned to read.

Howard Estes and his wife were of the same mind in raising their children. Though at a great disadvantage themselves, not being able to read, they taught their children to pray and observe the Sabbath. Sylvia never forgot the lesson her father taught her. One Sunday morning, their mother was working at the big house, and their father tended to the children. Sylvia had her new clothes on and could hardly wait for her father to finish combing her hair. She was so happy she skipped through the door. Quickly her father called her back, saying, "This is Sunday, now walk out with more modesty, not like a horse bolting through a barn door." Sylvia never forgot the lesson, even after she and her son had grown old. When their hay was out in the field on Sunday and the clouds threatened rain, she would wait until the morrow.

The Estes family went to church; of course the colored people were seated back by the door but they were allowed to partake of the sacrament after the white folks had theirs. And the sermon especially for the slaves was, "servants obey your masters." Every slave knew that part of the bible by heart.

Although Mrs Estes could not read, she was not deceived. She said no one could convince her that God was the author of slavery. Sylvia remembered on one occasion the taking of the sacrament became positively loathsome, changing her whole concept of the performance. The minister used the low language of a boss to his slaves, ending with "God knows you are a hard nation."

Life for the Leopold slaves would have been comparatively easy, but for the nagging disposition of Mrs Leopold. Perhaps she thought if her husband would not rule their slaves according to custom in a slave state, she would.

Mrs Estes usually went through these eruptions calmly, although they made her angry. It came to a climax when her mistress called her to make a fire in the kiln when her hands were in the dough. So she explained to her mistress that she could not make it at that moment as she was making bread and did not want to spoil her bread. Apparently Mrs Leopold was out purposely to start a row. She said, "How dare you disobey my orders." Hannah Estes was not afraid of the big German woman. Hot words passed between them. A quarrel was precipitated that nearly proved disastrous. When Charles Leopold came in he heard his wife's story which was very much distorted. He was very angry. He said he would be ruined if this went around, that he allowed his slaves to talk back. He held a menacing whip in his hand, but Hannah would have fought him with all the strength she possessed if he had attempted to flog her. Her wild Madagascar blood was aroused. It was settled at last with a sound lecture to both women, Mrs Leopold sobbing the while because her scheme to have Hannah flogged had failed.

At a considerable risk to himself, Mr Leopold had on one occasion quelled a race riot at an anti-slavery meeting. It made him very unpopular with the slaveholders. These eruptions worried Sylvia, too. What troubled her mother, troubled her ever since that Xmas morning.

Life for Sylvia was surrounded with terrorism. It was not safe for colored children to play outside of their own homes. They kidnapped colored children and sold them down south to the cotton fields from whence they never returned. Sometimes a stranger would offer candy to Sylvia. She always refused it and ran home.

> Look beyond, there's light for thee
> Streaming o'er a turbulent sea
> Soft it smiles though distant far
> The beautiful polar star

[In 1849, Howard Estes was sent to drive cattle to California, to supply the new gold rush there. While working in the gold fields, Howard managed to save over $2000 dollars to buy his own freedom, then returned to Missouri where he paid an additional $2,900 to Charles Leopold for the freedom of Hannah, Sylvia, and his son Jackson. The family bought farm land in Missouri, but were fearful of the "Ku-Kluks" who frequently terrorized and kidnapped free blacks. Howard decided to take his family west to California permanently on the next cattle drive across the country. They faced thirst, starvation, and Native attack, but eventually arrived and settled in Placerville, near a gold field where Howard and Jackson worked as miners.]

In 1858 Howard Estes decided to leave a comfortable home and go in search of greater freedom. The Colored people of California were becoming alarmed over general agitation under southern pressure to make California a slave state. In 1852 the federal government had passed a law permitting the return of fugitive slaves fleeing to Northern States to be returned to their owners in the South.

It was also required of all colored people in California to wear a distinctive badge. Furthermore the state legislature had taken what appeared to be the first steps against The Colored Race. The effect was to deprive them of the ability to protect their property from spoilation by the white men. By these acts colored people were disqualified from giving evidence against a white person.

B.C. Historical Quarterly

apr- 1939

Then in the mining district where Mr Estes lived certain laws governing mining operations were designed to protect the miners and seemed to clash with the homesteaders' rights.

The Starks and Estes both were preparing to leave California. They had heard about New Caledonia, as B.C. was then called. They longed for the freedom of B.C.'s fir-covered hills.

Stark sold all but 50 head of his best cattle and took to the old Oregon Trail with the help of Jackson Estes and others of a company, herding the Cattle on the Trail.

H. Estes sold his farm for what he could get, and took the women and children to San Francisco, embarking on the boat Brother Jonathan. The boat was old and unseaworthy, but it carried a heavy Cargo. When the Ocean was rough the boat rolled and creaked with every rising swell. Then they threw 40 head of fine horses over board, for safety. It was another pitiful sight that saddened the trip for Sylvia, to see those poor animals swimming after the boat crying for help. They were too far out to reach land. [. . .]

The Emancipation of the slaves in the U.S. was a burning political question. The Negro people were dis-satisfied with the laws of the country. They met at San Francisco to discuss how best they could improve their hard lot.

A committee was sent to B.C. to interview the Government. Governor Douglas received them and extended them a Cordial welcome to establish themselves on British Soil.

As a result of this favorable report by the committee, fully six hundred Colored people came to B.C. Some came up on two pioneer steamships, Brother Jonathan and Pacific.

from the Army & Navy Veteran
Magazine, Conventional Number.

Those pioneer boats carried hundreds of 49ers to and from the Gold mines. The Pacific afterwards was sunk in a collision off Cape Flattery with a loss of three hundred lives.

Some of those colored people went to Australia, some to the Cariboo mines, others to Victoria & Saltspring Island.

The Boat landed at a place called Stillicum, Washington. This place was sparsely settled with white people and Indians. The Family stayed in Stillicum more than a Month waiting for the arrival of Mr Stark with the cattle. They bought supplies from the farmer. These new settlers were poor, like most of the immigrants. One Family helped to solve their own problems. When they bought a sack of potatoes they ate the potatoes and planted the peelings, thus raising another good crop of potatoes.

When the men arrived with the cattle they went to Victoria B.C. in a sailing vessel. Much of what transpired from the time they left Stillicum and their final landing on Saltspring Island was not remembered. The first thing Mr Stark did after landing in Victoria, he secured Naturalization papers for all of the Family.

Sylvia Stark remembered that a delegation of colored people called on Governor Douglas requesting permission to form a colony of colored settlers on Saltspring Island about that time. But he refused saying it would be to the best interest of all to have a mixed settlement.

Some of those colored people remained in Victoria and some went to Saltspring and other places. Those who remained in Victoria acquired valuable property, and several took part in the City's municipal activities. Mr Estes and Family located in Saanich, Victoria, where he bought property.

That was a busy time for the Starks. They were preparing to go to Saltspring. There was a restless herd of cattle to keep in a corral and feed. It was no small task. Mr Stark located a place on the North west side of Saltspring, and built a cabin on it, during the Family's stay in Victoria.

It was a bright day in 1866 when the Starks moved to Saltspring Island. Sylvia remembered 1860 chiefly because John E. Stark, the second Son, was born four months after they landed.

They came to the North west side of the Island in a sailing vessel. The cattle were lowered into the water with strong ropes, where they swam to land, and took the trail leading up to their home, lowing as they went on, without any one to guide them.

The passengers clambered down the side of the ship on rope ladders, and into two Indian canoes, manned by two Indians, a man and his wife. A Hudson Bay Co. man landed with them, Mr Macauley. The Hudson Bay agent offered to stay with Mrs Stark and the two children, while Mr Stark went down to the settlement to get conveyance to haul their baggage.

While they were waiting for him the two Natives with their natural keen-ness of sight, saw canoes in the distance. As they drew nearer the Native and his Wife became very much excited, showing fear. They said it was the Northern Indians. They were hostile to the Tribes inhabiting the Islands in the Strait. Their Indian woman stole away into the bush near her canoe.

The Haida, or Northern Indians, had several big canoes, seven or more heavily loaded with furs. As soon as they saw the small group on the beach, they turned and headed for the spot. They beached their canoes then hauled the boat with the Stark belongings, high up on the sand, and examined its contents. Then one of the men who could speak English approached Mr Macauley and shook an ugly knife in his face saying, Are you afraid? He answered with a smile and a shake of his head. Sylvia could see that Macauley was trembling and very pale.

She had an awful feeling. She held her two children close to her as they sat on a log and prayed to God to save her children, with no thought for herself, only what will become of my children when they kill me.

Their Native pilot was sitting on the ground, not daring to look up. While this was happening, the local Indian woman who had hidden near her canoe was paddling swiftly away to inform her Tillicum at Penellekut Indian village on Couper Island. In the meantime the Northern Indians talked with Macauley. When they learned that he could speak their language they offered to carry the Stark belongings up to the cabin, but Mr Macauley explained to them that Stark had already gone for help.

When they learned that Macauley was visiting the Lineker Family at the place where the harbor house now stands, they said they would take him there as they were on their way to Victoria. Mrs Stark believed they would have all been killed if they, the Haidas, had not been going south to sell their furs.

Mr Macauley's story of his experience with the Natives. He accepted their offer to take him to the other side of the Island. When they were out on their way and he was feeling quite safe they saw a large band of local Indians with many canoes coming after them. Macauley thought this would surely be his end.

He begged the Haida Indians to put him ashore anywhere, but the Haidas tried to out-run them, but were too heavily loaded. They were soon surrounded by a desperate band of men on the war path heavily armed. We will not kill the white man, they said to the Haidas, but we will kill you.

So they agreed to let the Northern Indians take Mr Macauley to his destination, and they all paddled to the head of the Bay we call Ganges, and put Macauley out, then went out into the bay and fought a most desperate battle with hundreds of local men, to a comparatively small number of Northerners.

Another account of that Historical Battle came in a newspaper published in 1932. It read, only one of the Northern Braves escaped, and he was so badly wounded it was doubtful that he recovered.

That was the time the local Natives themselves were quite hostile. They held meetings with much Skookum pow-wow (Chinook: strong talk). As they saw their beaches and hunting grounds usurped by the incoming settlers, and the sight of carcasses of animals lying on the beaches, their hides taken and the meat left to spoil. When an Indian came to one of such, he made a clucking noise with his tongue which indicated disgust. It only served as fuel to an already heated situation.

Saltspring Island was officially named Admiral Island in 1859, but it still retained the name it had acquired in 1856, Saltspring, a self name because of its salt springs.

There were seventy resident land holders on the Island in 1860.

> The first white settlers were Mr and Mrs Lineker & Family.
> They came in 1858.
> > B.C. Historical Quarterly
> > 1851

As Mrs Stark remembered, there were six Colored Families on Saltspring Island in 1860 when the Starks came.

She said there were two old colored people known as Grand Pa Jackson and Grand Ma Jackson. Grand Ma Jackson was 112 years of age and Grand Pa Jackson was 114 years of age. They did not stay long on Saltspring.

Sylvia Stark's first sight of her new home on the Island was an unfinished log cabin surrounded by trees and thick underbrush. It was anything but encouraging. It called for work, in which she would have to take part, but one happy thought in this wilderness, it was their own, and it stood for freedom. And that all absorbing thought was all the stimulus needed for the Colored settlers in those days.

They hung a quilt up for a door, and the Neighbors came and helped Mr Stark to put a roof on the house to keep out the rain.

Sylvia had not recovered quite from the shock of their first landing. She found it hard to get use to their wild surroundings. It was so lonely being located in an isolated place quite a distance from the Settlement.

There was no Dr available then. She was yet in her teens, and felt the need of a woman's advice and companionship.

The first time she was left alone with her two small children she wept despondently. Her little son Willis tried to comfort her. Stroking her head soothingly, he said, Don't cry Ma, let's go home. The only home he knew was in California.

But a change was coming to Sylvia. She would know the peace of a Comforting Saviour. She would know why her Mother used to hide away in the old shed to pray. She was often left alone with her children. There seemed to be no other way. Their neighbors were in the same predicament, to some extent, when their men went to town for provisions.

Looking back over those dark days, Sylvia often made the remark, Now I can see the hand of God guiding me through all of my troubles, guiding me to a higher life. Her husband was not sympathetic, so she would steal out into the woods to pray, although wild animals roamed through the bush. Black bear, cougars, even wolves were on the Island those days, but she was serving Daniel's God. The bush had no terrors when the urge came to pray.

> Then one day as she lay on a couch tired and self aban-
> doned, these words came to her. Fear not for I am with thee.
> This passage may be found in
> Isaiah 41:10

It gave her joy, it was the answer to her prayer. On this wild Unconquered Island she had found new life. She could not read the Bible and understand it without the help of those faithful missionaries of the Wesleyan Methodist Church, who visited the settlers and read the Bible to them, giving much needed help those days.

Four months after their arrival to Saltspring, a second Son was added to The Stark Family. They named him John Edmond. He loved adventure. He took up the trail where his parents left off, and pressed further northward as a prospector & mineralogist.

It was between 1857 & 1858 when Mr Estes came to Saltspring Island to take care of the Stark family on the Mountain. It was necessary, not only to live on a pre-emption, but a certain amount of work must be done on the place to make it secure.

He brought a friend with him named Jiles Curtis. Mrs Estes stayed in Saanich on account of failing health. They went around together, and worked that way for safety, but the shadow of the Indian seemed destined to cross the threshold of that Mountain home with tragedy.

It was one Sunday, Mr Curtis felt indisposed, and did not accompany Mr Estes when he went to church. Very reluctantly Mr Estes left him alone and went to church. He never missed a meeting unless it couldn't be avoided. While sitting in church, a feeling of uneasiness disturbed him, so he left before the service was over.

When he came to the fence surrounding the house he saw the bars were down. He knew he hadn't left them down. Further on, a pillow had been dropped, as though someone had made a hasty retreat. He needed no further proof. Hastening to the cabin he found Curtis still sitting in a chair with his back to the door. When he called, there was no answer. Curtis was dead. The chair he was sitting in belonged to the Starks. I can remember seeing the mark of the bullet in the back of the chair as it took Curtis' life. The house had been robbed of everything worth-while.

If Mr Estes had stayed with Curtis, he too might have been killed, for the Indians went about in bands.

A Native named Willie was apprehended, the man who had pointed the gun at Stark. His wife said she would tell all she knew about the case, if the law would protect her.

She was left behind to mind the canoes, and could only tell of seeing the stolen goods brought back. She knew their intent, though not a witness to the slaying.

Willie had often been on trial for his life, but he seemed to lead a charmed life. He never came to the Gallows. After the trial his wife suddenly disappeared.

In the early nineties, I saw Willie paddling his own canoe selling fish. I was told by an old timer that he was the man who had made his boast of having killed thirty people.

After the death of Curtis, Howard Estes went back to his home in Saanich.

Dad and the Boys worked hard with axe, saw and auger, working the hard way, but they soon cleared the logs from around the house. They felled trees, bored holes on both sides of the tree, kindled a fire in the holes. The holes measured rail length. When they burned through, they were split in rail lengths for fencing.

They cut and dried the wild meadow grass for the cattle in winter time, but they soon raised a big field of tame grass around the house. Beef cattle were fed on turnips and bran. We never heard of mangles those days.

Then before our meadow around the lake was cleared it seemed to be a breeding place for cougars. One evening when the farm was still in the rough, we were sitting outside where it was cool. An eerie sound came up from the meadow in the distance. It was the cry of young cougars. They sounded like the weird cry we sometimes hear of wild animals on the radio, a sound you would not easily forget.

One Sunday when patches of land had been cleared, and smoldering logs and burning brush scented the air, my sister Serena and I strolled out to a moss-covered hill overlooking the meadow. We lounged at ease in the warm sunshine when we heard what we thought was our cat crying, and we answered. It cried again twice and we answered it both times. Then a long silence.

Suddenly from the bush just across the road came a loud and frightful Meow. We didn't answer that one. To use our brother John's expression, we got up and flew. We had been calling a panther. We never stopped until we got home.

A Colored man from South Carolina named Overton, who came west seeking to better his condition, landed on Saltspring Island with only 75 cents in his pocket, was helped up on his feet by Louis Stark; he also took a claim on V.I. where he could work with Stark. He felt that he was indebted to Stark for helping him in a time of need. He also had a claim with a lake and meadow, like Stark and the Richardsons, but Overton's meadow, where he raised his vegetables, was rather far from his house.

Sometimes he was late getting home. Often people who came to see him, and finding he was not in, would sit on his door step and wait for him.

One evening he was late coming home; the moon shone dimly as he was mounting the stile fence surrounding his cabin. He saw what appeared to be a large dog coming towards him; thinking that someone was waiting for him on the door step, he called loudly, "Please call your dog off." He got no answer; then he was scared, but before he could think the animal leaped upon the stile beside him and down on the other side and was gone.

Then he knew how close he had been to a panther; cougars were called panthers in those days. He passed a restless night. He lay awake early in the morning waiting to hear his rooster crow. Becoming alarmed he went to his chicken house; 20 chickens missing, including the rooster.

With the aid of Stark's dogs they found the chickens buried in the woods on his Farm. Their throats were cut and drained of their blood.

On more than one occasion Sylvia was forced to be her own nurse and Doctor too. Sometimes her husband gave much needed assistance. Then a friend whom she had known in California came to her assistance, and Sylvia in return went to the assistance of her Friend.

They were the only Nurses available at that time.

There were no stores on the Island. The settlers made use of the empty flour bags. They came in very handy in making various articles of clothing. When short of patches Sylvia would patch her husband's overalls with flour sacking. When that wore through, she would put another patch on top of that, until, in her own words, the pants would fairly stand alone.

They worked very hard in those days enduring great hardship as the price of Freedom. But it was with a joy of performance and pride of achievement.

There were no tractors; Stark made a homemade tractor, finding a v-shaped body of a tree. He put a coulter in the end and spikes along the sides. They called it a drag. Hitched to a pair of oxen it proved effective in tearing out roots and cultivating the ground.

Mr Stark was reared on a fruit farm in Kentucky. He grafted and planted fruit trees among the stumps. His plan was to have the fruit trees coming on while the stumps decayed. In time they would be easy to dig out.

They soon had enough cleared land to raise grain for their own use. They kept chickens, turkeys and pigs. The bears caught some of their pigs, the young ones, and the turkeys ran wild. When they wanted turkey, they had to shoot them from the trees. There were wild geese and cranes on the Mountains. They built their nests there, but as more settlers came in, these wild birds left for wilder regions. There was no regular Boat running to the Island. The settlers navigated in Indian canoes or flat bottom boats when they needed provisions.

On one occasion Mr & Mrs Stark with a Family of three Children were returning from Victoria in an open boat. A storm came up and nearly capsized the boat. It kept Stark busy with all of the strength and skill he possessed to hold the boat abreast of the waves, while Mrs Stark bailed frantically to keep the boat from being swamped at each swell.

They were soaked to the skin when they finally landed, glad to be alive. Mrs Stark collapsed, and Stark had to take the children home and bring a chair to carry her home. That was in 1863.

The first boat running to the Island was the S.S. Douglas. It came once a month. Not many months after that perilous trip, the youngest son of the Family was born. By that time a retired English Dr was on the Island. He said this boy would always be weakly.

Only a Mother knows how it feels to bear such a burden. It called for Abundant Faith.

The Starks were in their mountain home when an epidemic of smallpox in B.C. spread to the Islands. The Indians became a prey to the disease. When one Native in the camp got sick, the rest fled the camp, as they had no way of combating the disease. That served to spread the epidemic.

Mr Stark had himself and all of the family Vaccinated; about that time the cattle came home from the woods. As it was his custom, he went out to feed them to encourage them to come home of their own accord. While he was out it began to rain. He was nursing a sore vaccination and felt damp and chilly.

He came to a nice warm fire his wife had made. While sitting by the fire he became delirious. His wife put him to bed and gave him hot drinks, and for several weeks he was so delirious she could not leave him alone with the Children to go for the Dr.

There were 14 cows to milk, pigs and chickens to feed, aside from her other duties, and tending to the Children. One wonders how she managed to carry on. Her Husband's arm was swollen out of all proportion. She tried every remedy she knew of to no avail, trying to reduce the swelling when he regained consciousness. He thought the swollen arm was a log lying beside him. He told Sylvia to go for the Dr.

She told Emmie who was six years old to mind the baby, and not let her Brother Willis leave the house for fear of panthers, then she took the trail down to the settlement.

A Colored man named Buckner was living where the golf course now stands. He took the Dr and Mrs Stark in his cart up the hill to the Stark home. Dr Hog said Mr Stark had Variloid. He ordered cold clay from the bottom of the spring wrapped around the arm. It brought quick relief, as the swelling disappeared.

Thereafter the arm was smaller than the other; however, Stark became strong again.

Dr Hog was a retired English Dr. As far back as Sylvia Stark could remember, he was the first Dr on Saltspring. Doubtless, he practiced because of the people's great need, but he proved to be a first class Dr, though handicapped by having only one arm.

He lived alone in a small house overlooking the meadow adjoining the property where the Harbour House now stands. He had planted turnips down in the meadow across the road. One day, looking from his high elevation down into his garden, he saw a Native pulling up his turnips. When he objected, the man chased him and would have killed him, but the Dr ran into his house and locked the door. He saw the Native shake his fist at him through the window. Some days later they found the Dr's lifeless Body outside of his cabin. He might have saved his life if he had only left the cabin for safety. A man by the name of Willie was responsible for that Crime, a Native of whom they said, he led a charmed life. It seems strange that they never captured him.

Mrs Stark seemed to be tireless in her efforts to make their home life enjoyable. She made hominy from the wheat and corn of their own raising, sometimes boiled wheat had to be a substitute for bread. When the Missionaries came they ate boiled wheat too, but hominy was a rare dish with Venison to those Ministers. Then she tried grinding the wheat in a coffee mill. It made good whole wheat bread.

The work of those early Ministers, like that of the settlers, was fraught with hardships and danger. Long voyages across the water in stormy weather, frequently in Indian canoes, taking what accommodation their poor parishioners were able to give gladly and thankfully, adapting themselves to hardships with their parishioners.

Here are the names of some of the first Wesleyan Ministers to Saltspring.

Mr Thomas Crosby, for many years Missionary to the Indians at Port Simpson B.C., Rev. Sextsmith, Rev. White, Mr Cornelius Bryant, Mr Ebenezer Robson, who came to the Island in 1861, was another outstanding Minister of the gospel. When he came to the Stark home he refused to take the best bed they offered to him. He said it was wrong to rob Peter to pay Paul, he preferred to sleep on a straw mattress on the floor. He made himself generally useful, chopping wood, bringing water from the spring, even churning the milk, when Mrs Stark was busy with the cooking. He loved fried clams. He would sit on the beach waiting for the tide to go out so he could dig clams.

Mr Cornelius Bryant was the first man to join the pioneer Methodist church in Nanaimo. He brought his Credentials with him from England. He also organized a band of young people as helpers to the church. They were named the Band of Hope. Sometimes he brought his wife to visit the Stark Family. He took great interest in the young people. He taught Emmie, the oldest of the Stark family, to play on the organ.

Not the least of all of those early Ministers was Mr Raper. He was not an ordained Minister, but he kindly took the pulpit in the absence of the Minister. When Stark offered to black his boots for him before he went to Church, he took it as a great joke when he discovered that his boots were blacked with panther grease.

An unbarked log cabin School house at the crossroads at Central Saltspring Island served as a Church for the Methodist Ministers. A Colored man named Robinson taught the Sunday School, and another Colored man, John Jones, taught School during the week.

The three oldest Stark Children had their first schooling in that log cabin School. They had to walk in a trail through dense woods up to their mountain home. Once the two oldest Children were coming home from School when they heard an angry Growl from the bush on the roadside. It might have been a panther; they couldn't see it, nor did they have any inclination to look. They ran all of the way home, but when their Father took his gun and went in search of the animal, it was nowhere to be found.

During the thirteen or fourteen years the Stark Family lived on Saltspring Island the slaying of the settlers by Indians continued. Several colored people lost their lives that way.

Two colored men, Mr Robinson and Giles Curtis, were both slain about 1867 or 1868. There is a tombstone in the pioneer graveyard, marking the grave of Giles Curtis in 1868.

Mr Robinson, a very devoted Sunday school teacher, often sang this old sweet song to his pupils, "Children of the heavenly King, as we journey let us sing," sung in the old tune with all of the quavers of a spiritual. I have often heard my Mother sing it just as they sang it in the old log cabin school house where she first learned it, and kept it in mind down through the years. One Sunday he sang it to those brave children of the brave pioneers for the last time. He told Sylvia Stark next Sunday would be his farewell meeting. He had written to his wife asking her to come west, but she refused to come to a wild country where the Indians were hostile, so now he was going back to her.

When next Sunday came, he failed to arrive. They waited with growing uneasiness, then a party went to his house at Vesuvius Bay. They found him slain in his cabin where he had lived alone.

One evening five Indians came to the Stark cabin on the mountain side. It happened to be on a Sunday when Mr Stark was at home. The three children were asleep, the youngest a baby in the cradle. They walked right into the house and began to examine everything in the house. They even counted the blankets on the bed, and talked among themselves. Then one of the men took a gun from over the mantle where Stark kept several guns, ready loaded, and began to examine it. Stark shouted to him to be careful, as the gun was loaded, and grabbed the muzzle, turning it away. "I know it's loaded," the Indian said, and tried to wrest it from Stark's hands.

Sylvia was praying silently, as she felt that the Indians had come to kill them. She knew that they were too many in number for her husband to have a chance. In the scuffle Stark held on to the gun turning the muzzle upward. Suddenly there was a terrific blast, the bullet going through the roof. Immediately, to the surprise of the Starks, the Indians left quickly. It is quite evident they were afraid of Stark, who was known to be a good marksman. And he was not afraid of them.

An Indian going by the name of Willie had made an attempt on Stark's life, but the latter had seen the gun sight glistening in the sun. The gun was pointing towards him in the man's hands. Instantly, Stark shouted to him, calling him by name. The man was afraid when he saw that he was detected. He knew if he missed Stark, Stark wouldn't miss him. He was trembling when Stark came up to him. After that, Stark was very careful. He always took his dog with him when he went into the woods.

After the appearance of those five Indians at their home, the Starks felt that it was quite unsafe to live in that place, so they took a claim on the other side of the Island, and moved to a claim by the seashore. At their new home they could get plenty of seafood. Herring and smelt came up on the sand during the shoaling season. The Farmers raked them up with garden rakes. The mussels were very large then. They hung in thick clusters on the rocks.

Very often, the Farmers lived on clams and potatoes when other necessities were scarce. However, living so close to the sea had its disadvantages. It was not immune from prowlers. One day a Native, without knocking, he asked in Chinook, "*Ka mika man*" (where is your man). Sylvia answered in Chinook, "*Wake syah*" (not far away).

The dog Watch was lying asleep on the floor, but when the man spoke, the dog jumped up, and would have caught the man by the throat when Sylvia prevented him, though with some difficulty. That stopped the prowling.

But as a rule the Indians were quite friendly. They sold their commodities, Salmon and all kinds of seafood, and berries in their season. They needed the *chickeman* ("money" in Chinook).

There was one man whose name was Verygood, Captain Verygood. So named, he gained the respect of all who knew him. W.O. Stark learned from him something about the Customs of the early Natives. He said there were *hiyou* snows on the Islands in the early days (*hiyou*, big snows). The Indians wore nothing on their feet more than moccasins. They went through those heavy winters without catching cold. And they lived to see many moons. Now, after their contact with Civilization, they caught cold the same as the White man. [...]

My recollections of those early days on Saltspring Island are like a dream gone dim with age. I first saw the light on a farm near the seashore. The place finally took on the name Fruitville. When Captain Scott bought it, he enlarged it and made it a fruit Farm.

Louis Stark was the first man to the Claim. He moved his family there to be safe from Indian trouble. I remember that a little white pig used to come into the house and they would feed him there, also the noisy whales that came into our small bay.

A small unbarked log cabin stood inside the yard. It was a temporary shelter while the big cabin was being built. It was then occupied by a pioneer family from the Hawaiian Islands. They were Colored Hawaiians, perhaps the first of their country people to come to the Island. They occupied the cabin until they located a place of their own. They were the first family to take the claim now known as the Mansel Farm.

Whenever I went to their cabin, Mrs Frederson would always give me a cookie, and one to her grandchild Rena. That was why I enjoyed going to see Rena. Then our Dad Louis Stark took a claim on Vancouver Island in Cranberry Dist., so called at that time. I was too young to remember my age, but I remember well the day we left Saltspring. I carried the memory of that scenic path leading uphill through blue grass to a fence with bars to pull down and pass through. It was of no importance, just a memory.

Since then I have seen many hills leading up from the beach on Saltspring where the sea has made its bed. And there is a petrified log on the beach at Fruitville, black and hard as though in transformation from wood to coal. It has been chopped and left as though the attempt had been made by a dull axe, perhaps a stone axe.

[1966]

Nora Hendrix [1883-1984]

from Opening Doors: Vancouver's East End

When I came there was no church. What few coloured people were here had some kind of little club, you know, that they used to gather and have a little affair, like, meeting and singing and whatever they did. They used to have it down on Homer Street, was a hall there, they had that going when I came here. Them fine years different people was coming from Alberta. There wasn't very many come direct from the States like I come, right just crow-flying like that. Of course, there used to be different little people, missionaries, come through, but they'd always get some little store place or something, you know, rent it, and have a little church or something like that. But nobody had ventured out to try and get a church for their own. They commence getting together, say, "Well, we should get a church of our own." Yeah. "Ain't got any other business of our own, so got to get a church anyway, if nothing else."

So, let me see, it could be back in 1918, as far as I can think back, when we first taken that church over on Jackson Avenue. I don't know who had it before,[1] but when we saw that we could be able to get this church, well everyone then started in, working together. All the families and everybody that wanted a church, we all got together, and commence working for it to get this church started. And some of the men, they intercede and got a hold to the high-ups in the States, and they always from the States, we got all our preachers and residing elders all come from over in the States. That's where the head office of that church was, the AME it was called. So then we got together and so they said, "Well, if you raise $500, we'll raise $500." So all of the sisters and brothers and everyone, we commence getting busy then, to start to having entertainments and bazaars and suppers and everything we could have, to raise the money to buy this church. So when we worked around and got our share of money together, well, they let the residing elder know that we was ready, and so they came over and then set up our church, so then we had our own church then. So it was $1,000 we had to pay down. Getting dollars together them days was hard. When you went out to work, all you got was a dollar and a half for your day's work. And your carfare. That's what you got in them days. So, you see it taken us a little while to raise up $500.

I think Reverend Robinson[2] come from the east of the States, the first reverend we had here to work in our church. Then after 6 years we commenced getting different preachers every year pretty well, after he was here. And we had a Reverend Wright.[3] He was here for quite awhile, he was a kind of settled man. He was a good preacher. Well I finally, after awhile, after years going by, well, I kind of pulled myself out and of course, a lot of my old friends had gone. After the younger bunch came in the church and commence working, well I said, "I'll let these young people take it over now, and I'll just get on out and kind of rest myself. Let *them* run it."

Of course, you see, we was supposed to *pay* the preacher, he isn't supposed to do any work at all, he don't have to. But most of the preachers we had that come here, they all were pretty handy, they'd do things around the church, you know, if they see something to be done. Sweep up, if it happened to be we didn't have no regular janitor or nothing. So we always was kind of lucky to have good preachers, that would do anything that was around.

We used to go around and sing. There was one musical man come here, named Bartley. He came here and got about 50 of us and got a big choir, and we used to go around and sing in all different theatres or churches. I guess that was in the Twenties where we put on all these singsongs. And the old Avenue Theatre, I think we sang in that with our choir.

On American Thanksgiving the church used to always have a big turkey dinner on that day and then other nights we used to have the chitlin dinners. Them chitlin suppers – we'd sell out so fast, why, they wouldn't last no time. You see, 'most all those sporting people, they like that kind of food. We often wished we could have got more, you know, but you couldn't always get the amount you wanted, and when they cooked down, you see, they cooked down so small. There were chitlins and corn bread – that had to go along with it – and with the cabbage slaw and whatever other things we'd put with it. But we'd sell it so fast, oh, make your head spin. Just put the word out. Somebody'd just go around down in the district where all the sporting fellows and what not, and tell them the sisters going to have chitlin dinner over at such and such a place. Why they'd be there setting in the hall. If they didn't come eat it, they'd send plates and buckets and things to take it out, and then you'd turn around in a little while they're all gone, just like that. Ah! You can't buy no chitlins now. No, they run out of chitlins, I don't know how many years back.

Well, we used to have a minstrel show around here that this club put on every year, for about 5 or 6 years there in the Thirties. I didn't belong to it, but I used to be in the minstrel show every year with them. Mrs Pryor[4] was the head of that and this girl Chaney-belle. It was only 15 belonged to this club, but one year, Mrs Pryor said to me, she says, "Next year, Mrs Hendrix, I want you to be in our minstrel show." I said, "All right, I'll be in it." So the next year come and when they got ready to do the rehearsing and the piano, well, she let me know. So I went to the rehearsal and get lined out what I was going to do, because I was going to be one of the end men. You would crack jokes to the interlocutor – he's the interlocutor that's sitting in the middle there, you know, the dressed-up guy. And of course, we the funny guys on the end and we ask all kinds of funny questions, you know, and say, "What made the chicken cross the street?" Well, any old funny something, any old thing. 'Course, we had it all lined up. We done practised it, you know, when we went to rehearsal, we done rehearsed and had all of them. Then we had to sing songs, too, in-between, and then the whole bunch would sing. Oh, all the people used to enjoy that, and they'd fill up that hall. I kind of missed it myself, when they give up.

Down in the 200 and 300 block Prior and Union and Keefer is where most all these chicken places were. Mrs Pryor had a eating place on Keefer[5] and then there was a Mrs Alexander had one on Union Street[6] and there was Mr Soldier Williams,[7] he had one that used to be a funeral parlour. Well, there used to be different fellows around down on Prior Street and Keefer Street that had little clubhouses and things like that, years back in the Twenties and the Thirties. George Paris used to teach the policemen to box, and of course, he used to be around Mrs Pryor's place a good deal. He'd be around there for any disturbance, or anything that come up, he could be around there, you know, to look after, like, bouncing a fellow, I guess. He's pretty good size, yeah, and he didn't wear no hair on his head, and his head was skinny. Yeah, kept his head bald. That's the first place I saw him was around Mrs Pryor's. And as I say, Dode Jones, he had some kind of club. And this Mr Holman, I think he had a club, too. And Buddy White. They was all around down in that category, close to Main Street. The railroad fellows'd go down them places you know, play their games and gamble and whatever, like men like to. And 'course, oh yeah, the city and the mayor and them know a lot where all the different places was. That's why they could keep things so straight, like, 'cause if the railroad men come in, they know just where to go if they want to play their games, and gamble, go right to these places, as though they were right there for them. So that's why I say, that they could keep all the different things in the spots where they supposed to be. And they wasn't a whole lot of carryings on, nor a whole lot of fighting going on.

Everybody liked Mayor Taylor[8] 'cause he was one of those kind of plain man, he looked like he was for everybody. And he had the town fixed so that the sporting people lived in one part of the town and the other class of people live in another. He had them all separated. And they had a red-light district, you see? That was what a lot of people liked about Taylor, having this red-light district, because it did help to keep the people, you know, the what-you-m'a-call women was all in this one category. And when the boats come in, when those fellows want to go somewhere for a good time, well they knew where to go. See, they'd go to this street in this neighbourhood, 'cause it was all set for them. And the women had these houses and they had these girls in there and they had doctors that looked after them and all that, you see. All that was when Taylor was in.

Then the Chinese used to have their gambling, playing their lottery, and everybody'd want to play it. A lot of people – it was a dime – and sometime they get $18, just all according to the way they marked the ticket. Well a lot of guys that didn't work or didn't want to work, why they just spend 10 or 20 cents and they'd have something to live on again, then they'd always keep a ticket in there, so they didn't have to beg, you see. Sometimes a law used to come around and pinch them, because the law would get money out of them, because they'd take them in and fine them so much. If you happened to be caught in this place when they come get the head man, and you happened to be in and the law grab them and grab you, and take you downtown or wherever they take you, well, the Chinaman, he paid the fines for everybody and they go. And he's home, he gone and go on back to his little place and start all over again. Yeah! Got right back and the people would be *waiting* there to come in!

Chinatown was just a real dull place then. It wasn't built up and lights all around like it is now. I used to go down there lots to buy different things, especially when I want to get some black-eyed peas. Oh yes, I used to go down there and trade, sure. But sometimes, some of the Chinese would look at you so funny, you feel kind of funny when they look at you. 'Course, I couldn't blame them for looking. That's what their eyes was for.

The people, they didn't bother you on the streets like they do now. You could walk all around and didn't nobody bother you. Men wasn't grabbing women and all that stuff. 'Cause a man coming out of the woods or something, well he'd know where to go. He didn't have to bother you or any other lady walking up and down the street. No. It was a good thing to have that red-light district. I know a lady and her daughter used to do the washing for the girls that worked in them houses, and they made all kinds of money washing them women's clothes. Them girls didn't have to do nothing. They had people, maids, to come clean up the house and all that. There was a lot of coloured girls that used to love to go there to work, 'cause it was good money. Sure. Go there and cook. I know a lady who cooked there and she made a thousand dollars, in a little while, and she sent back to the States and brought her family here. Yeah. A woman that's looking for a job, to cook or to clean up, that's where you could make your money. And nobody'd bother you. 'Cause the men that come in there, they wouldn't bother *you*, you were just a working woman around there.

Most of the men worked on the railroad. Except only those that worked in the buildings downtown, down in the big buildings, they had coloured men janitors down in there. I know one man, Mr Wallace, he was a kind of overseer. Well, he was a little bit richer than the rest of us, and 'course he had a job of overseeing, getting men to go around and do the janitor work, you know. Like they give him the job to go to get the help for these different buildings, you see, and he'd get the men to do the janitor work and the cleaning up. He worked some, but he didn't have to, because he'd have all these men that, work under him like.

It was hard for coloured men to get just the ordinary jobs. One year my husband was supposed to get a job working in a gents' restroom but when that policeman got shot, there's a lot of stuff come up, and he didn't get the job. There were this coloured fellow and this sporting woman who was a friend. Marjorie Earl, her name was. And all the policemens liked this woman too. 'Course, she run around with anybody, and this sporting fellow, this coloured boy, she was friends with him. And this policeman, he jumped on the car when they come in from the race-track and raised the devil, and one of these policemen got shot. Well, they blamed this coloured fellow, and they send him to jail. But they said that they didn't find no gun on him.[9] Everybody was all mad about this coloured boy shooting a policeman. Well, you know, that put a damper on where the coloured boys were working in different places, it made it hard for them, they want to bar them out. So then my husband didn't get this job. There was some excuse.

The few families that lived here, they had certain kind of jobs. There wasn't a whole lot of shoeshining stands, because the Italians had a lot of those. Oh the Italians, leave it to them, brother. They come in here and they commence to getting rich, I'm telling you. 'Cause they had all the streetcars running and the streets had to be fixed, and the Italians would do all that work. They had a night shift, day shift work on them streets, and keep men all night working. They'd be out there, working like sixty. Oh yeah. I think the Italians had the taxis, too. 'Cause they was pretty smart, when they arrived here. They got busy and commence building up their part. Yeah. Like I used to tease a friend of mine when we'd go into the bootleggers. I says, "You see all them nice carpets and things we're walking over? You helped to buy them," I said. "You helped to buy them a good solid carpet that you go way down in you can't hear you walk. You helped to buy it. And don't say a word," I says.

[1979]

NOTES

1. From 1903 to 1913 it was the German Lutheran Church. 1913 to 1918 it was the Norwegian Lutheran Church. After 1918 it was Fountain Chapel, American Methodist Episcopal (AME), the favoured church of Strathcona's black community.

2. Reverend Ulysses S. Robinson.

3. Reverend J.W. Wright.

4. Rosa Pryor.

5. The Chicken Inn.

6. Mother's Tamale and Chili Parlour.

7. Martin Luther Williams.

8. L. D. Taylor, mayor of Vancouver, 1910-11, 1915, 1925-28, 1931-34.

9. Daphne Marlatt and Carole Itter: "According to contemporary newspaper accounts, on October 9, 1922, at 2:30 AM, Police Constable R. G. McBeath was fatally shot on the corner of Davie and Granville Streets, after boarding a car and arresting its driver, Fred Deal, for drunken driving. Marjorie Earl was the other occupant of the car. After shooting McBeath and Detective R. S. Quirk, Deal escaped but was rounded up by other officers called to the scene. At his arrest, he was unarmed, but a revolver identified as Marjorie Earl's was found on the staging of a billboard in the vicinity. This killing caused public outrage because McBeath was a young World War I veteran who had been awarded the Victoria Cross for heroism in France." *Opening Doors: Vancouver's East End* (Victoria: Aural History Program, 1979), p. 63.

Rosa Pryor [1887-?]

from Opening Doors: Vancouver's East End

That winter I saw the people just dropping dead on the street. I never seen nothing like that flu. And I never caught it at all. The man that ran the undertaking business, Mr Edward, down in the half block where I lived, why, he had bodies just dead laying out in the alleyway, and he couldn't take them in to get them ready to bury. He'd put a canvas over them till he could work on them. And I used to have to go down that alley at night. I'd see people, and they'd say, "Well, I'll see you," and then I'd wake up the next morning and it was the same Mr so-and-so who died last night. They just died so fast they'd be just standing talking to you and just drop dead. Oh, it was awful.[1]

About that time I opened up the Chicken Inn, and I was there for 42 years. I thought, well I'll get those live squabs in the Chinatown, make little squabs and maybe people around there, close to the Stratford Hotel . . .

Well, when I first opened up the Chicken Inn, I didn't have a nickel. Didn't have a quarter. I got everything ready to open and I looked around and I didn't have any money. And I had to have $20 for a licence. I didn't know what I was going to do. I looked at my husband and you know, I'd just as well been looking outdoors. He sat right there and looked at me. I said, "Well, why don't you get out and maybe you'll find some money on the street, 'stead of looking at me, 'cause I don't have nothing." All I can do is to write to my mother and get the money. Well, I knew that my mother didn't have any money, but my mother lived in the country where she was acquainted with the rich white people around there, because she worked for them. So I had to write to her, because the man was waiting for my $20. Well, my mother wrote me that she didn't have the money at first and she was around trying to borrow it from different places. There ain't nothing on earth that a mother won't do, you know. So she borrowed the money and she wrote me in a hurry on a paper sugar sack, some kind of sack which she split open. And it said, "Rose, I'm sending you some money. I have had a hard time getting it. I didn't have any money in the house and I went from place to place and it's hard times here."

But by then I had *borrowed* the money. I'd found a woman running the racetrack and she took me to the races every day with her. That woman said, "You want to buy? Here, you take $2." I didn't want to put it on a horse, I wanted it myself! But I'd put it on my horse, you know, and I'd lose every time I'd bet. She was paying away and she just had a pocketful of money. She came from down in California, but she said she just liked me – she liked to talk and she didn't know anybody, and I'd do the talking, but I wanted some of that money. I wanted $20! My God, that woman had so much money and was just buying stuff for me. She was drinking, and buying. I couldn't drink. I couldn't do nothing. I wanted that $20. Well, I couldn't get no money from her, she was a *stranger* to me. But she said she liked me, so I just asked anyhow. I said, "I'm going to open up a Chicken Inn . . ." She just looked at me, said, "Well, you don't know me. I don't know you. I'm just spending my money. My husband came up here to bring this money and just have a good time. But I don't know anything about you." Well, she *didn't* know anything about me. She said, "If I give you the money, when are you going to pay it back? How are you going to pay it back if you don't have a nickel?" I said, "If you give me the money, lend me the money, I'll pay it back in 2 weeks." Oh, she bawled me out like a dog. She talked bad, too. She said, "Well, if I loan you this money, then don't you frig off with my money." So by God, she lent me the money. Oh, she had a great big thing of money.

On the first day, I asked the different people to come and I didn't really expect they all were coming. A man came in and said, "Ain't you got them chickens ready?" I said, "Yes, I've got them and I'm *just* ready to open up. Come back in half hour – you'll get your chicken. I couldn't afford to buy but 2 chickens at a time – I'd run my husband over there to buy the chicken and he'd just cut them up right quick and I'd wash them and I'd get them on frying. Oh, he liked the chicken. I gave him a good dinner. I kept saying to my husband, "Now you stay right here in the hall so you can run quick over to the Chinaman's and buy another chicken." And then I'd commence talking, "Oh, yes, yes, so and so and so," and I'd talk to take up some time until I'd see him come in, then I'd say, "Well, I must get those chickens on." Then I'd get him to pay and I'd say to my husband, "Now, you get 2 more." So, I got by that way. And that night, the woman who lent me the money came there and was fooling around, watching me. But she was alright, that woman. On the next day, I just paid her the money. "That's alright," she said, "I knew you'd pay me or I wouldn't let you have it." I thought to myself, "No, well, I had to *beg* for it."

And about 2 weeks later, the money came [from my mother]. The doorbell rang, said, "Registered letter here for you." It said, "Rosa, I had a hard time getting this money. I had to send all over everywhere to get it." And shoot, I had about a hundred dollars then all saved up and plenty of chickens and everything. I was a big person. I just took the money and got it together and put it right in the envelope and sent it right back to her. And I've never had to borrow a nickel from anybody since that day.

I was the first person who ever owned a "Chicken Inn." First person who ever fried any chicken. They didn't know much about fried chicken here in this country like they did in the States.

I remember lots of funny things happened. I've done lots of fighting in there, I know that, with every damn fool coming in there and one thing and another. There was lots of people who were going to fight me but I'd fight them back. I never went for no police the whole time I was there. Oh, and fight! But I had a husband that weighed 200 and some odd pounds and I wasn't bad myself, and so if they'd start the fight, well, we'd always win. I had a stick. Always. Right here under my apron. By God, I'd draw that out – they'd leave. I never lost a fight. Had some bad ones, too.

It was awful bad in the Thirties, but I just kept one girl and then me and my husband done the work, and so we got along pretty good that way. Didn't have to have no outside help. But it was a long time. But I know we didn't take in nothing – we sat up there and played whist all night. You weren't getting any money then, but you weren't spending anything. Oh Lord, it was hard. When you get a dollar, you better hold on to it. 'Cause they all make out like they are going to give you this and do you that, and one thing and another, but oh, God, when you ain't got it! And then you are looking at a bare floor or looking at a man and he's doing nothing. Oh, I haven't ever been broke since, no.

[1979]

NOTES

1. "The provincial government estimated that 30 per cent of the people of British Columbia were sick. In Vancouver there were between 28,000 and 30,000 cases of influenza. In 1918 there were 618 deaths and in 1919 there were 329 deaths." Margaret Andrew, "Epidemic and Public Health Influenza in Vancouver, 1918-19," *B.C. Studies* 34 (Summer 1977), pp. 21-44; quoted in Marlatt and Itter, p. 109.

Austin Phillips [1910-1979]

from Opening Doors: Vancouver's East End

Corner of Main and Union was the Bingarra Hotel which has been torn down since the new viaduct opened.[1] Then you went down the alley, down Park Lane, to this place called Scat Inn which was, oh I'd say they cooked a few chickens and steaks and played a lot of music and people danced. They cut a few walls out of an old house, sold drinks, a regular bootlegger at that time. Whisky was 25 cents a drink, beer was 25 cents a drink – that's bootlegging prices. Then the real part of Hogan's Alley started right at Park Lane and it ran right straight up between Prior and Union, ended around Jackson Avenue – that's when you were out of Hogan's Alley, the rest was just called an alley. Oh, the things that used to happen there! I came out here in '35 and that's about the first place I run into. I didn't know anybody in town and I just got off a freight train somewhere out here by the ocean and started to walking. Just walked right down as though I'd been in town before and ended up in Hogan's Alley. Going through the alleyway, you'd see some people laying on wagon wheels – they had a bunch of old broken wagons out on this old-time lot with the grass maybe growing up around it about a foot high, 2 feet high. And people, some of them bums, would just sleep in the wagons, sleep in the grass.

There was one thing about it, none of them were big boys around there. They'd act all the play mostly from everybody coming in and out getting their drinks, and they'd have a room where you'd have a dancing space. Then there was Buddy's over on Prior. The Chief of Police remembers him from now. He was the only man that was known to take a set of square dice and throw from 2 to 12 on 'em and never miss. When he died, the Chief of Police made this statement in the paper. He says, "He's the only man I ever saw say dirt to me because I bet him 2 bucks he couldn't do it." He had an ex-fighter, most everybody knew him, Joe Wilson, and he used to play piano for him.

Another one down there, the big boss of the place, was Lungo. This was the big Italian, he was 310 pounds, 6 foot 4 inches. His house was in the middle of the alley and they called him "The King." He made homebrew wine, you know. He'd make this wine and he would sell it for 40 cents a quart and the fella across the road from him, this West Indian guy, used to buy from him and sell it for 10 cents a glass. So you can imagine the profit he was making.

There was nothing but parties in Hogan's Alley – night time, anytime, and Sundays all day. You could go by at 6 or 7 o'clock in the morning, and you could hear jukeboxes going, you hear somebody hammering the piano, playing the guitar, or hear some fighting, or *see* some fighting, screams, and everybody carrying on. Some people singing, like a bunch of coyotes holler – they didn't care what they sounded like just as long as they was singing. Oh, I used to go from one place to the other playing guitar. They never paid you a salary. They had what you call a kitty, a little tin box with a horn like a phonograph on it. People wanted to tip you, they'd want to throw a buck, 10 cents, whatever it was – well, they'd throw it in the kitty. That was *your* money, that's what you made. Then if you didn't want to drink whisky, well you'd ring for the houseman, the boss, and he'd bring you Coca Cola for rum and tea for whisky. Then you'd get that two bits for yourself, see.

So I can say, myself, I was making my money going from place to place, you know. There used to be a bunch of chop suey houses on Pender Street – always, has been – and I would go from restaurant to restaurant and play from booth to booth. I've seen myself make as high as $25 a night in those days. And then go down and go into the bootlegging places again. I was playing the songs that come out then: "East of the Sun, West of the Moon," and "Don't Get Around Much Anymore," and, oh, just mostly all those songs. "Stardust" was pretty well famous in those days, and "Am I Blue," that was one of the favourites. And "Beale Street Blues," "St. Louis Blues," and "Beautiful Lady in Blue," "Paper Moon." Those songs all got famous around '36, '37, then they died out. There's been thousands of them. I can't remember them now until somebody requests them, and then I try to remember all of 'em. I would take my guitar, throw it across my shoulder and go from one place to the other. I play all string instruments – piano, guitar, banjo, steel guitar, ukelele, mandolin, violin. Somebody want a party played for, I'd go all over town. I'm a pretty good singer in my time, and I always dressed pretty well, always ready for an occasion, and I've made a lot of parties.

Back in '38, that was after McGeer was out and Taylor was in,[2] anything went. [Prominent people] would come in a place, and if they didn't want anybody to know, they would buy it out, say $100 or $200 a night – just whoever they wanted to stay there and drink with [them]. And Mayor Taylor used to come down and drink if he went to Buddy's or Dode's, or Mother Alexander's for chicken and steak.

There weren't too many guns around Hogan's Alley, it was more blackjacking and mugging and stuff like that. There was more killings in the West End, even at that time, than there were in the Alley. I can't recall of anybody except this one guy getting killed. Another guy was shot in there, and some of them was stabbed in there, but they all lived. But this guy, this Lungo's son, never knew his name – he's the only one that was really killed. Coloured guy killed him with a wrench over a dogfight. What happened was, this guy they called Ernie, he was setting back near the Scat Inn in the summertime you know, and he was strumming away on my guitar. And the dog starts a fight down the alley right in front of Lungo's place. His son was hitting the other dog that was fighting his dog, and he hit him with a stick. All of a sudden, Ernie goes down and he says, "Don't ever hit a dog around me," he says, "dog saved my life overseas," he says, "you hit the dog again, I'll hit *you*." So the guy kicked the dog and, well, he hit him with a wrench – very light tap it looked to me like, but it was enough to kill him.

Well, there was always somebody in fights, or threatening. But then again, you take all the other guys bumming, no matter what nationality they was, they was on the bum for dimes and nickels – and some of those fellas was bumming could stand on a corner and they'd bum more than the average guy working a day. They could eat cheap too, but nobody would refuse. These people that had the money with them, they'd give them 10 or 15 cents, a quarter. Some were generous, some made a winning and they'd hand a guy 2 bucks, tell him to "Go git your clothes cleaned" or something like that. But they was always good that way. Unless a man was something really out, like he was considered an informer or something, a stool pigeon. Then he wasn't liked, he wasn't welcome around that part. Even the police didn't like him. They'd use him til he was no more value to them, then if the crowds want to get him let them get him, he's served their purpose. But that's the way it run, off and on, like the fish in the sea: the big ones eat the little ones, if they could have them. You never know when that little guy might come into the luck and make something, might be able to get it back.

There was a guy came out of the logging camp – I think he was a donkey puncher, 'cause he was making good money. But he came down in this Hogan's Alley with a girl I knew, a regular clip-artist. She picked him up, or he picked her up, in the beer parlour there, and on a foggy night he comes down with $800 in his pocket. Well, she give him the knockout drops in the drink, and he walked outside and she rolled him, and when he finally did come to, he was on a pile of rubbish out in the alley. He went down and he made a complaint to the police, and they says, "Have you ever heard of Hogan's Alley?" He says, "No, I really haven't." He said, "You've heard of the East End, haven't you?" He says, "Oh yes, I've heard of the East End." He said, "You mean to tell me you didn't have any more sense than to come down here?" He said, "I'm a policeman, I wouldn't pack that kind of money with me in this part of town, and I've got a gun." He said, "If you're stupid enough to go down that end of town with that kind of money on you, I would say you deserved it, and we're not wasting our time looking for nobody we couldn't find anyhow."

There was gambling going on practically every place. Sometimes there'd be guys over from the American side, and I seen as much as 2 or 3 thousand dollars on the table. And some of the little places had penny-ante games you could buy into for 25 cents, and they'd play as hard for that as they would for the big stakes. Practically every house around there, they'd just start up a game, but there was only a few of the houses that had big games. Old Buddy, he was quite a man on the dice game, and he used to get all the big shots from across town, big-time gamblers, and he gambled them. They were shooting 200 up to a 1,000 bucks a shot, rolling dice. But he was one of the rich men there, he was top bootlegger, and that's all he did was bootleg and gamble.

There was junk that passed around there too. But maybe out of a 1,000 you'd see one dope-fiend in those days, that's how few they were. Not because some of them couldn't afford it. Because it was so cheap in those days they could go down and get a prick of morphine for about a dollar and a half. But very seldom you'd see dope-fiends.

But every place you went to, practically every place in Hogan's Alley boot-legged. If you could afford a high-class place, you went to the Scat Inn, you went to Buddy's Beer Garden. He served beer and he'd serve hard stuff – rum, gin, whisky. Then there was the two Macaroni Joe's, one guy was a little one and the other a big one. The little guy, he sold everything from wine to whisky, anything at all, right up until he died he was still a bootlegger. But this other big Macaroni Joe – I'd been buying wine off of him for probably a couple of years, and he had good wine he was making out of apples, it was sweet, and I like sweet wine, and it was a little bubbly, you know. So I was setting in his place one Sunday morning, right on the corner of Prior and Park Lane, and I said to him, "Joe, how do you make this wine?" So he says, "I got some mash on now, I go show you. I making with feet." Well, I seen pictures of girls running around with their feet to make wine over in the old country – that's girls, they wash their feet. But this guy, he pulled off these blue woolly socks and his feet were sweating, and in between his toes you could see this black he called toe-jam. He rolled his britches up, and he's got apples in a tank about 4 feet high, and it's bubbling up, and he just stepped right in there. He never washed his feet and he weighed about 250 pounds. Oh God.

We used to know a few of the police in town. They used to come down – they liked to get in on that gambling. One night 2 of them was off the beat and they'd come in and they'd put their money in the bank together, and they were dealing. Blackjack. They had a whole stack of money and everybody was betting the table, as many people could bet. All of a sudden, in comes the Chief of Police. What he was doing there I do not know but he drove up, I guess he must have seen the car parked on Union and wondered where they were at. So when he walked in the door, he said, "What are you guys doing here?" They just *dropped everything* and went out, left their money on the table, they just went away! Well, everybody had a ball with the money, everybody was grabbing away. They used to be pretty good, pretty good. They didn't pay any attention to prostitutes or pimps, they didn't bother them too much. What they were really hot on was dope-fiends, and there wasn't many of them. If they caught them, bingo! And anybody that was selling it, well, that was it, because they're worse against that than they are on murder. They didn't bother about gambling.

This town, it just run itself practically. Some of them were paying off. That's before Gerry McGeer took over. When he got to be mayor, he closed everything in town up, everything. He tightened on and he chased all the prostitutes out of town, all the bootleggers he was clamping down on them, he just cleaned up the place. The only good thing that he done, that I said to myself, was when he put Joe Celona[3] in jail. That's a guy you couldn't even be decent with – the guys he was paying off to, the cops he was paying off to. And he was just a young man but let go long enough he'd of become another Al Capone. But he ended up with a 20-year rap on him. He got that time just before I come out here in '35, that's when he first got sentenced. He did half his time and they finally gave him parole and he was out *one week* and the church people, all the people, signed a petition to put him back in. He did his time.

There was quite a few black people around. That old Mrs Pryor, that big woman, she used to weigh about 350 pounds, I liked to see *her* come in. She'd come down about once every 3 months. She used to bring a sack, one of them leather bags, and she'd have it full of silver dollars and 50-cent pieces. And she would set me on her knee, and say, "Play my song! You come on and you play 'Maggie.'" I did-n't know "Maggie," I'd just sing what I knew of it and everytime I'd sing "Maggie" for her, she'd give me a silver dollar. And curse me out, curse me out all the time! "Oh, play me that song 'Maggie' again!" Probably have to play it for her about 15 times a night, but if you got through, you got a dollar for every time you'd sing it.

Most everyone from Hogan's Alley is dead. I'm about the only one that was ever around there that's still living. And that is the lowdown rundown on the way it went at that time.

[1979]

NOTES

1. The Georgia Viaduct.

2. Louis D. Taylor actually last served as mayor of Vancouver in 1934. In 1938, George C. Miller was mayor of Vancouver. G.G. McGeer was mayor 1935-1936, 1947.

3. "Joe Celona was born in Italy in 1898, immigrated to Canada in 1913, and came to Vancouver 6 years later. He was shot in an incident in his home, 1933. A year later he was arrested on white slavery charges. At his trial in 1935, he was convicted of living in part on the earnings of prostitution, and of keeping a 'disorderly house' (the Maple hotel at 177 East Hastings, the top floor of which was said to be a brothel). He was sentenced to 11 years, but after serving 5, was released on parole by the Justice Department. Public outcry resulted in his being returned to the penitentiary to serve the remainder of his sentence. After his release, he turned to bootlegging. He was a witness during the 1955 Royal Commission investigation of charges of bribery and corruption in the Vancouver Police Force. He died in 1958. (*Province*, April 12, 1935; *Province* July 9, 1940; *Sun*, March 5, 1958.)" Marlatt and Itter, p. 143.

Leona Risby [1911-1991]

from Opening Doors: Vancouver's East End

My parents moved from Texas to Oklahoma, and from Oklahoma to Alberta in 1911. They brought most of their materials and all their furniture and their horses, and they even brought a dog. They chartered a wagon train, I remember my dad saying, him and 4 other men. They chartered this car and they brought all their belongings in it, and the menfolks slept in this car, but the women and their children they stayed on the train. They came to Edmonton and I was born in a tent there. Then they took us all to Athabasca and most of my childhood was spent in Athabasca, 100 miles north of Edmonton. My mother's Indian, a southern tribe, Cherokee. My father's black. Oh, there must have been tons of coloured people that came up from Texas. I don't like to go into that because it hurts and I won't talk about it, but I heard my father tell these stories of why he came to Canada. It makes you feel hurt inside, it makes you feel bitter, and you don't know who to feel bitter to, so it's best not to talk about it.

I was frightened when I first arrived because Vancouver was rough – when I came to the coast here it was *rugged*, really rugged. It was a sort of a red-light district in there on Main and Hastings. All around Hastings and Main and Alexander, but it wasn't down in Japtown. I was scared to death. I used to take the streetcar up as far as Woodward's and then I'd get home as fast as I could because it was *really* rough. I think it deserved to be cleaned up. They were not giving the young girls any protection, and there was so many young girls in that type of a mess, just to get a dollar. Kids, young kids. I knew girls that were 14 and 15 years old that was in such stuff as that. Some of 'em got there for the money, some of 'em got there to help support their family, sometimes their parents put 'em there, and sometimes the men put them there. The girls in that type of work wore these clinging satin pyjamas, they had these big wide legs to them, these pyjamas did, and they'd have on these beautiful pyjamas and all made up. Then you'd just pass a little house, there'd be a man across the street, and you're walking across the street, and there'd be "ping, ping, ping" – they're knocking at the man to come in. That's an awful thing. Now I think the town has cleaned up from that. Whatever they do now, you don't see it. Mama Pryor[1] said when she came here, you didn't go in that part of town that was a red-light district, but the red-light was all over Vancouver when I came out here – those bugs were lighting up everywhere! Well, the law got in there and they closed up *all* of those places. It was Mayor Telford that got in, and it was Telford because all of the people were fussing at Telford. They didn't like Telford, but he is the mayor that cleaned up the city.

Most of the black families lived out [of Strathcona] and not too many that lived downtown. Maybe the old pensioners that couldn't get around much, and didn't have much money for carfare, so they'd get a little room and crawl in it or something. Our people never lived close together, only with the people that lived down where we say the slums are, across from the church.[2] They lived in those little places because they couldn't afford to get any other. But the black people did pretty good for themselves here. They used their money well, most of our people used their money well. I won't say all of 'em 'cause some of them wouldn't have a job if you put it in bed with them. When they could buy something, they got it, 'cause they hadn't been used to getting money – just like myself. I've never had too much in life, but everything that I got, I earned and I earned it the hard way, and I pinched pennies.

When we lived around there, there was a lot of people living there, the odd drunk, and a few winos, but it wasn't rough. Nobody got robbed. And you could go to work safe – walk to work and back. I lived on Prior Street, in the 300 block Prior, used to walk back and forth to work in the early parts of the morning and nobody bothered me. Most of Mrs Pryor's business came from the Stratford. A lot of the loggers used to stay there and they were all clean-cut working men. You'd see the odd old wino laying around sleeping some place, but actually they don't bother, too weak to bother and they just want a little wine and they go out on a sleep and their face is all red and they look pitiful.

Then there was Hogan's Alley where they danced and they sang. Maybe one person was pretty high that would want one song sung all night and the same song, because it reminded him of something, and they'd be putting money in the kitty, and then when they get "Will you sing that song?" "Yeah," they'd say, and they loved that old song, and they would be wanting that played, just some song or 'nother.[3] And it was a small place, there would be a few around dancing, and a few sitting around at the table drinking until they fall on the floor, and pick 'em up and drag 'em and lay 'em out in Hogan's Alley.

Later [in the mid-1950s] I owned a place on Powell Street that was a Japanese fish market Mother Alexander bought, and I bought it from her son after she died – old, old place and it was between two big stores and it was kind of falling under. Well, my husband and my daughter, they didn't want it. "Oh, this old place will fall down. You don't want it. You're just wasting your money." So I said, "I'll call the city building inspector and ask his opinion." Well he came and he looked and he said, "Well, one thing I can tell you – that it will never fall down, because there's a building to hold it up on one side, and one to hold it up on the other." So I took the place, and honest to goodness, I never knew what I was going to do with that place. I sat downstairs and hour after hour I shut my eyes and visualized how to fix it. So I called the inspector and I told him what I wanted to do, and he looked at me and he said, "Well, I'll tell you what I'll do, Mrs Risby, if you'll fix it, I'll pass it." It was the worst looking building inside that you ever saw in your life. So I just sat down and I drew some plans, and it took me about 3 days to visualize how it would look, with my eyes shut. So I just got me a bunch of gyproc, and I just – schzoop – right over one side of the building just closed up all those windows, windows up and windows down, you never saw such a place. And the other side, I did the same. Then I painted it, put the rough ceiling on, and we built a nice little log cabin front. When I called the inspector, he came and he shook his head again, "Well, I don't know how you did it, but," he said, "if you think you would be able to open up on New Year's night, you go ahead and open up – I'll pass it."

We landed a nice business there. Had a lot of nice customers, and we had all sorts of banquets. We had banquets for A. Phillip Randolph,[4] we had banquets for the baseball teams, we had band banquets, and we did a real good business. My husband was a good cook and so was I and we worked together. Sometime I'd have as many as 6 people – I'd have to employ that many. We usually opened about 5 in the evening, and we closed around 7 in the morning, and sometimes we'd have a house full of guests at 3 o'clock in the morning. When the other nightclubs would close up, they'd come over to our place. And then we used to sing gospel songs. We got a write-up in the paper you know, the only nightclub in town that when they're not doing any work, they sing spirituals! We would all sing together and it was like a real big family – everybody knew everybody. We had most all the taxi drivers, people from the sugar refinery, longshoremen by the carloads.

You've got to *earn* what you get in this world and I feel that our people, some of my people, not all, some of my people are very good at going ahead and doing and helping and getting places – but there's a number of my people that just sit back for Providence to send them a flag. And if they don't get the flag, then they don't like it and it's "because we are coloured." If you get out and *do*, then there's no person born with nothing, like myself, no education, that can't go ahead and do – like Mrs Pryor and so many other people. You've got to have a *will* to want to do a thing and if you make one step forward, the other nationalities will help you.

This play *Roots* crucifies me! They speak of religion, our people are supposed to be the most religious people in the world. Yet they don't forgive nobody. Now the people that *caused* slavery – all those people are dead. There's not one person living that was in slavery. Now why should you go around and be mad at their offspring because of all this slavery? I think the quicker we get all this out of our minds, forget it and live in the future and not in the past, the better. I say I'm not worried about where I come from – I'm worried about where I'm going!

[1979]

NOTES

1. Rosa Pryor.

2. Fountain Chapel.

3. "According to Doris Lawson who worked for Mrs. Pryor for 9 or 10 years beginning sometime in the Forties, 'We always had a piano player there. Shebo'd be before Joe Wilson, Shebo and then Joe Wilson and then Mac, and Beau Panky stayed the longest, and Hilda Sing, a white girl who played the piano – she was married to a Chinese fellow. Black fellow, Joe Wilson, he's dead. And Beau Panky's dead. Well, everybody knew Joe Wilson, he was kind of famous, he was a boxer, you know.'" Marlatt and Itter, p. 139.

4. A. Phillip Randolph (1889-1979) led the Brotherhood of Sleeping Car Porters (BSCP) from 1925 to 1968, and was active in the American Federation of Labor and the Congress of Industrial Organizations. The BSCP was the first black union to successfully negotiate a contract with an employer. Many men in Vancouver's black community worked as porters during this period.

Dorothy Nealy [1917-]

from Opening Doors: Vancouver's East End

When I came here, this district was Negroes, from Main Street to Campbell Avenue, like you see the Chinese here now. Whole apartment blocks that were all full of Blacks. In '44 it was a ghetto. They had never realized that they could move out of this area, because if they went some place to rent a house, they wouldn't refuse them and say, "We don't want you here because you're Black" – they'd just mention some exorbitant price for the rent, you see. And they knew they couldn't handle it 'cause the first thing they'd ask them, "Where do you work?" Well they worked on the railroad, you know, and they just earned a certain amount of money. And then they had 4 or 5 kids to support, so they couldn't pay rent like they can now.

When they realized they could get other jobs, then they quit the railroad. Some of them went longshoring, and some of them started driving trucks. There must have been at least 400 people lived down here. And now there's only a handful of Black people left in the neighbourhood.

In 1938, when I came out here for a visit, they had a terrible riot down in Hogan's Alley. Apparently, some college kids came over here, slumming, and one of the girls got stuck on a coloured fellow, and she came back down to the East End, to the night spots. They had dance halls and cabarets all over, you know, and she liked to dance. I mean, there was nothing, she wasn't a prostitute or anything like that. She was just a nice young lady. Well, the white men just used that for an excuse. They said she was down here someplace and they were going to put a stop to it. They came in 3 carloads and they went down Hogan's Alley. So they sent out a call, the Black people did, and they came from all over here. Well, they almost killed them, and there was about 18 of them, they just beat them insensible. And they never came back down here. But every now and then, a gang would come down here, just for kicks. Even now it happens once in a while, at the Stratford – bunch of white kids come down. And they'll call somebody a "nigger." Out of a clear blue sky, you know. And the fight is on. You can't wait for police protection, because, if the police come and drive them off, they're only going to come back again. We just settle our own accounts. We have to, because I think in their subconscious mind they feel a white supremacy attitude, these kids that come down, you know. So the only way to let them know that one man is just as good as another, is just to beat the shit out of them. And then they'll let you alone.

Fountain Chapel was really the whole hub of this ghetto. If you wanted to meet anyone, the thing to do was to go to church. And that little church would be just packed to the doors. They had a beautiful choir. The preachers didn't stay here long, they were mostly American ministers.

Ten or 20 years ago, we didn't know anything about Africa. We were all Canadians and all we knew was British history. Like, I never knew Hannibal was a Black man till after I was grown and married. What I was taught was about all the great explorers and the seafaring men and how the British Empire was won. But we didn't know at *what cost*.

It's just in the last few years we've really become aware of what's happening. And then we started reading. There was a time we couldn't even get these *Ebony* magazines in Canada. We had to get the American railroad porters to bring them in. When the BCAACP[1] first started out, over 20 years ago, it was the NAACP,[2] and then they changed into the BCAACP because we're all Canadians. They more or less felt like our situation here is quite different, because, in the United States, the Americans are so blatant about the racial prejudice. You can fight it, because they call you "nigger" and they segregate you out loud and clear. But the racism in Canada is so subtle, and so elusive you can't really pin it down. Like finding jobs. They would tell you, "Oh, that job was just filled 15 minutes ago, and if you had of come a little earlier you could have had the job." They would no more have hired you than shot themselves.

But when I came to this East End in 1938, oh! I thought I was in something like Hollywood, because every door was sitting wide open, and you could walk right in, you know. It was just like walking in the beer parlour today, but these were bootlegging places. And they all had music, and they all had something to eat – fried chicken, hot tamale, bowl of chili.

I think the first big shake-up they had here was when McGeer became mayor. And they said, "McGeer's put the lid on Vancouver and he's sitting on the lid." Because before that, these people ran these places like they had a licence, but they didn't, you know. Like all the sporting houses – they had to pay the police, because if any strange women was hustling out in their block, in front of their house, they phoned the police and had her arrested. They had so many houses on Union Street, and all up and down Gore Avenue. They had all kinds of women. Some of them had Chinese, Japanese, white, coloured, all nationalities. None of them specialized. Because the girls were moving from place to place across Canada, or going into the States. One girl would say, "I'm tired of Vancouver. I'm going to see if I can get in a house in Calgary." So they'd contact a landlady in Calgary, which was wide open too. Or they'd go to Nelson, or Prince Rupert. Some went to Toronto. All the landladies knew each other, clear across Canada and down through the States. I've heard the girls saying, "I'd like to go to Kimberley. I've got a friend, she told me she made a lot of money up at Kimberley." And the landlady would say, "Don't go till I get someone to take your place." Some houses had 2 girls, some had 5. Well, they got tired of living in a house maybe for 5 or 6 months or a year, you know. Maybe she'd want to go to Kimberley, and then they'd phone the landlady in Kimberley, say, "Can you send me a parcel?" "Yes." "Well, I can send you a parcel in 2 weeks." "Well, I'll send you mine in 2 weeks." So that meant that when that girl came, the other girl left, so the landlady wouldn't be out of a girl.

And then when the heat was on, well, the girls would disperse. Like a new mayor or a new police chief, they'd come in and they'd close all the sporting houses and raid all the bootlegging places, and then everybody'd have to scatter, especially the girls. The landladies stayed and they would try and get them places to go to in different parts of Canada. 'Cause the police chief as a rule, he gave them 30 days notice. And then maybe the sporting houses would be closed down for a month or 2 months. And then they'd make a donation, to the firemen's or the policemen's – some benefit organization that they had going, you know. And then they'd have a talk with the police chief, or the mayor. Then pretty soon they'd start to get 1 girl, then they'd get 2 girls, then they'd get 3 girls and start all over again. The sporting houses, they finally closed down in the Fifties. But the bootleggers they never really shut down until the last few years.

Practically every Black woman in Vancouver has worked for Mrs Pryor's Chicken Inn sometime or other. Some of them has worked there for years and years, from the time she started. And when she first started, she couldn't afford to pay wages, so everybody worked for their tips. The Chicken Inn was just like sitting in your own kitchen, you know. It was kind of primitive: she had plain tables and chairs, with oilcloth on the tables, and she had ashtrays there for a while, glass ashtrays, but everybody kept stealing them, so she just put sardine cans on the table. The food was very good. She sold hot tamales and chili and fried chicken and steaks. Her coal and wood range was about the size of that bed, a huge great big black monster. I think there was about eight eyes in it. And she had those big black cast-iron frying pans, and they were huge things.

I was the day cook. I'd come on at 2 o'clock in the afternoon and work till 10 o'clock at night. I'd go out and chop kindling and get 2 or 3 cardboard boxes of kindling, and bring in several scuttles of coal, and I'd start the fire and I'd make the soup, and then sometimes, I'd make the biscuit dough, or the cornbread dough. In the daytime it was usually very quiet, but if it got busy she was there, 'cause they lived upstairs. And she'd come down every day, sit and talk with me, and when it got crowded she'd cook and I waited table.

Then there was a lot of poultry houses too, in this part of the East End. I worked for 3 years at Visco Poultry packing house in the 300 block Keefer. We used to dress chickens and turkeys and geese and ducks. And then there were 2 places on Georgia Street and a lot of places on Pender Street where they killed and cleaned chickens. The trucks would come in and the chickens were squawking and the ducks were quacking and there'd be trucks lined up and down the alleys, waiting to be unloaded. Chickens were killed by hand, and then they went through a scalding tank, then they went through a buffing machine which buffed the feathers off them, and then they were on an assembly line and everyone of us had a job to do. My job, 'cause I had small fingers, I'd slit a hole in the chicken and draw the craw out, and I'd do that all day long. I know there was 22 of us Negro women working there, several Japanese, Chinese, East Indians – not very many East Indians. They stuck to the mills in those days, and they didn't allow their women to go out working, like they do now.

There was the New Station Cafe, on Main Street between Union and Georgia, and it stayed open 24 hours a day. It was world-renowned – anything you wanted to find, go to the New Station. People would come from all parts of the city, used to come off the ships, the merchant seamen, and they'd stop you, "Where's this New Station?" You ordered something to eat, and you had your bottles with you, and you drank, and you met people and laughed and talked and danced up and down the aisles. Chinese owned and operated that restaurant. I don't know how they stood it, but they made money, and I think their whole attitude was, well it was no Chinese making a fool of themselves. If you started a fight, well they'd just call the police, and the police came with the wagon and threw in whoever was going in there, and the party went on. They had a jukebox in there, and they had one of those pinball machines. And they had 2 rows of booths and then they had a long counter. If we went to the New Delhi,[3] well they closed at 4 o'clock in the morning, and everybody would just pour out of the New Delhi, those who were still on their feet, and we'd go down to the New Station. And they'd be walking bootleggers, up and down the aisle. Then you'd just call them, "Give me a mickey." They'd give you a mickey, you'd call the waiter, "Give me a Coke, Seven Up, glass of water." And you'd be pouring, and if the police came round, you'd just put it down, and they'd come round with the flashlight, "Is that your bottle?" "No, *I* didn't . . . is that a bottle under there?" 'Cause you had to pay a $50 fine, you know, if you claimed a bottle and nobody claimed the bottle.

As soon as they walked out, "Well, they've gone to Hastings Street." Well, call the bootleggers, and the bootleggers would have their booze stashed around out in the garbage cans and different places. They'd go out there and open the garbage can and come up with a half a dozen bottles, then serve everybody and the party would carry on. We got a thrill out of the cat-and-mouse game with the police, you know. We were always trying to find some way of stashing our liquor. Like one time we were in the New Delhi and they says, "The law's at the door." So I took the 2 bottles of whiskey and I put 'em in the toilet waterbox, and came back proud as punch, thought I had defeated the police. They searched the building. Finally they went to the bathrooms and opened them, took all our whiskey, and we'd been just so smug 'cause we figured they wouldn't *think* of looking in the women's room.

When I first started working at Canadian Fish, there was whole families of

Indians, the mother and the father right down to the grandchildren, all working. This lady, she worked there for so many years she was the top seniority woman, and to me she looked quite young. So I said to her, "How could you get so many years seniority? You must be 65 or 70!" She says, "No, I came in here as a child." She says, "When we started, my mother stood me on the box and I put labels on the cans." Then she said, "That's the way we worked in all the canneries." Steveston, Queen Charlotte canneries – they did that throughout British Columbia, years and years ago.

And then, in the early days, the Chinese used to contract. One Chinese, he'd be like the foreman and he'd hire all the Chinese and they would pay him by the month. They weren't paid by the hour like the rest of us. But now the union has stopped all that. They're more integrated in the everyday workings of the cannery, they run the machines, or they're mechanics, or engineers. They're qualified.

On Dunlevy Street, before they fixed up the neighbourhood, there used to be a row of houses from Union to Hastings, and on both sides of the street the old Chinese men all summer long, they chopped wood in stove-sized pieces. And they'd pile them up on the side of the house, they'd fill the basements, then they'd fill the side of the house, and then they'd put pieces of tin to keep the rain off of it. They'd do that every summer. One old man, when he told me he moved into the housing project, "Oh," he says, "I miss the house. Nothing to do. Just sit down. Nothing to do." But they'd all talk and they'd stop and smoke their cigarettes and their pipes and they'd laugh and talk, and then they'd go in and have a cup of tea and they'd come back out. And they were there from dawn to dusk. They chopped cords and cords of wood, all summer.

When we heard of city council's plans for the neighbourhood, we were horrified, we just screamed. They intended to put high-rises all over here, like the West End. But the people that lived here, we just took up a petition. We got thousands and thousands of names. And we stopped them. The Vancouver Resources Board met with city council and they met with different organizations. They met with SPOTA.[4] You see, it wasn't just SPOTA that fought for this East End. There was the churches and all kinds of people got involved. The whole neighbourhood got involved. Because *we* were satisfied with our neighbourhood. But the people from outside came in, and told us we shouldn't have these houses, we should live in housing projects, we should live in high-rises. But what was wrong with living here? *They* didn't live here, I don't know what they were so worried about. As I said, I've lived here for 33 years. I wouldn't want to live anyplace else. But somebody comes over from Dunbar district, looking down their nose at this end of town. It's just like the Christians going to Africa, trying to convert you to Christianity when you already have your own tribal laws and religions and everything else. And that was their attitude when they came down here.

[1979]

Notes

1. British Columbia Association for the Advancement of Coloured People.

2. The American-based National Association for the Advancement of Colored People.

3. The New Delhi Cabaret.

4. Strathcona Property Owners and Tenants Association.

Rosemary Brown [1930-]

from Being Brown: A Very Public Life

In 1955 Black students were a rarity at UBC and Dr Gordon Shrum, who was in charge of student housing, found that he had to give them priority in university housing, because the neighbours of the university were certainly unwilling to do so. However, because we had not anticipated a problem, by the time we realized how critical our situation was, we were too late for university housing that semester, so our name went on a waiting list and Bill kept searching. It was desperate, depressing work and after many failures we decided that job-hunting and house-hunting were draining too much of our time and energy. It was clear that the racial barriers in the city were too intact to respond to our feeble assault, so we accepted defeat and agreed that we would stop trying to find decent, good quality shelter and live wherever we could find housing, whether it was suitable or not. Clearly this was not our town so we would remain here only as long as necessary, then arrange to leave this province within five minutes of Bill writing his final exam, never to return.

Despite the efforts of white friends and classmates who themselves had no difficulty finding housing, since there was actually a glut of apartments on the market, we found that we were not welcome in the West End, nor in the neighbourhood around Vancouver General Hospital. We finally managed to rent a bachelor suite in an old converted house at the corner of 6th Avenue and Spruce overlooking a dirty and sluggish False Creek, which at that time gave no hint of its trendy, fashionable future. The rent was $40 a month and accommodation consisted of one room with cooking facilities and a bathroom down the hall that we shared with two other tenants on the same floor. That experience was the beginning of our bathroom fetish – we swore that if we survived that situation, we would never share a bathroom with anyone again. We furnished our suite with a double bed, two bamboo armchairs, a coffee table and a small kitchen table with two straightback chairs. We had received dishes and saucepans and linen and everything else as wedding presents, so we were very comfortable as we settled in to get through the next three years of our life.

A week after we moved into our apartment I answered an ad placed by the Registered Nurses Association of B.C. for a clerical worker. When I arrived for my interview, I was introduced to Miss Alice Wright, the president, who spoke happily of her visits to Jamaica and of the friends she had made among the nursing community there. She asked why I was applying for such a junior position despite my clerical experience and university degree. I explained about the difficulty I was having in securing employment. She was genuinely upset by my story and offered me the job although she felt that I was overqualified for it; she insisted that I treat it as a temporary placement until something better came along.

I worked at the Registered Nurses Association office on Cypress Street for one year at $130 per month, until I was hired to work as a library assistant at UBC for $181 monthly. I remained in that job until a month before the birth of our first child and only daughter, Cleta.

As employment goes I was lucky; other non-white immigrants with more skills and better education have had to work a lot harder under worse conditions for less money. I have always been grateful to Miss Wright and the RNABC for being 'the one person' willing to employ me despite the colour of my skin.

Over the years I developed the 'one person' theory, on the basis that no matter how many people in a situation are willing to discriminate against you for racial, religious or other reasons, there is always 'the one person' who will refuse to go along with the pack. So the secret to living with discrimination is to hang on and keep fighting until 'the one person' in any given situation is found – because that person always exists. Certainly the story of my life in Canada is the history of these 'one persons' who always marched to a different drum when prejudice and discrimination surfaced.

A friend once asked me whether the Jamaican McGill graduates who encouraged me to attend university in Canada had discussed Canadian racism with me, and I realized with some surprise that no one mentioned the topic even once during all of our briefings. Even more surprising was the realization that on similar occasions when I had spoken to students planning to attend Canadian universities, I had never raised the question of racism either.

Everyone knew of and spoke openly and at great lengths about racism in the United States; everyone spoke openly and at great length of our sense of betrayal at finding racism in the mother country – England – but for some strange reason we did not discuss racism in Canada.

Part of the reason, I guess, is because of the subtle and polite nature of Canada's particular brand of racism. We often found it difficult to describe to each other racist experiences because, except in the case of housing and employment, their form was so nebulous – a hostile glance – silence – being left to occupy two seats on the bus while people stood because no one wanted to sit beside you – being stopped and questioned about your movements by the police in daytime in your own neighbourhood – the assumption of every salesperson who rang your doorbell that you were the maid. How do you protect yourself against such practices? How do you tell someone to beware? How do you explain that sometimes you feel ashamed to be the recipient of such treatment and that the reluctance to acknowledge its existence is somehow linked to lowered self-esteem and self-worth?

I believe that if you are going to be a Black person living in a racist country, it is best to be born a middle child. The sense of humour you develop to compensate for the fact that you are neither the first-born (with the attendant privileges of that position) nor the youngest and pampered, stands you in good stead when racial stupidity intrudes on your life. I developed humour as an armour and I learnt in time how to use it as a teaching tool to turn insensitivity into a crash course in tolerance. When the saleslady in the exclusive dress shop who was waiting on me as I tried on a very expensive ultrasuede suit asked with a smile whether I was a singer, I replied with a smile that no, I was not, neither was I a boxer! We both laughed at my response, and the message was sent and received that Black people earn their living like everyone else in a variety of different ways. Humour doesn't ease the pain or deflect the hurt of the victim, it just penetrates the mind of the perpetrator because her or his defences are down.

After two years in our bachelor pad, my pregnancy precipitated the need for us to seek larger accommodation, and once again we were faced with the tedious reality of anti-Black and anti-children landlords and landladies. Pregnancy compounded our dilemma: now we could be refused housing, not because we were Black but on the ground that we were about to have a child. Many landlords were relieved to be able to tell us how much they wished they could rent to us because they really like 'our people,' but unfortunately the other tenants would rebel at the prospect of a baby in the building. That experience was the beginning of a fear that has grown over the years, namely that Canadians as a people do not like having children around and often just barely tolerate their own.

In any event, once again just when it seemed that there was no hope, 'the one person' in all of Vancouver willing to look beyond our colour and my pregnancy and rent us accommodation appeared. In this case, it was Margot Ney, a school teacher who had given birth to her daughter in July, one month before Cleta, our daughter, was born, and her husband Phil, a medical student in the year behind Bill. They described themselves as Christians, who believed that because all people are created in God's image, no one person or group of persons was inferior to any other person or group, and that to hold a prejudice against anyone would be to hold a prejudice against God. We had been discriminated against by so many Christians over the years that we had ceased to think of Christianity as having anything whatsoever to do with humanity.

Phil and Margot were truly special. We became their tenants. Our daughters became and remain fast friends and, despite differences in belief and commitment on very basic and fundamental issues, we all remain part of a loving and extended family – a really strange fact considering that Phil, a psychiatrist, is opposed to feminism and the right to reproductive choice; that Margot returned to university to study law at age forty and is one of the leading legal supporters of the anti-abortion movement in B.C. I remain firm in my belief that the control of one's reproduction is an inalienable right that should not be wrested from women by government or law – and that, if women lose that right, their enslavement will be complete. The Neys and the Browns never discussed abortion during the years both families lived together, and during which our respect and love for each other grew. So, by the time the abortion debate began to divide friends and relatives, we already had too much respect and love for each other not to accept the right of each of us to her or his personal belief and commitment. Even today, although we oppose very strongly each other's opinion on this controversial issue, and even though we would dearly love to convince each other of the rightness of our positions, we accept our differences and our love survives.

By 1956 the Black population at UBC was increasing, albeit slowly. More students, especially from Trinidad, were coming to take advanced degrees in agriculture and other sciences. They were also coming to understand and appreciate the similarity of their on- and off-campus experiences. Bill and Ozzie Dawkins, the Jamaican medical student who had planned our wedding reception, decided that the time had come to organize a West Indian Society. They were both disappointed that there was no centre to the West Indian community, and, although they appreciated International House for the haven that it was, they longed for the peculiar rapport and camaraderie of a West Indian Society like the one at McGill and other eastern universities. They hoped that such a society would create a place where consciousness-raising as well as political debate would combine with fun and socializing, bolstering the self-esteem and combating the loneliness of being a 'foreign' student.

The Black West Indians flocked to join the organization, but they soon made it clear that they were primarily interested in the social aspects of the club. The legacy of Senator McCarthy hung heavy in the air and everyone took great pains to steer clear of any political discussion or involvement. In the Caribbean, the Federation of the West Indies had disintegrated, and individuals were focusing more on the politics of their own particular island than on global issues. Bill and I were desperate for political debate and discussion and we really missed the engrossing and stimulating discussions that had been so much a part of our life in Montreal. It seemed that in Vancouver, everyone was caught up in studies and personal or superficial concerns as well as the nationalistic chauvinism that is so much a part of people from small countries. The West Indian Society was not our only social contact. We also became part of a small group of the married classmates of Bill's year who partied together and shared our concerns about children, mounting debts and the future. After our daughter was born, I stayed home until she was six months old, then returned to work, this time for the Faculty of Commerce at UBC. For us, life revolved around our daughter, my work, Bill's studies and our friends.

Although we occasionally saw other Black people in the city and would always smile and say hello, it was not until Bill's third year in medicine that we actually became acquainted with any members of the British Columbia Black community. During a hospital rotation at the Vancouver General Hospital, Bill met a patient named Dolores Collins. He was so excited that he phoned me on his lunch break that day to tell me of this first meeting with a real live Black Canadian in Vancouver. Mrs Collins seemed genuinely pleased to know him, and they chatted every day that she remained in the hospital. On her discharge we were invited to her home for dinner and there we met Frank, her husband, and their children, and learnt about the B.C. Association for the Advancement of Coloured People, which was just in its formative year – Frank was the president.

It was the beginning of a truly wonderful friendship that changed our life in B.C. Bill was especially happy. He was tired of being surrounded by West Indians, much as he loved us, and he longed for contact with American Black people. He found that the Collinses and the Holmeses, two couples in the Black community, and their friends had more in common with him than West Indians did, and he embraced the Black community of Vancouver with eagerness and joy. We joined the BCAACP immediately and became very involved in its struggle against racism in British Columbia. In the process we learnt much about what it was like to grow up as a true visible minority person in this province.

The BCAACP was patterned after the American NAACP. It was neither the oldest nor even the most powerful Black organization in B.C. at that time. The Union of Sleeping Car Porters had a larger membership than any other Black organization. The Marcus Garvey Movement, although still in existence, was small and not very active. The Black American Church had lost most of its members, and its preachers, like its congregation, drifted away to join other mainline churches. There was no highly visible Black ghetto as in Montreal and in many American cities, but with one exception all of the Black families lived and owned homes in the east end of Vancouver. The exception was Mrs Ruby Sneed, who lived with her husband and two daughters on West 8th Avenue near Alma and taught piano lessons. We soon came to know that many members of the Black community were members of one large extended family that included the Ramseys, the Sneeds, the Collinses and others who had migrated here from Edmonton, Alberta. In the late 1970s when I was invited to speak at a reunion of the Alberta Black community, I discovered that just about all our friends in the Vancouver Black community were in attendance.

The BCAACP under the leadership of Frank Collins was an active and aggressive organization. It established a few priorities for itself and pursued them vigorously. It was determined to open up housing and employment to Black people and to ensure that young Black people pursued education and professions as one means of fighting discrimination.

Over the years I sat on the executive of the organization, and both Bill and I worked with it in its efforts to force the provincial government to introduce human rights legislation and a human rights commission. Neither of these goals was achieved until after the election of a New Democratic Party government in 1972, an election in which Emery Barnes and I became the first Black people to be elected to any provincial parliament in Canada's history.

The BCAACP was responsible for raising the consciousness of the Vancouver community around Black issues and for increasing the pride of the community in itself. It was not a radical organization and it enjoyed a lot of support in the white community. The daily newspapers were very cooperative in reporting its activities, and in time it became the organization that spoke for all Black British Columbians, its opinions being respected by all levels of government. In later years more radical Black organizations took over its place in the limelight, but none of them has equalled or surpassed the BCAACP and its lasting impact on the quality of life of the Black people of this province.

By the time Bill graduated in 1958 either our painful memories were fading or Vancouver was changing. In any event we were expecting our second child and planning to purchase a house and put down roots in Vancouver. I still longed to return to Jamaica, and especially so that my children could grow up in a warm and loving Black environment, and Bill had nostalgic longings for the stimulation and excitement of Montreal.

Bill's career plans ruled out both options. At a time when internships were becoming difficult to secure he was fortunate to have been accepted at the Vancouver General Hospital. By that time, also, he had decided not to return to research but to pursue the specialty of psychiatry. When in addition he had been assured of a position in the UBC residency program under Dr. Jim Tyhurst, we accepted that we would be living in Vancouver for a long time.

Before marriage, Bill and I had spent hours exploring the options of where we would settle down. We desperately wanted to live and raise our children in a Black environment, I because my experience had been such a positive one and he because growing up a Black child in the southern United States had been so fraught with anxiety and tension. Despite this, wherever we looked, it seemed that political insta- bility, economic underdevelopment and lack of social resources were the lot of English-speaking Black countries of the world. Bill believed that we owed our chil- dren the best education, the best health care and political stability. He was convinced we could compensate for their minority status through teaching and example.

I disagreed on every point except the one of political stability. I was not will- ing to expose the children or myself to civil wars and violent uprising. However, I believed that the building of self-respect and self-esteem that comes from living as a member of a majority group was more important than health care or educa- tion. Also, because I came in contact with racism later in life I knew that there was a qualitative difference to life for a Black person in a white community. Because that Black person is always 'on guard.' A seventh sense is developed that is always alert, a radar scanning for hostile signals. I remember reading somewhere that Black women in North America never let their babies out of their sight when away from home – not in a shopping buggy or on a playground swing – not because they were afraid their children would fall, wander off, or get into mischief, but because they feared that someone would hurt them.

Black people have a sense that one is always in danger. And conveying to one's offspring at the earliest possible time the importance of always being 'on guard' had always been the primary responsibility of Black parents raising children in a white environment. Black parents overprotect their children in the same way that women overprotect their daughters. They know that for them the world is a truly dangerous place.

The discussions about a place to live escalated to arguments, but Bill was adamant. He believed that it was important for our children to live and survive and excel in this country. I have always felt that there was no substitute for a Jamaican childhood and that my children were deprived because they did not have that experience, although I must confess that they seem none the worse for the lack. Eventually, the compromise we worked out was that at the completion of his medical training, we would return to Montreal. He would complete his residency and establish a practice there, and I would return to McGill to study law. We would be close to Jamaica and to his family in Georgia and our children would have easy access to both these Black communities. Like so many of our life plans, the future took on a direction of its own. The subtle magic and beauty of British Columbia, combined with the FLQ uprising in Quebec, convinced us that British Columbia was home and that we should put down our roots right here.

My second pregnancy, in 1959, also precipitated a rethinking of my own career goals. I rejected the study of law as no longer feasible for a number of reasons. For one, I would be quite old by the time Bill completed his four-year residency, and each year that I was away from university my doubts about my ability to handle a long, rigorous academic program increased.

With each passing year Bill had contributed less and less to responsibilities around the home since his studies were so demanding, and I began to doubt my ability to juggle parenting, homemaking and studying. So I decided that I would have to pursue a program that was shorter and less demanding than law, but I had no idea what it would be. Bill repeated his commitment to support me during my course of study in return for the four years I would have to work while he pursued his psychiatric residency, plus the four years he had studied medicine and interned. I found myself negotiating for eight years of educational support, even as I was deciding that I would have to restrict to less than four years the time of study I could pursue.

We accepted that B.C. was home – in 1959 we applied for and received our Canadian citizenship. For better or for worse this was our country now. We were Canadians and what happened to this country was part of our responsibility since we now had the right to become actively involved in its workings.

[1989]

Lily Spence [193?-]

Koopab . . .

1

Ekute mwen bien, ish-mwen, ekute mwen.
  Mwen di u ekute mwen bien!

Pa fe sa, ish mwen, pa fe sa!

Ish mwen, mete dwet-u en zawye-u paz

Bateau mun-blanc-en en la-ward-la

ke fe denye kri-li. I ka renfle-glo fos i vle chewé pat.

Pa ekute-li ish-mwen pa ekute-li paz

i ka kriya-u pu i voltege-u en jam d'aut peyi.

Ish-mwen, si dwet-u pa assez, mete ka-ka-bwef-sec en

zawye-u. Pa ekoute-li. Se pa blag ish-mwen. Se pa blag!
  Pa fe sa ish mwen, pa fe sa!

2

Koopab!

Ekute mwen bien, ish mwen, ekute mwen.
  Mwen di u ekute mwen bien:

Pa fe sa, ish mwen, pa fe sa.

Ish mwen, la pa ni l'or en lawi d'aut peyi-on!

Ish mwen, en-kondwi, d'aut peyi ky vale-u tut-a-fet
  mwen di u tut-a-fet kon u mete go zotyi-u en lawi-li

Ish mwen, ler sa-la, u ky mande kestion enityl u pa te jamen
mande-kow-u. *Kote mwen ye en???*

  Se pa pi-tet, ish mwen, se pa pi-tet.

Ah! Ish mwen, pa fe sa. Mwen di u pa fe sa!

3

Koopab!

Ekute mwen bien, ish mwen, ekute mwen!
  Mwen dit u ekute mwen bien!

Pa fe sa, ish mwen, pa fe sa!

Asiz-kohw-u asu wosh anba campeche-yse
      bord viya maman-oo
Mete tet-u asu jam maman-oo

Tiwe lide-u asu bateau-a en la-ward-la
  ki renfle-u . . .
  Pa fe sa ish mwen, pa fe sa!

Koopab!

We-bien: *Tuju*, soliel-la . . . la en tet ciel Bondya-ah ky fe mi tut
              giyave-li avek fe bet-ani-fe danse en bois-campeche-la . . .

We-bien: *Tuju*, Kas-u repose amba kalbas-la en borde lan'mer-ya-la
              ky espaya-u, ish fooben mwen . . .
              Ek asu lan-mer-ya, i-mem soliel-shoo-ah, ky tuju
              fe zin-yan-yan ek vegle peche a midi . . .
              ki tuju vegle Papa-u osi, en shaloop-peche-li. Mé, ler la-lun
              kiewe, jen-mun ky tuju fe vis-yo asu
              do sab-i-mem . . . ah-mem-tan, la leun, mem, ky tuju klewe asu
              visag ti-garzon kon yo shashe kwab-tu-lu-lu-yo; mwen
              dit-u, mem-assu boosh viya-nom kon yo valé ti-lo-lo-yo . . . *Tuju*

129

We-bien: *Tuju*, Jamb piton-en, mem-kon jamb fam-sho ky
            trampe en glo-vé pu fe nom we-yo . . .

Etan bien: *Tuju*, closh eglise-la ky sonde midi le nu
            valé ti salé-nu ek konfiti-patat-nu . . .

Etan-bien: *Tuju*, van-en en piye brapen-en ki epe avek senti-mi-li
            mem, ky wule mer-foo-ah en gorge *Bal-am-boosh*-la . . .

Santi-bien: *Tuju*, Kan-kupe-ah, banan-mi-ah, fle-immortel-ah ki
            pawfiti bord morn-la ky hapé lazier-labowe-ya, yo ki
            kase wosh en fond morn-la . . .

            en-fen, en-fen . . .

Ish mwen, etan bien, we bien, senti bien ek pense bien
avan-u hape kow-u volteje d'aut peyi mun blanc. Mwen di u
is mwen . . . *Moosh ki te viv on sezon pa retournir on lot sezon* . . . BON!
Ish mwen, ler sa-la, u ky mande kestion enityl u pa-te-jamen.
Mande-kow. *Se mwen, Koopab, sa-on?* Mwen dit u, se pa pi-tet, non!

            Pa fe sa ish mwen, pa fe sa!

KOOPAB EN LAWI D'AUT PEYL
Meh, eheh! eheh! Se mwen Koopab-sa-on
avek tet-wed sa-la, mem kon pima-noir-ah
anba shapoo-feuille-cocoa-ah? We papa!
Gade nez-sa-la ki sam boosh zofi-ya . . .
Me, sa-mwen-mem
kon kosol-mol shival te trampe!
Meh, eheh! Eheh! Aquedi toot zye kule-vari ka
reproche noir-mwen! Pu ki?
Wi-i-i man-man!
Aquedi gendam-la avek baton-bwitalize-li
ka kriya . . . Aquedi J ka hele: "Antansoin! Antansoin!
Me Neg Mahwon-la?" Aquedi, aquedi . . .
Vit! Vit! Se pu mwen, Koopab, mete pye-asu tet
ek chew pat . . .

Later, plenty later,
a fella wid waistcoat
wid panama
wid briefcase
wid umbrella
come back to 'im island
'im mouf *chewing rags*, fer so,
Bot, unfortunate-ly,
di scents, sights, sounds stan'
way back of 'im
    and
from whence 'im come
back of 'im, too.

[1997]

The Return

1

I tell you!
It was just the same
Hot day,
That . . . going-to-town . . .
That same old thrill
Resurrecting from
My sweaty feet bottoms
Right there on Main Street:
The same Stores
The same Bank
The same Bridge over
The same Ravine
Spat in
Over which
Marched corps in

WWII. It had been those same some
Bacchic wooing bands and pans . . .
Those same some
Woeful funeral hands flipping sweat
Off slim crepe-crimped-rose-wreaths . . .
Those same some
Rum'd masqueraders
On Boxing Day
Waylaying high school girls
In faded-blue pinafores;
Flaying boys in alpargatas
Clapping "Rar-Rars."
Same some sad donkeys dragging
Their drays down town:
"Balah-pah-ta . . . Balah pah-ta . . ."
Burdened with jute bags
Squared with ices;
Obese with spices.
Rotund raffias swollen
On sweet potatoes
Squashed onto clipped-
Eyed crabs: vine-bunched. Now,

There on Main Street
Buicks revving it up . . .
Toyotas and Mitsubishis
Mixing a piccalilli heating
that hot alley at 5 PM

2

I tell you!
It was just the same old Main Street . . .
Where office clerks, self-conscious
On New York spikes, throw
Perspiring legs over
Shallow drains.
Where men still stand at the same
Tight street corner
Women at another,
Some talk and laughter caught
In gears of motorcars
Now
Stopped by foreign

3

Lights.
Ahead, the same Mount fronting sun.
The same old dormer'd-balconied-jalousie'd shysters
Paying their deference to the same bougainvilleas
Upon lavenders upon hibiscuses ever
Unaware of tall palm trees'
Windhungflung dun fronds.
The same ordinary ordinance station
At right,
The same sundry cement crucifixes
At left
Leaning on drubbing time; on earthquakes; on hurricanes.

4

"I tell you!" It was
Just the same
Hot day, there on Main Street,
With bells at midday.
But, now, those hawkers bawling their wares
... up ... down ... a dust-sweat wind.
Sellers too seated too stiff-necked
On sweaty stools: suppliants
To straw'd Bermuda'd outlanders,
Sun-seared-altered, and
Me!
Who cares to remember
Long, long time ago
Gone with cockerels
No longer heard at 3 AM

[1997]

Mourne Fortune, Castries, St. Lucia

Ever escaping memories'
    loophole:
Mourne Fortune and you, Opportune.
One: a self-conscious
volcanic obtrusion
scrambling its every
ambitious rise and fall and rise
to nudge God's blue cheeks.
The other: her fingers
an ecru grip seizing mine.
Each day, we followed the same
hot macadamized road where
the wasting shybush withheld
Road's discrepancies
from other unleathered
soles;
she and I grudgingly
heaved our efforts
to home among guavas
mangoes sapodillas . . .

[1997]

Fred Booker [1939-]

Powell Street Conspiracy

There's a hotel on every corner
A café and a dock
When you get up near Nanaimo
Dundas makes a stop
There're cracks in the pavement
Because of the deals in haste
There's a flaw in my character
Since the first time I took a taste

Of Powell Street at midnight
Nobody taught me wrong from right
Hey now, there ain't a thing on Main Street
To keep a black cat out all night

The factories are a one-man show
To make things for the sea
When they're hammering there is no relief
It's a red-hot canopy
Timber from the mountains
Salmon hatchery
Tell me, if I'm not a stevedore
They ain't got no time for me

Powell Street at midnight
Nobody taught me wrong from right
Hey now, there ain't a thing on Main Street
To keep a black cat out all night

The immigrant on the jukebox
Singing 'bout Vancouver slums
Put 'em down on Powell Street
Till the Judgement comes

Don't you look for the answer
You do just as well
To take a stroll at sundown
To watch the merchants sail

Powell Street at midnight
Nobody taught me wrong from right
Hey now, there ain't a thing on Main Street
To keep a black cat out all night

The drunks are a dime a dozen
Scrap metal heaps for free
The train tracks cut Powell Street in half
Like it does the Japanese
I wasn't born on Powell Street
Fire's not my sign
But the black cat is my brother
And the music's right on time

Powell Street at midnight
Nobody taught me wrong from right
Well, there ain't a thing on Main Street, y'all
To keep a black cat out all night

[1974]

One Road to the Sea

to Ruth Wheeler and Sylvia Stark

I caught the blues train
I left the noose behind
Holes in my pockets
Bad habits on my mind
Driven on by freedom
But never knowing why
I had to run so far
When I was running off to die
I left Satartia suddenly
'Twas on the sabbath day
Started driving cattle
From Missouri to L.A.
In old Midas mines
There were riches that could show
I could buy my freedom
And a hard way to go

I was running for my life
I was running to be free
I got stopped for speeding
In Sault Ste. Marie
If I get to Saltspring
For the bell tolls for me
I won't mind dying
Where there's one road to the sea

A thousand and nine in gold
To free my wife and child
A lumber camp in Oregon
Kept us for a while
We heard about a place
North of Puget Sound
Where free men and the lion
Leave their prints upon the ground

Homesteading spinning wheel
Bringing in the hay

My wife, she's threshing grain
The old fashioned way
We're digging clams and saying
By the end of the day
New Caledonia's gonna be
A fine place to stay

I was running for my life
I was running to be free
I got stopped for speeding
In Sault Ste. Marie
If I get to Saltspring
For the bell tolls for me
I won't mind dying
Where there's one road to the sea

[1978]

from "Blue Notes of a White Girl"

On Burnaby Mountain: Summer 1978

ENCOUNTER

Spider-web silent
sun-warm placid
diamond-hard dry

the trees hiss
coniferous curses

their stout boughs fan the air
as smoke from charcoal fires
rises with the clamour

of people –
excited insects
who flit after frisbees and
soccer balls –

a simple scenario to paint
I think
until Adam's black head
emerges on the canvas

a looming bust
coloured ivory and gold
hanging in the trees
among the spruce cones.

I gasp
as my hands paint me into the picture –
a series of identical blonde figurines
clinging to his Zulu neck.

TREE SEED

I draw Adam to me

from his sprawl by the duck pond

using my finger to gauge the distance
lining him up
in the cross-hairs of my brush
until I catch his eye

our interests connecting.

He looks over my shoulder
asks what I have done
unable to discern his features
painted in the boughs of tall trees.

"The mountain has stolen your soul,
I claim it back with paint."

My words spoken
with the cadences of a guardian
not a thief

hoping he's flattered
that I see him as an expression
of living things

that endure.

A FAMILY CIRCLE

As Adam speaks of
his black Canadian ancestors
encircling him
I paint as if eavesdropping

OLIVIER LEJEUNE
slave in New France
touches Adams wrists, ankles,
exclaims, jerks away
as if from a scourge

baffled
that no chain, no manacles
bind Adam's hands and feet
a free man

Olivier's face full of wonder
as if he's touched the dream
he always believed was real.

JOHN WARE
Alberta rancher, bronco buster,
touches Adam's heart
wonders why all hearts are not broken
after a cruel prairie wind
took the life of his young bride

his fingers probing Adam
to discover the link
between heart and will
the answer to
a life and death question –

how could he have prevented
his horse from falling,
crushing him to death
when he found it so difficult
to stand, walk, go on
without his one true love?

JOSIAH HENDERSON
entrepreneur of Canada West
touches Adam's eyes
to discern
through his sense of touch
the miracle of literacy

how does one translate
ink spots on paper
into ideas and action,
make a book speak
fill the silent ache
with words and meaning?

Henson touches Adam
promises to contend with Beelzebub
if Adam will teach him
to read his name
even if it appears only on
a crumbling page of history.

CAN YOU DIG THAT?

I paint Adam talking of black music
his index finger puncturing the air
an emphatic interrogative
can you dig this?
can you dig that?

I work quickly, capturing
zealous eyes
when he describes

the musical humour of
Thelonious Monk

then splash on sepia tones
as exciting now as
the mahogany sound I heard
coming of age in Niagara-on-the-Lake
beneath a solid-gold cloud
Top 10 Soul records
broadcast on AM radio from Buffalo

Al Green, Aretha Franklin
Marvin Gaye, Chaka Khan
Earth, Wind & Fire
back to back

names rolling off my tongue
easier than
"William Lyon Mackenzie King"
ever did

to my sister's grief
who accused me of
"going *black*"

the same as
going *bankrupt*, going *crazy*
going *her own way*

what a furor!
over something as tiny
as a black musical note:

now I ask,
can you dig that?

ATAVISM

I paint Adam with a target skin
the bullseye at the centre of his back

after he placed my fingers
into a pair of indentations
in his scalp

a birthmark

carried by one male
in each generation of his family
as if left by a midwife
at the birth of the primal ancestor
reluctant to deliver him
into the carnage

the white rape of Africa
the lynching of faith, hope and charity.

Paint falls on canvas
like running footsteps in a night
of violent death

Adam emerges
seated with his kinsmen
their heads in their hands
fingers in the ancestral grooves

uncertain whether to pull or push.

A POOL OF HONEY

Adam serves camembert
green grapes
white wine.

Johnny Guitar Watson
swirls in a Panasonic wind
hangs himself on the walls

with Degas prints
of women at pianos
men with guitars
others holding points of view.

The conversation
falls from grace to
liqueurs
cigarettes

candlelight, flickering on
truth, beauty, coffee,
and hot kisses melting
crushed ice, etiquette,

into a pool of honey.

POND BED

Eiderdown heaped
our bodies sprawled on the bed
elbows linked
thigh-pillowed heads

nostrils flat
faces cleansed with sleep
love won.

His black body my shadow
elongated
poured at my side

my white body
his splayed reflection on the pond

we are symbiotic –

tongue to clitoris
mouth to cock
hand on buttocks
lips on hair
fingers on cheek
breath on face
fire on brain
cry against eardrum

a howling marked our leap
throats opened to our surrender
and down we fell
in head-to-feet spirals
onto the fitted sheet
sleep

the stillness
of mallards on the pond
indistinguishable from decoys
until we move

glossy coats of oil and water
unsinkable objects bobbing

man and woman on pond bed.

[1989]

Arthur Nortje [1942-1970]

Waiting

The isolation of exile is a gutted
warehouse at the back of pleasure streets:
the waterfront of limbo stretches panoramically –
night the beautifier lets the sights
dance across the wharf.
I peer through the skull's black windows
wondering what can credibly save me.
The poem trails across the ruined wall
a solitary snail, or phosphorescently
swims into vision like a fish
through a hole in the mind's foundation, acute
as a glittering nerve.

Origins trouble the voyager much, those roots
that have sipped the waters of another continent.
Africa is gigantic, one cannot begin
to know even the strange behaviour furthest
south in my xenophobic department.
Come back, come back mayibuye
cried the breakers of stone and cried the crowds
cried Mr Kumalo before the withering fire
mayibuye Afrika

Now there is the loneliness of lost
beauties at Cabo de Esperancia, Table Mountain:
all the dead poets who sang of spring's
miraculous recrudescence in the sandscapes of Karoo
sang of thoughts that pierced like arrows, spoke
through the strangled throat of multi-humanity
bruised like a python in the maggot-fattening sun.

You with your face of pain, your touch of gaiety,
with eyes that could distil me any instant
have passed into some diary, some dead journal
now that the computer, the mechanical notion
obliterates sincerities.

The amplitude of sentiment has brought me no nearer
to anything affectionate,
new magnitude of thought has but betrayed
the lustre of your eyes.

You yourself have vacated the violent arena
for a northern life of semi-snow
under the Distant Early Warning System:
I suffer the radiation burns of silence.
It is not cosmic immensity or catastrophe
that terrifies me:
it is solitude that mutilates,
the night bulb that reveals ash on my sleeve.

1967

[1973]

Immigrant

Don't travel beyond
Acton at noon in the intimate summer light
of England

to Tuskaloosa, Medicine Hat, preparing
for flight

dismissing the blond aura of the past
at Durban or Johannesburg
no more chewing roots or brewing riots

Bitter costs exorbitantly at London
airport in the neon heat
waiting for the gates to open

Big boy breaking out of the masturbatory
era goes
like eros over atlantis (sunk
in the time-repeating seas, admire our
tenacity)
jetting into the bulldozer civilization
of Fraser and Mackenzie
which is the furthest west that man has gone

A maple leaf is in my pocket.
x-rayed, doctored at Immigration
weighed in at the Embassy
measured as to passport, smallpox, visa
at last the efficient official informs me
I am an acceptable soldier of fortune, don't

tell the Commissioner
I have Oxford poetry in the satchel
propped between my army surplus boots
for as I consider Western Arrow's
pumpkin pancake buttered peas and chicken canadian style

in my mind's customs office
questions fester that turn the menu
into a visceral whirlpool. You can see
that sick bags are supplied.

Out portholes beyond the invisible propellers
snow mantles the ground peaks over Greenland.
What ice island of the heart has weaned
you away from the known white kingdom
first encountered at Giant's Castle?
You walked through the proteas nooked in the sun rocks
I approached you under the silver trees.
I was cauterized in the granite glare
on the slopes of Table Mountain, I was baffled
by the gold dumps of the vast Witwatersrand
when you dredged me from the sea like a recent fossil.

Where are the mineworkers, the compound Africans,
your Zulu ancestors, where are
the root-eating, bead-charmed Bushmen, the Hottentot sufferers?
Where are the governors and sailors of the
Dutch East India Company, where are
Eva and the women who laboured in the castle?
You are required as an explanation.

Glaciers sprawl in their jagged valleys,
cool in the heights, there are mountains and mountains.
My prairie beloved, you whose eyes are
less forgetful, whose fingers are less obvious
must write out chits for the physiotherapy customers
must fill out forms for federal tax.

Consolatory, the air whiskies my veins.
The metal engines beetle on to further destinations.
Pilot's voice reports over Saskatchewan
the safety of this route, the use of exits,

facility of gas masks, Western Arrow's
miraculous record. The flat sea washes
in Vancouver bay. As we taxi in
I find I can read the road signs.

Maybe she is like you, maybe most women
deeply resemble you, all of them are
all things to all poets: the cigarette girl
in velvet with mink nipples, fishnet thighs,
whose womb is full of tobacco.
Have a B.C. apple in the A.D. city of the saviour,
and sing the centennial song.

1967

[1973]

Hope Hotel

Dawn light over my hotel notepaper
with a bird's alert incursion breaks
in softly potent rhythms to the simple provocation
of rain's splashy dissonance at windows.

Wet threads against the blue glass gleam:
this street that will be full of honeymoon soon
awaits today's invasions as I exorcise
the stigma of my own inexactitudes.

In a book of nudes the tortoise of the mind
feeds in isolation, and against the flesh horizons
of curvaceous models, voluptuous stone,
thinly stand those pyramids, hang those gardens

through which meanders the river bringing
pesticides from upland farms, the effluence of our lifeblood.
The rain-forest now still breathes though
the chimneys of the pulp mills belch sulphur.

Depressed confessions come through normal channels
with the word-order wishing not to change
as I watch the river and the snow runnels
where the fire sun will melt the wounds of winter.

The lush woods luminesce in green explosions
and the rich valleys regiment with ease
my scope, confined my art: it is not worth
consideration even now to win back selfhood.

British Columbia, 1968

[1973]

Yvonne Brown [1943-]

from "The Literature of Africa and its Diaspora: Black History Month, 1997"

I want to start by asking you a question. How many people know anything about the Middle Passage? One, two, three . . . four. And I noticed the people who put their hands up. Three of the four people are of African descent, and one – are you of African descent? Not quite, no. You see? This is interesting.

I'm going to tell you about the Middle Passage. I want you to look at this map. See that map? Isn't it a beautiful map? It looks like a patchwork quilt, does-n't it? Well, it is not. I want you to look at the legend. What does that map tell us? I don't really want an answer, I'm just talking to myself. What does that map tell you? Everybody was down there havin a good time. And guess what? After about two hundred years of a triangular trade, involving all these people up here going down for a little trip on the coast, and in the meantime you bring back a few peo-ple – and you say, "Here's my booty" – and if you want more you can go back and get them. And then about two hundred years through this triangular trade peo-ple left Europe here, went down here. First of all, when they left, they didn't leave with an empty ship. They filled it up. Guns, liquor, you name it, whatever. Then they came down and when they got to the coast of Africa they sold what they wanted to sell, then they filled up these ships with guess what? What did they fill up these ships with, do you know? People! You ever buy a can of sardines? I'm not exaggerating, they pack em in there just like the sardines. And that book I brought, that's an artist's rendition of that experience.

And then they brought the people across over here, and they came into the Central America here and dropped some off in Cuba, in Jamaica. They didn't just drop them off, they sell them. And down in Brazil, South America. And down here they pick up the gold and whatever else they got up there and they went back up here. That was the triangle. This map doesn't show it so well, so it went from here, along there, over here and back up here. Got it? That's why it was called a triangular trade. Well, this end of the triangle was called the Middle Passage, this part that brought the people from Africa down to the Caribbean and South America was called the Middle Passage. And it's a horrible, horrible, horrible, horrible experience, I'm telling you.

In the most recent history we have the Holocaust. Six million Jews were killed, and the Gypsies, and the homosexuals, and the Jehovah's Witnesses. But preceding the Holocaust was the forced captivity and transportation – get ready for this – of twenty to sixty million African people. The conservative estimate, that it was twenty million. The more realistic estimate by historians is that it was sixty million. Fathom that.

Now I have to tell you a personal story. I had gone to school all my life – I never left school. Cause I was a pupil, then I went into education. All my life. And for all my formal education, even in Jamaica where I grew up, I never read a single book written by a black person. Not in elementary school, not in secondary school. I read the Shakespeare and all them – I can't remember them now, my brain's filled with something else – but all the classics and all the showpieces of Western civilization. I read them all and I can spout them all. If you wake me up certain times of the night I'll recite them perfectly. But not a single word. And we were told that black people didn't have intelligence in writing in any form.

But I came to a point in my life just short of fifty when I had this sort of empty stuff in here, and I needed to hear the voices of *my* experience. And the crowning experience came in 1989 when we had a Black History Month public forum, and somebody was looking for somebody to speak about black women, and I thought, gee, I'm one, but I don't know anything about myself. I can't go in public and speak. And so the guys, as usual, were gonna tell us, and I thought, that's pretty good courage, but I sat there and I heard some things that made me so mad, I said next time, no damn way. I'm going to do it myself. But in order to do it intelligently, I had to go do my homework. So I started reading. And I'm telling you, I hardly sleep since 1989! I sold my car because the car compete with the money I spend on books!

And so tonight I want to let you know that the Middle Passage is the single most horrendous historical experience that has connected people of African descent in the so-called New World. And you ought to know something about it. It is also the experience that has brought from Europe all the negative stereotypes about Africa and its peoples. Some of your most celebrated philosophers like Hegel – last week we had a wonderful presentation by an African philosopher, we were trying to bury Hegel's ghost. Now, he didn't quite bury Hegel's ghost for me. It was raised from the dead. But nonetheless, all those things – that Africa has no history, in the African we find the relics of humanity, Africa is the end of the road, all of these horrible things, all of that came with the Middle Passage and has survived till now. And 350 years of plantation slavery. Did you hear me? Three hundred and fifty years of plantation slavery on the islands of the Caribbean, South America, United States. It was twelve generations. When you see images of black people in the United States, those who are shown to you as criminals and so on, step back and consider this history of the Middle Passage, and all that followed that. Complete dispossession and disgrace. And this is why I'm doing this presentation. I have two, I have another one – but it's the teacher in me now – that's more political, that one will be for March 21st when I face off with two vice presidents at UBC. So I can't do that one now, because I want each one of you to go away from here tonight with some commitment to reading some of this history and literature. So tonight I want to say to you, think of the Middle Passage and its implications, and think of how that has translated into certain issues around your education, as well as the education of children and peoples of African descent.

I have identified these six things. There's a problem of identity, and there's all kinds of things around identity which will come up later. There's problems around curriculum. Tonight this room is almost full, and I ask how many people have heard about the Middle Passage, and there were only four people. That is a fine example of the omissions that have happened, that a history that involved those fourteen European nations could be omitted completely, an event that lasted for 350 years – omitted completely. Never happened. When I read about the psychiatry and the psychology of slavery and enslavement of African peoples, it's called collective amnesia on the one hand by those who want to forget, and collective trauma on the other hand for those people who just can't forget, and are not allowed to forget. There are all those stereotypes. My God, you imagine black kids who are in school are afraid to read the novels and stuff because they are afraid of the images that come out. Then there are things to do with interpersonal relationships and social relationships, and I think Evelyn[1] gave a fine exposé of what that has meant for her as a law student. Those interpersonal and personal relationships. And it's the same in the workplace. Then there are things around learning theories and black underachievement. I was doing a class and I asked, "What did you learn in Ed. Psych. about black folks?" I said, "Did you learn about how we don't have any intelligence?" No, no topic, no. They don't talk about it anymore, it's just not there. And I'm not sure whether that's a good thing or not, but it's a non-issue now. Because, as one of my vice presidents at UBC told me once in the corridor, "Well, Yvonne, race has been disproven as a scientific concept, so race doesn't exist." So we will have a second round on the 21st, because as a teacher I have to do something about that. Then the other thing about representation. Africa and its peoples are represented in certain ways in the texts that are read. They're represented a certain way in the talk that you hear from people, about who African peoples are, and about the continent of Africa. And that map. When you hear people talk about Africa being a "basket case," please remember that in large part, if it is indeed a basket case, it is because of that map. In 1884, in 1885, when all these fourteen nations were down there scratching around, not only capturing the people but digging up the earth and taking out the minerals, they began to meet each other in the bush, and realized that they weren't speaking African, but French and German and Dutch and so on. During colonial times I discovered that even though the nations in Europe competed, they had strategic alliances when they wanted to do their little business. So what they did, the civilized people that they were, they gathered at a table in Berlin, and decided in a gentlemanly fashion, how they would divide up the continent. And it was called the meeting for "the scramble for Africa." So that's something you will see in history, "the scramble for Africa." And they didn't quite settle it in 1884, so they met in 1885 again in the Hague, and they did it all. So you have Portuguese Africa, you have German Africa, you have Dutch and all of this kind of stuff.

When I was a kid in school I thought that was natural because they brought civilization. It was only later that I learned it was a grand theft. And because it was committed in the name of kings and queens, it wasn't called "theft." It was called "annexation" and "discovery" and all those nice terms. Euphemisms. Those are marvelous lessons in euphemisms.

And the sixth one has to do with school-community relations. I mean, you only have to have a kid in school to know school-community relations. And I'm speaking not only from the literature, but my own experience of putting three kids through the system. They're not kids anymore, they're grown adults. And one thing I haven't told you is that most black parents have to do something called dual socialization. You socialize them how to deal with the system and how to take care of themselves, and you socialize them at home about certain values that they ought to have and preserve, and certain values that build their identity. After school, suppertime, that was one job I had to do frequently with my kids. After they had experienced the curriculum, after they had experienced the interpersonal and social relationships, sometimes they came home, and pretty sore from it all. And I had to pick up their egos and start all over again. So those are some of the issues.

Now here's something nice that you can do. You can start reading, because one of the nicest things about living in Canada is that there's a high level of literacy. Everybody can read, right? Contrary to what the statistics say, that you can't read, most of you *can* read, and at Kwantlen College[2] I would hope that you're here because you *can* read. I want to invite you to start a reading habit, and when you get an assignment, when you're reading for pleasure, go find something about black folks. That *they've* written. And you'll be surprised, even an article or a book, how interested you get after that. And here is the map to take you through it.

Now, I got this picture from reading black folks' stuff. Not only did I read the literature, but I went and read the literary criticism, because I wanted to know, what do the intellectuals in the humanities talk about when they analyze a work of art written by their own people? I wanted to know what vocabulary they use, I wanted to know what themes preoccupied them, and so I went and researched. And of course they have a Western category of literature because they do write, and I think they were writing before the Europeans came too, because one of the oldest universities in the world was in Timbuktu. There was literacy there before in parts of Africa. I discovered this whole long list of stuff. But this is the neatest part of the whole thing. Look, you see that word – "orature"? I'm sure you never met that word before. Have you? How many people have? No, you never. Yeah, you? Tell us about it.

Audience member: The spoken word, not written.

Yeah? Does it have anything to do with the oral tradition?

Audience: With the spoken word, not written, you pass stories from person to person. It's kind of like if you had a communication that's social, as opposed to people sitting down with their books, then going off to individually study. A social thing.

Social thing? Yeah. Passing on history, passing on values, wisdom. Well, I'm impressed to know somebody did hear about it. I'm not so smart after all. Good for you. Orature was what I picked up from reading the African literary critics, and they use it to include more than we have come to understand from anthropologists as the oral tradition. It's the sum of all spoken word. The expression I use is picked from all the extensive reading I've done, I speak about Africa and its diaspora, because that's a connection. That Middle Passage brought about the diaspora, African diaspora. And when I read the literature, I go back and forth, around, and I even went to Africa, Michael,[3] I did. Because I wanted to see for myself. I'll come back to tell you about my trip in a little while. But included in this, when I think about the diaspora, there's a relationship with the spoken word and colonial languages. This one only focused on English, but the same thing would happen for all the other colonial languages. The Dutch, the German, the French, all of them. The African peoples bend the language to suit their own purpose. Both in the spoken form and in the written form. Those of you who take French, go find some black French writers, and you'll see what they do to the president's language. Well, in English we know what they do with the king first, and then the queen's, language. They bend it in all sorts of ways. Expressed in dub poetry, in reggae, in calypso, the whole thing. They make that language work and they bend it out of shape. And it doesn't matter how much it is described as deviant, we have a good time making it deviant! What do they call this stuff right now, what is the new name for it?

Audience: Ebonics.

Oh, yes. That's another story.

Between these extremes of orature and literature, there are all of these forms here. I nearly flipped my lid when I understood we wrote symphonies and we wrote operas, and I thought all we were good for was the blues and jazz! Can you imagine? I said to my friend Richard, "You gotta show me that symphony," and he did. My eyes just bulge out, never mind my ear. Those are some of the wonderful things I discovered. And then, in terms of orature, some of the most brilliant political speeches, political oratory, is in a class by itself from black folks. Especially those in the diaspora. Black pain and all that stuff has to be expressed. And you know which is the one I think is fantastic? Preaching. You've watched those movies. Those ministers that you see, those are caricatures of the real stuff. I've heard many of those sermons in my day. That's why you can't shut me up. I've been programmed for years. But speaking and story-telling all are a very rich part of the orature.

[1997]

Notes

1. Evelyn Achah, a lawyer who spoke on her experiences as a black law student.

2. A college in Vancouver, B.C.

3. Michael Acku, a mathematics instructor who gave a talk on perceptions of Africa.

Truman Green [1945-]

from A Credit to Your Race

CHAPTER 3

The Bakers got home the following Sunday just in time to take Mary to church. After the service Mr Baker took her up to talk to Reverend Phillips about her immorality. Don't get me wrong. It wasn't about her going bare naked in the barn. He wanted to show Mary that the church didn't approve of mixed couples going out together. Now the Reverend was my Sunday School teacher and I was sure that he wouldn't say anything bad about me. But I was wrong. It wasn't that he had anything against me personally. In fact he told Mr Baker what a fine young man I was and how I had won the merit award in grade one and what a fine future I had ahead of me. But going around with people of different colours was defying the word of God. The Reverend said that it was right in the Bible that people should stick to their own kind. He read some passages to Mary and her father looked at her meaningfully.

Now we really had to sneak around. Sarah wasn't much help either. She'd see us down at the park and tell Mom. I was absolutely forbidden by my own mother to go out with Mary. And Mr Baker was going to get a big police dog and come after me if he ever caught me out with Mary or heard that I had been out with her.

Then I thought of a foolproof plan. Mary and I would pretend that we had had a big fight and split up. She'd tell her father that he was right about that dull-witted nigger (meaning me). She'd say that she was going around with Dickie Williams of whom her father approved.

"You gotta be kiddin', Billy. If I pick her up she's going out with me. I'm not lying to her old man just so you can sneak around with her. Why don't you pick her up?"

"Come on, eh Dickie. Her old man doesn't like me."

"Oh yeah. Why not?"

"He says I'm a bad influence on her."

"If he doesn't like you, what's he going to think of me? You're the suck-hole of Fraser High. He knows I been caught stealing hub caps."

"He doesn't like me cause I'm coloured, and you know darn well, Dickie. Why you trying to be so smart about it? How would you like me to just kick the shit out of you instead?"

"Jiggers, here comes Teach."

Mr Hatfield, our socials teacher, was coming down the aisle, shaking his finger at me. "Why don't you just get out of here if you want to talk, smart guy. We're supposed to be learning about *your* people, not gossiping with Dickie Williams." I opened my book to the page about Bushmen and Hottentots.

So that's how it was with me and Dickie and Mary. He'd go by every night after supper and call on her and I'd wait out in the orchard for them to come out. One night I waited out there for about an hour. When they finally came out it was raining so hard that Mary had to go back to get her coat. But Dickie had gone home and Mr Baker wanted to know why he didn't come back with her. He stuck his head out the door and called, "Dickie, Dickie Williams, come on in for a minute." But of course, no Dickie. So he decided he wouldn't let Mary go back out until Dickie came in. I waited another hour in the cherry orchard. But Mary never did come out that night. I walked home fighting back the tears. What a hell of a way to have a girlfriend.

After that I started to spend less time with Mary and more time practicing for the track team. Sarah and I went to see some real good movies too. Mom wanted me to spend more time with Sarah because she didn't have many friends. But what Mom didn't know was that Sarah didn't have any friends because as soon as somebody said something about her colour she just smashed them right in the face.

Soon I started looking around for another girlfriend. I mean . . . Mary was really nice and I loved her and all, but I couldn't take this sneaking out with her all the time.

I was a leader in Scouts two weeks after I joined up. Scoutmaster O'Reilly wanted to see me box so bad that he said he'd let me be a leader if I'd put on the gloves and "have at it for a coupla rounds with Jamie Watson."

Jamie was a great big kid and I was scared of him. But he said he wouldn't hurt me so I stripped down and put on the gloves and me and Jamie performed for O'Reilly and the rest of the kids. Jamie beat me pretty bad but I got to be a leader so I could really pick on him when I was inspecting fingernails and unpolished shoes and crooked neckties. That's how I came to be called a nigger for the first time. (I mean by a white person. My sister Sarah and Mom called me a nigger every time they got mad at me.)

"Get those shoes polished, Watson," I said, really smart as I passed Jamie in the lineup.

"Why don't you shine 'em, Billy. That's what niggers are for isn't it?"

I stood there staring at him, taken down off my high horse. But that wasn't fair. Leaders were supposed to talk smart like I had to Jamie. Some of the other kids thought it was really funny. I guess that's what upset me so bad. I took off my yellow and green troup kerchief and threw it at Scoutmaster O'Reilly.

"Here," I said, tears streaming down my cheeks, "you can keep your old scouts." Then I ran all the way home.

Mary was sitting on her front steps when I went by her place but I didn't stop because I didn't want her to see me crying. But then I dried my eyes on my shirt sleeves and ran back to the front of her place and stood whistling softly on the road. When she came out to me I told her that I had quit scouts.

"That's good," she said. "They're just a bunch of sissies, anyway."

"I had a fight with Jamie Watson."

"What for?"

"He called me a nigger."

"Oh."

"The other guys thought it was real funny too. They just laughed."

"Marabelle says the word is Negro. Niggers don't like to be called niggers, do they, Billy?"

"Mary! What are you trying to do . . . make me feel bad? You just called me a nigger."

"I did not, Billy. How come you have to get so mad? Is that all you can think about? People calling you names?"

"Do you still love me, Mary?"

She hugged me real hard.

"I'll always love you, Bill. Why?"

"Cause I don't love you anymore, that's why."

She stopped walking. "Why not Bill? What did I do? I didn't do anything. Just cause you had a fight and got called names doesn't mean you have to take it out on me."

"It's got nothing to do with being called names. I just don't love you anymore's all. Betty wants me to go around with her again. Her father's not prejudiced either."

"I can't help it if my dad's prejudiced, can I? That's got nothing to do with you and me." She was crying now and the tears were falling on my scout shirt.

"Why do you have to be mean to me?"

"I'm not being mean. I could sneak around with her behind your back. But I'm telling you instead. I can't help it if I don't love you anymore, can I?"

"What about us getting married and everything?" she cried.

"Well I guess that's all off now, Mary."

"I'm knocked up, you know, Billy."

I was shocked out of my skull.

"What? You're what, Mary Baker? But you said you couldn't get knocked up. What the hell about your period and everything?"

I was really shouting at her.

"I don't know nothing about that, Billy. I just know I missed my last period."

"Oh boy, that's just wonderful. I guess you know your dad is going to kill me. Good-bye, Billy Robinson. Holy Christ! What am I supposed to do now, shoot myself? I haven't even got my driver's license yet, either."

"Don't worry, Billy. He won't know it was you. I been going around with Dickie Williams, remember."

"Oh sure and what's Dickie going to say about that? You think he wants your dad to kill him?"

"Daddy won't be mad at him cause he's white. He always said if I ever got pregnant he'd want to look after the baby and everything. But if he finds out it was you, he's gonna go after you."

"Mar-yeee." It was her dad standing on the front porch, calling her.

"I've got to get going, Billy. Do you love me?"

She was squeezing my hand real hard and big tears were running from her eyes.

"Sure I love you. I was only fooling about Betty. But I sure wish my dad was here to help fight your old man."

CHAPTER 4

"You know, Billy, you're starting to get a bad complex about being a coloured boy."

"A what?" I said, eating my supper with Sarah.

Mom looked up from *Gone With the Wind*. "A complex," she repeated.

"Oh. What's that?"

She put down the book and put her arm around my shoulder.

"Don't you even know what a complex is?" said Sarah. "I knew what that was when I was nine. Boy, are you ever dumb."

"Eat your food, Sarah," interrupted Mom. "A complex is when you're always thinking about one thing. Can't you forget about your race for awhile?"

"It's pretty hard, Mom. Every year now since I started school I've been the only coloured person in the whole school."

"What about Xavier Wilty. He was in your class in grade four," said Sarah, looking at me like I was lying or something.

"He wasn't really coloured, though, Sarah. His dad was Spanish and his mom was Hawaiian."

"You've got to quit thinking about it so much," said Mom.

"I don't think about it, Mom. Somebody's always reminding me." I started to cry, then got up and ran into my room.

"Jamie Watson called me a nigger, Mom," I pouted, wiping my eyes on my shirt sleeves.

There was silence in the kitchen.

Then: "What for, Billy?"

"For nothing, that's what for. He said I should shine his shoes 'cause that's what niggers are for."

"Come in here, Billy," called Mom.

I sat down at the table, still wiping my eyes.

"Billy, you're just going to have to handle it as best you can. I can't run and bawl somebody out every time you get your feelings hurt. You'll have to work it out, son. Sarah does."

"Yeah, but she doesn't even have any friends. Every time somebody says something to her she just smashes 'em right in the face."

"You liar, Billy," screamed Sarah. "How 'bout you making Mary Baker go bare naked in the barn?"

I thought Mom was going to faint.

"Billy Robinson," she managed, "you what?"

"Nothing, Mom. Sarah's just lying 'cause I told on her."

"Don't lie, Billy. I saw both of you and you know it."

I got up and ran out of the room, giving Sarah a good slap in the face as I passed her. In a minute we were both running across the field, jumping all over Mr Hoffman's strawberries. Luckily for me, Sarah couldn't run as fast as I could.

"Wait'll you get back, Billy. You're going to really get it now," she yelled after me.

I kept running right down to the creek and sat down in the grass feeling like the whole world was breathing down my back. Boy, if mom ever found out Mary was pregnant . . . I didn't like to think about it. Sarah wasn't much help either.

CHAPTER 5

Mom liked to get dressed up on Sunday and take Sarah and I to church. She had been raised in a devout community full of praying coloured people who worshipped the Lord every day of the week. It wasn't that they were pious people, but they liked to call on the words in the "scriptures" for just about everything.

Grandpa (Mom's dad) didn't believe the earth was round and I used to argue with him when he'd come over to bring us fresh vegetables. Of course, Grandpa never really listened to anything I had to say in the name of grade nine science. He knew the earth was flat because it said so right in the scriptures.

"Sonny," he'd say, spitting into whatever it was we had fixed up for a spittoon, "these fancy flying machines ain't nothing but some riggin' they got fixed up in some Hollywood studio and I'm a bit disappointed in you for believing them Russians actually got dogs floating around up there in space."

Then we'd really argue until Mom got mad at me for being disrespectful.

"There's enough disrespect in the world without you arguing with grandpa over what he believes in. You're just trying to be sassy."

I had this kind of mother and this kind of grandpa.

When Mary got pregnant I tried to have a real good talk with grandpa about coloured folks and white folks mixing.

"Grandpa, what do you think about intermarriage?"

"That's one thing I try not to think about, Billy."

"Oh."

"Tell him, papa," said Mom. "He's all mixed up about it."

"Well sonny, I'll tell ya." Then he sat contemplating the thing for about two minutes.

"Billy, tell me, do black cows marry white cows?"

"Grandpa, that doesn't make too much sense, you know."

"Well, answer me, sonny. You must have learned that much in school."

"Grandpa . . . cows don't even get married."

"Yeah, but if they did white cows wouldn't marry black cows."

That was enough!

Pretty soon I was running again, up the street past Mary's house, fighting the tears. Mr Baker called me from the field where he was fixing his white posts.

"Hi, Mr Baker," I yelled back, trying to be calm.

"Billy Robinson, will you come here for a minute? I got something I want to talk to you about."

The sweat started dropping from my armpits.

"Uh . . . Mr Baker . . . I uh got to run an errand for my mother."

"This will only take a few minutes, Billy."

I imagined a quick death. Maybe a blow from his axe or a short wrestle with a police dog.

"Billy, c'mere, will you."

Mr Baker was a great big man – at least six foot two. But I was sure he couldn't run as fast as I could. I walked down to the fence where he was working. I stood a good fifteen feet away from him, leaning on a fence post.

"Billy, are you afraid of me?" said the giant man whose only daughter I had knocked up.

"Whatdja want, Mr Baker? I got to go to the store for my mom."

"Bill, you like Mary quite a bit, don't you?"

"Yessir, she's a pretty nice girl."

"I guess you think you might marry her when you're older, eh?"

"Oh no, sir. We never talked about anything like that."

"Well, Bill, I thought I'd tell you before you got any such ideas. We don't believe in it in our family."

"Oh no, sir. My grandpa doesn't either. He says it's one of the worst things you can do."

"Well, he's right, you know, Bill. It's a pretty terrible thing. The children suffer. Half black and half white. People hating them everywhere they turn."

"I guess so, sir."

"I don't want you to think I got anything against you people. I think your mother's a very fine woman. And your sister's the best babysitter we ever had. But it's you and Mary I'm thinking about. I don't want you making plans for something that can never happen. I was young once myself so I know how it can be."

"Well, thanks, sir. I appreciate you telling me this."

"Just thought you should know how I feel about it. That way we won't have any misunderstandings."

"Well, thanks again. I guess I should get up to the store now."

"How old are you now, Bill?"

"Almost sixteen, sir."

"I guess you get kind of, uh . . . horny sometimes, eh, son?"

"Mr Baker?" I figured this was it. He dropped his tools and looked straight at me.

"I think you know what I mean. You'd like to sleep with Mary, wouldn't you?"

"Mr Baker, I . . ."

"No use hidin' it, son. Mary's an awful pretty girl. But let me tell you one thing, Billy, don't you ever do it. 'Cause if I ever find out you and Mary been foolin' around I'll come after you. You hear me?"

"Yessir. I got to go now." I turned and ran from the place.

"You remember that, Billy," he called after me.

I didn't get to see Mary for a week or so after that little talk with her dad. She was off picking beans every day and I was helping Sarah cut cascara bark in the woods. (They make medicine out of it). That was a pretty good way to make a few extra dollars in the summer. We stripped the bark from the trees and sold it to the co-op in potato sacks for about sixteen cents a pound.

So there we were stripping cascara bark and something's coming through the brush making a hell of a racket.

"It's probably a bear, Billy. Let's get going. I'm scared."

"Naw, Sarah, there's no bears around here. It's just a dog."

Then Mr Hoffman came trudging through the bush.

"Hey, you pickaninnies, what you doing stripping the bark from all my trees?" He was carrying a big double-barreled shotgun.

"We're only trying to make a few bucks for school's all, Mr Hoffman. We only stripped about ten trees."

My voice was unsteady as I eyed the shotgun. But I was sure tired of being pushed around by white men. I threw my bag of bark at him, grabbed Sarah's hand, and we started running through the woods at a breakneck speed.

In those days it seemed like I was always running for something or from somebody. I guess that's how I got to be such a good runner. If I wasn't running from somebody making me feel bad, I was running from Mr Hoffman, our neighbour, or running to win races at school. It wasn't that I particularly liked running or anything, but it sure was a good way to solve problems. But knocking Mary up! Wow! There was no place to run from that. If her dad didn't get me, the Mounties would. But honestly, I really didn't know what to do about it. I couldn't tell anybody. I mean, there wasn't anybody I could tell that I'd knocked up a fourteen year old girl. And a white girl too – which was twice as bad. I would have gone to talk to the minister about it like I usually did when I had some real bad problem. Like the time I got caught taking Mr Hoffman's prize pumpkins and smashing them against his barn, or when me and my cousin Eddie stole those cherries. But this was something *real* big and the Reverend wasn't on my side anyway. But then I got the idea of seeing if Dickie would take the rap for me. I mean . . . I wasn't a coward, but if I told I'd get killed or put in jail.

"Look, Billy, everybody's gonna find out sooner or later anyway. You might as well fess up now." Dickie was riding with me to school, steering his bicycle in and out between the white lines.

"If her old man finds out she's pregnant, he's gonna get a big dog and go chasin' after somebody. It might as well be you. I'm too young."

"Listen, Dickie, you gotta do this for me. You don't have to say you knocked her up. I just want you not to say you didn't so Mr Baker'll think maybe you did. He won't be able to come after me 'cause he won't have any way of knowing if I did it for sure. Please, Dickie. Or else poof! Goodbye, Billy Robinson."

"Kee-rist, Bill, I seen this movie where some guy got a chick in trouble and he just got a bunch of his friends to say they all screwed her. Nobody could do nothing about it 'cause they couldn't figure out whose baby it was."

"You trying to make a slut outta Mary, Dickie? She loves me, you know. She's not like that."

"What makes you so sure? She went out with me a coupla times, you know."

"You want me to hit your face, Dickie?"

"Aw, don't get sore, Bill. I'm only kidding."

I stopped pedalling and got off my bike and leaned against it, gazing down the road at Mary's bedroom window.

"You know, Dickie, there just ain't no way I can get out of it."

"Why not, Bill?"

"'Cause I'm coloured."

"Aw, come on. You just think everybody's picking on you. You ain't the only one who ever knocked somebody up, you know."

"I'm not saying that. I mean . . . it's not fair. If I was white, I'd just get a bunch of guys to say they mighta done it. But that baby's going to be a coloured guy. And I'm the only coloured guy in this part of Canada. Boy! Talk about discrimination."

Mary seemed to love me all right. At least I didn't have to worry about her not being with me on this thing. She even said we could run away and elope or something if her dad threatened me. But at least I wasn't that dumb. They'd find us in a few hours anyway. Where's a fifteen-year-old coloured boy and a fourteen-year-old white girl going to hide? I mean you'd be recognized right away and turned in.

Mom and Sarah couldn't help either. In fact, I was afraid to tell them 'cause if they knew they'd want to go and sit down with the Bakers and talk the whole thing out. But you couldn't talk to Mr Baker democratically. Soon as he got mad, he'd want to rent a dog and make him bite me. Or maybe he'd beat me up himself. School was coming pretty soon too. How was I going to study with this on my mind all the time? And I didn't know one thing to do about it either.

[1973]

Christopher James [1948-]

out of order / talk'n about them folks jimi –
a tale of black male of black mail

and, now i see a million of them /
laughing in accord with the fool,
about an amusing comedy of sadism,
lemon scent on the lips of the clowns
talkin politely and feeling each other
in the amusement park, to the mock and
snarling disfigurement of the animal faces
spitting and throwing thoughts at the playground's attendants, dissenting the fantastic
horniness in the forum. the speakers address
themselves to the complacent, sitting hands folded
and grinning, shocked out of their minds at the language
that has changed them through the years. they have seen
some things, and the only expectation is the burst of
games to their hysterics, as the jubilance carries
everyone to a high of defiance. between the teeth
lies the sneer that leads in a funny way to war.
oh what a freak i must be amongst you!

[1971]

christopher's blues

and so these hours, that creep up on the soul when
it's sleeping. a sleep that lies silent in the body, dead,
though it moves, speaks and tears in an unyawning descent.
two bodies dead, hustled together in the same grave, not knowing
one is black and the other is white. two bodies buried in the
same grave, forever brothers, deadly brothers in death
and though life may be divided into two different
paths one bearing "to each his own," then what is more yielding
than two uncommon brothers striking the death toll upon a free
way, "who knows."

and, now the weather turned with the falling
of the little rubber ball. bouncing back and forth like the
heartbeat of any anxious individual; the silence of dreams
engulfing the ideas of all alive; so we all move towards the
awakening of thought, reluctantly, knowing the nature of failure
and the meaning of passing far away into the unknown, where it
is said that the bad dwell and the good await; where christ descended and ascended on the third day, in the death fathoms of
his dreams, that he might save the world's people from their cal-
amity. the lord whose unveiled face cries from the stake to the
grave on the rise of courage and the fall of reason. and, now all
days seem to be like this one, construction of figures of lines
drawn grey and blue, chaotic focuses overshadowing the grave.
there in the midst of this grave stood an ailing man, who said he
was the oldest man in the land, standing in the graveyard, tired
of dying.

[1971]

talk'n about ho bo'n it jimmy

early in the morn'n she's mourn'n
time i wake up she's groan'n. when i'm at work
she's phone'n. i walk outside the door and she's
horn'n. try'n to keep a close watch on me ooh wee
close security, that's my baby.

i step out into the street it's about ten,
i decided i'm gonna drink me some gin, yeah. i slip
into the side door of uncle ben's, there a narc sipping
on a soda, i dug him. i slide into a seat i'ma peeping
in comes my woman she's a weep'n, tellin me that the night's
a creep'n all around her mind, it's about time that we be
leavin

we split to the lady's car
i'm slinkin; we get to the woman's pad and she's a
pantin all over me, ooh wee loving me, that's my baby;

because

early in the morn'n she mourn'n
time i wake up she's a groan'n
when i'm at work she's a phon'n
i walk outside the door and she horn'n
tryin to keep a close watch on me,
ooh wee, close security,
that's my baby

[1971]

Hope Anderson [1950-]

1980

for George Stanley

description:
an event. still the 30th year
nothing / everything changes

green light in the far corner
long maple tables / 'the pips'
circa 1972
'i betcha wonder how I knew
'bout your plans to make me blue'

the lines are drawn.
in Jamaica, an american-born
syrian is instated, proposes
a puerto-rican model of government
discredited since 1948

an enemy of humanity / this B movie
actor goes to washington
an act so secure in its imperfection
& moby dick sits next to me
american excess squeezes me
into the corner

my fifth 'blue'
in my forehead
'i heard it thru the grapevine
i'm just about to lose my mind'

design;
I WANT
a movement of language
beautiful in its selflessness
up through the cold floor
a power so pure
it gives food & shelter

refrain;
with other voices
coming into the world
with much less information
than we need
a nervous laugh / the danger
of this inadequacy

& can't remember
the aphorism
of an old wise black man
the miserable alienation
unarticulated anger
we share
more conversation; story be direct

they consolidate power
in retreat

we get sluggish
any fluidity of motion
stalls
on the way thru Pasadena county
a racist banner reads
'niggers who can read beware
niggers who can't read better beware'

yes there is brutality
in all the gods
& everywhere there's an overlapping
& here the dancing unruly
I'm another domino falling
& cannot tell how we feel
until that moment, i become
the speech of the other
the one to which i speak
the cry a prolonged cry
of despair

[1987]

landed

not much to clip
the heart

the ride to you
colours seas & elevators

in sleep sheets
are given their portions
ache

one faces
the light green detail
of *the luncheon*
& might have made
all preparations
& then removed
from its celebration

when i find you
in some distant terminal
city, become diehard
in the service of your thunderbolts
& resonance
name the towns your ancient
name, united hearts of the possible
then refuse to fold tents
or pull anchor

[1987]

repatriation

my love & me
are in a mood indigo
of a thousand thumb pianos

these days are longer
less time for the vanguard
who will plant poems
of explosions in the houses of parliament

less time for us
to walk the rococco avenues
in our talk along
terraced gardens of babylon

skip over shrines of bourbons
& tudors
the catholic conscience
in the quarters of bujumbura

although it's prospero's cup
a nubian will lace it
with lye

later at approximately
40° longitude
caliban unravels his perpetual plan

ten chains of mountains
interconnecting tunnels
to protect my love
from further political bamboozlement

deposit the idiotic movies
of american bliss & violence
hammocked in the archipelagoes
into the accommodating arms
of the chase manhattan
& baron de rothschild
enliven the natural *bandung*
bury the 1885 insipid berlin air, further
before you turn out the lights
leave our coal in the basement

[1987]

Tongues in memory of Bob Marley

for Michael Paris & Lama Mugabo

1

we are stretched, body & mind
      we descend
      into it, black holes
      around us

(ejection into ergo-sphere)
      schwartz child

two of him, one with wild
flashing earth brown, coils of hair
play the black keys, Rahsaan Kirk says.

going against movement of earth
speed of the heart
      abt 5,000 miles
      air & water

as if you've carried yourself
millennia in a knapsack
& nothing disappears
      only waves
      billow
all the blue, blue
      sounds of it

they dazzle & you won't see
barracudas
as if buried deep
      in your luggage
      with the jellyfish

2

a sensualist
the dreadlocks
floats into portantonio
      of strange colonial beauty

so easily the raft
      slips into the lagoon

imagine hair
      like seaweed

we enter the city
no less memorable
garbage does swim in the ocean
or flies to miami in terror

'i am a revolutionist'
      on the radio
suddenly eyes like
      pearls
      beyond description
he's deep in his pocomania self
      tongues like
      hailstones
the knowledge that nothing is like
      anything else

it's now only how the music gives it
it's now whether words have force or power

3

you find the mind not ordered
so we order the mind, call
things up
   how can i be
   in this for you

as no monuments are built
to the dead or wounded
in these undeclared wars

& we are dancing rubbing bellies
in the dim, dim light
of Orchid's birthday

4

we are a few left, we are gone into the bush
& Burning Spear is meditative chanting
'remember Marcus Garvey' & so on
thru brambles, all crackle & break
the tongue slides over the juices
of the mango carp, releases its sweetness with its worm
we are still edging, anticipating the beat
holds attention
full moon ahead, so
   when you feel it
   you're gonna say it so nice

5

stir it up
   in the air, ear
   still true in its simplicity

6

a thousand eyes
the voice, scream from the gun court
sky of buzzards, uniforms of low, low
speech
when he came thru as that one
it was that he played the music
play the music
        just this way
        till the final breath
        till the rock hurled at you
        oh sarcophagi, flesh eating stone
        that burn the skin
        like wax
        in the sun's ultrasonic heat.

[1987]

Into Consciousness

for doug beardsley

1

a companion whose dream
i broke, leaves this with me
'if it were not for these words
i would not return from the waters'
beaten down with loss

lately this opens the world
dons us in clothes of a new
movement, a plague of desperate
& frantic citizens, flailing
our skinny arms at flags
& christmas

2

while i'm sure
my ancestors counted
ten thousand yams & cows

not enough time to sit
with makumba e.g.
deep in the couch, unhinge
the larynx, decipher the white man's
great trick, this *a* this *b*

or forward to the centre
attend that angle of speech
of a warm harlem, trenchtown's
rock in the lattice work

where everyone is out of doors
with work

as here / i hear
speech awash
ocean spray

truly say
lately i've come to think
of this

[1987]

C. S. Giscombe [1950-]

from Into and Out of Dislocation

GRANDE PRAIRIE, ALBERTA

Sometimes when I'm driving up Veterans Parkway, the boulevard that traces the eastern and southern edges of my city, Bloomington, Illinois, if the light's right or close to right, I'll suddenly remember Grande Prairie, Alberta, where I spent a night at the beginning of the summer of 1995. I'm never startled, really, to recall Grande Prairie at those times – the road into that town had made me think of Bloomington when we arrived there dirty and tired after several days on the various northern highways – and I *like* remembering the place, Grande Prairie, and will tease the memory, once it's arrived on its own, and pretend instead of downstate Illinois and that I'm heading for the Peace River instead of Kinko's copies or the Schnucks superstore; or that I'm driving out to Fort Dunvegan or Fort St. John instead of off to teach my afternoon class at Illinois State University.

I was with my wife and our nine-year-old daughter. We'd been in northern Alberta for two days and I'd been surprised to discover how flat that part of the province was. I didn't know Alberta well (and still don't): before this trip, I'd only crossed it by train once, thirteen years earlier, and all I'd recalled of the province from that trip was the railroad track snaking through the incredible snowy mountains west of Calgary – Katherine and I had sat up at the top of the carpeted stairs in the coach's observation dome for hours staring into the infinity of white peaks. And here were planted fields, the look of agribusiness, a landscape that should have been familiar to me because of Illinois. But until we came into the little city, Grande Prairie, it hadn't felt like Illinois – the light we were encountering in the country was different from the light I was used to cutting through on the drive to Peoria or the drive to Champaign: there was a hazy quality to it, probably owing something to the forest fires that year, but that quality was disconcerting because I could see a great long way *through* the haze, out to where the horizon did blur into the sky. The surface of the earth there in Alberta seemed to be dishy, slightly concave in its flatness way into the distances, and the light seemed to exist not as a series of gradual, far-off wanings but as an ever-present, if less distinctly visible, entity. It seemed to be pooling in the fields.

We'd driven into Alberta – from Fort St. John, British Columbia – through that and come eventually to the Peace River at Dunvegan, where the landscape changed; we went down into the forested hills that rose above the water and camped in a provincial park. We spent the next day, which was cloudy, in some small towns along the Peace River and along the Smoky. Katharine was constructing a photo-essay about our travels along these rivers, and this low grey day was a challenge, she said, because of the kind of film she had in the camera. She photographed the Smoky from the spindly girder bridge at Watino and the Peace from the five-car ferry on which we crossed it for a third time – the first had been on the peculiar, curving span at Fort Dunvegan itself and the second was the long bridge that led into Peace River, Alberta, the town named for the water. Then we got over to Rycroft, where the rain started, and followed the straight road to Grande Prairie, dropping into town from the north.

At the eastern edge of Bloomington, Veterans is the long artery of upscale commerce. The east side's the most profoundly white side of town and there Veterans Parkway is garlanded with frontage roads and has a grassy median strip and "smart" traffic signals that allow you to turn onto the access roads for the malls or for one of the McDonald's or appallingly ridiculous Jumer's Chateau, the huge restaurant-hotel built according to a fantasy of stuccoed Europe. Beyond Veterans the "good" suburbs are extending – town marches farther east into the cornfields and soybean fields each year – and the boulevard's swath is a rough boundary between the older upper-middle-class neighborhoods (giant maples, straight streets, Prairie-style houses with recent additions) and the stark, newly built homes of surgeons and people in the insurance business (Bloomington's the corporate headquarters for State Farm), these in neighborhoods with names like Harbour Pointe. Unlike other urban boundaries the parkway doesn't separate discrete socioeconomic communities – its several lanes separate only styles. The sky, though, seems to well up above Veterans more than it wells up at any other place in Bloomington. Hardly anything is tall on the horizon and perhaps because of that the sky is simply most visible there, from along Veterans, from one's automobile – during the afternoons, the light and clouds are incredible, nearly static presences, towering in fat vertical contrast to the divided lines of traffic. But the *location* of the light is different there: it's specific and diverting and profoundly a thing. Yet even so, Veterans Parkway looks like a lot of places I can think of, effortlessly, in the East and Midwest – Far Hills Avenue in Dayton, Ohio, for example, or Erie Boulevard in Syracuse, Adlai E. Stevenson Drive in Springfield, Illinois, Central Avenue between Albany, N.Y., and Schenectady, etc. Some days I remember Grande Prairie but usually, if I'm thinking about location at all as I drive up Veterans, I think about how I could be at the edge of anywhere.

And because of that I *had* been surprised – as Katharine and Madeline and I came into Grande Prairie that evening in June – to be reminded so strongly of Bloomington's strip; it had rained, as I mentioned, earlier in the afternoon, but that had stopped and the day had cleared and the air was bright and free of haze and here we were coming into an unexpectedly big town with a lot of traffic lights, restaurants, and motels. The sky was a presence. We were grubby – we'd camped the night before, as I said, at old Fort Dunvegan on its wild little hill above the Peace and we'd spent the night before that camping in the Rockies, in prosaically named Summit Pass, in B.C. The previous evening we'd tented at Mighty Moe's Campground in the Cassiar Mountains near McDame Creek; that was one of the nights during this trip that it never quite got dark – twilight had lasted and lasted and swelled outside the tent. The air had seemed to become increasingly granular but it never really got dark.

We were actually making a long, wide circle – a two-week car and ferry trip – and Grande Prairie was the last stop before we arrived back at the starting point, Prince George, British Columbia, where we'd been renting a house near the Nechako River. Prince George is in the geographical center of the province, it's the place where the north-south highway and the north-south railroad cross the ones going east and west. The Nechako flows into the big Fraser River at Prince George; the confluence is visible from Cottonwood Park downtown. It's a hub, a lumber and railroad town, the only city of any note for several hundred miles in any direction. I had a Fulbright that year and this was where I needed to be – I'd wanted to figure out some ways to document the travels in northern British Columbia of the Jamaican miner John Robert Giscome. He'd flourished there, as they say, in the latter half of the nineteenth century and he was, perhaps, a relative of my – and Madeline's – ancestors. He'd arrived in Prince George in the November of 1862, when it was Fort George, a Hudson's Bay Company outpost; he was on his first prospecting trip north from Quesnel, the village seventy miles south of Fort George where he'd been living, and he was accompanied by Henry McDame, a man from the Bahamas. They were headed for the Peace River country, where there was supposed to be a great quantity of gold, but the ice on the Fraser River stopped them and they hunkered down for the winter in Fort George. He was thirty-one years old then, I don't know how old McDame would have been.

We'd arrived in Prince George in the winter too, or part-way through it, in January, and were due to go back to the States at the end of June, so this would be our last trip out of town before that. Madeline was missing a little chunk of third grade but her teacher had agreed with us that this would be a worthwhile experience for her and that she could learn to multiply by seven later. It had been a pretty good jaunt – we'd taken the Yellowhead Highway west to the Pacific at Prince Rupert and caught the ferry from there up past Ketchikan and Wrangell and Juneau to Skagway, Alaska. From Skagway we'd made a detour to Whitehorse, the nearest city, the capital of the Yukon Territory, because Katharine was sick and needed a doctor and maybe was going to need a hospital. But it turned out all right and we were able to get back on the road after a couple days in a motel and drive down into the Cassiar and through the Rockies and so forth. The Cassiar and the Rockies and the Peace River and Wrangell, Alaska, were important to the project because they were places John Robert Giscome had got to; Grande Prairie was not – it was a convenient juncture for us to clean up in and relax for the last evening before the last day of travel, before we'd drive over Pine Pass and come down the Hart Highway back into Prince George. (And then we'd start packing up to really go home, to return to Bloomington.) Grande Prairie was on the flats, as its name suggests, on a high dry plateau devoid of the sorts of undulations that rivers provide, and John R. had gotten everywhere he went by water.

After the ice broke up on the Fraser in the April of 1863 Giscome and McDame had set out for the Peace River goldfields on the roundabout way that was standard then – eighteen miles on the winding Fraser north to the Salmon's mouth and then northwest for twenty-some miles up the Salmon to a short, marshy portage to what's now called Summit Lake. From there they were going to descend the Crooked River to McLeod Lake and the Parsnip River and eventually get to the Peace. But when they arrived at the place where the Salmon River flows into the Fraser they found the Salmon high and dangerous and their guide – a local man, an Indian – suggested that they go a little farther up the Fraser and take a short path he knew to a lake from which they'd be able to reach McLeod by canoe. That was in April. Much later, around Christmas, John R. would be down in Victoria talking about all this to the *British Colonist*, the newspaper there. The long front-page article, "Interesting from the Rocky Mountains," in the December 15 issue is the main source for my knowledge about his trip; it's the main print source for what I can begin to know – or guess, really – about him. The paper notes that he and McDame "made a portage of about nine miles to a lake, leaving canoes behind," and at that lake they picked up another canoe – "from an old Indian Chief" – and came down the Crooked River (as it's called now), getting eventually to McLeod Lake. There were no towns, then, of course, only those forts dotting the landscape, sitting on the shores of lakes and rivers. At the fort at McLeod's Lake "a salute of about 20 shots was fired, with firearms, in honor of the arrival of that party through that route which had never been traversed by any others than Indians." The route that Giscome and McDame used – that "portage of about nine miles" – was a more dependable route to the north than the standard, one not subject to the vagaries of high water; by 1871 the path was known as the Giscome Portage and it appeared prominently on maps until the age of highways began after the First World War, at which point travel past the new city, Prince George (built at the townsite adjacent to old Fort George), began to stop meaning travel via lakes and rivers. Up until that point it was the *way*. That first lake that the partners came to after the portage, Summit Lake, is the beginning of the Arctic watershed; the Fraser flows south and enters the Pacific at Roberts Bank in Vancouver, but Summit Lake drains into the Crooked and the Crooked flows north into other rivers and lakes and, eventually, all that water gets to the Arctic Ocean. According to the *Colonist* story, John R. noted, as he and McDame left

Summit Lake, that they were in a north-flowing river – he must have known he'd crossed the divide. The two of them did eventually make it to the Peace on their 1863 trip but found little there in the way of gold and, after some adventures, moved on to other sites in B.C. where they fared better.

Now, there's something black people, or American black people of certain generations, say: we say that no matter where you go, no matter how far, no matter to what unlikely extreme, no matter what country, continent, ice floe, or island you land on, you will find someone else black already there. (In Fairview, Alberta, when I went into the 7-Eleven to ask where we might camp in the vicinity it was a big chocolate-colored man in blue overalls who said that he'd just driven his truck over from Fort Dunvegan, where there was a provincial park, and that we could be there in twenty minutes.) And maybe white people do something similar but on a grander scale, make a similar claim but one so unironically tied to civic identity and national consciousness as to be invisible, as to require no particular thought or *self*-consciousness: the local case in point is that most histories – casual and published – of B.C. start by mentioning the same fact, the same luminous detail, they all start off with Alexander Mackenzie being the first white man to enter what is now the province. The story is not indicative of some vicious racism on the part of its tellers but its presentation as a flat fact reveals the tendency that we all have to go along with things, to not question the conventional. When John R. and Henry McDame strolled into Fort McLeod, the Hudson's Bay Company lads there at the fort fired off shots in their honor, or in what John R. *reported* as honor, "in honor of the arrival of that party" over that trail "which had never been traversed by any others than Indians." I imagine that when people read that description in the newspaper they assumed that our heroes were two white guys; and I imagine John R. smiling as he or the newspaper reporter, or the two of them together, came up with that phrase, "any other than Indians." I imagine him smiling; I don't know if he did. Who was the first black man to enter B.C.? Who was the first Giscome and how did he or she spell the name?

And all my life I've been struck by how the world's staked out by names – that the path between the Pacific and Arctic watersheds became the Giscome Portage, that's the thing that brought me to Fort George a hundred and thirty-three years after John R. had wintered there. Of course, the name's a spelling variation of my own family name, Giscombe, and all the handful of Giscomes and Giscombes I'd ever met or heard of up to the point of my own arrival at Fort George had been, as I am, black Jamaicans (by birth or ancestry); Giscome or Giscombe is not the sort of name that one associates easily with the Arctic, with ice and snow. And British Columbia is a land of white people (who've written the place's history, starting that book with A. Mackenzie), Chinese people, and Indians – that's the standard racial breakdown in the province and white history in B.C. is an even more recent series of events than it is elsewhere in North America; "pioneer" appears with great frequency in the names of businesses and organizations in the province and various other white firsts (after Mackenzie's) are casually mentioned in most conversations about the landscape. Photographs abound of the early days of the province – history is close by. But into that history, from the Bahamas and Jamaica, come Henry McDame and John Robert Giscome. They came into Fort George that winter and the latter's black name got affixed to the geography around there: the portage wasn't the only thing named for him – there's also a town, thirty miles out from Prince George, and a canyon and a rapids, both on the Fraser, and a spate of other designations as well. And into that history – and into the land of ice and snow – came I and my little family; it wasn't the first time we'd come to Prince George but it was the first time we'd arrived to dig in.

Prattville, Jamaica, West Indies

I finally went to Jamaica for the first time in the spring of 1996, after we'd been back from Prince George for almost a year. I went there rather specifically to interview John Aaron Giscombe, Jr., who was ninety-three years old then and who is the great-nephew of John Robert Giscome. He lives just outside of Prattville, a tiny place which is itself in the hills above Mandeville, a big market town in the center of the island. There hills are no region of Giscombe family origins, they're where his wife's people were from. All the Giscombes trace back to the parishes of the northeast coast, the northern side of the Blue Mountains: Buff Bay – where my grandfather was born – Belcarres, Portland Parish, etc., places I've still never seen. Or that I've not seen yet. I suspect there's a blood connection in all that geography, a link that's out there waiting to be found between my grandfather's people and that family, John R.'s. Or I imagine that there is; names rise in a number of different ways and if we do share some ancestry – if the same coupling long ago produced both John Robert Giscome and myself – I've certainly not discovered it, marked it, located it; I've been concerned, so far anyway, more with the peripheries than with a core.

And John R. is himself, in Canadian history, a peripheral character – that is, he appears, or his name does, in a variety of contexts, but almost never as the central focus. The articles and descriptions and paragraphs are rarely about him – they're about the countryside or the route through it that bears his name or about the business ventures of a white man for whom he's reputed to have worked once. There are a couple of exceptions to this, though – one is that long article in the *Colonist*, "Interesting from the Rocky Mountains," and the other is a videotape, made in summer 1994, at a Giscombe family reunion in Melbourne, Florida. The tape contains an extensive interview with old John Aaron and it was sent to me a year or so after the fact by Lorel Morrison, who lives in Maryland and is himself one of John Aaron's great-nephews: there's a relatively tight family group descended, it turns out, from John R.'s brother Peter, who stayed in Jamaica while

John R. went on to Canada, and Lorel's part of that group. I don't know whether or not I am: there's a coincidence of some first names but they're fairly common first names and there are enough holes and guesses in the family trees to make me dubious or at least cautious and qualifying in my embrace. But on the tape the old man was sure about some things – he called the names of people long dead and told stories about John R. and Peter, who was, of course, his own grandfather.

My grandfather, for whom I am named, left Bluff Bay suddenly one afternoon near the turn of the century and never went back: the story goes that one of his brothers was shipping out on a United Fruit boat to Costa Rica and that he – my grandfather – had gone down to the docks to see the brother off and decided or had decided (impulsively, that is, or by design) to join him. He picked bananas for a while in Costa Rica and saved money and came to the United States and went to Clark, the black school in Atlanta, and then on to Meharry Medical College in Nashville. He settled in Birmingham, where my father was born, and practiced medicine there until the week before he died in 1962, when I was eleven. He was a short man with coppery skin and high cheekbones, he was fierce and calm at once in his demeanor; he had an accent, of course, and I can remember the sound of that much more vividly than I can recall anything he ever said. He said rather little. When he died we all went down to Birmingham on the overnight train (from Dayton, Ohio, where I grew up and where my parents still live) and I played with the neighborhood boys while my father closed up his office. Small mysteries were discovered among the papers – nothing scandalous but things he'd never mentioned: a medal and an accompanying citation for his work with the Selective Service signed by Harry Truman, a handful of stock certificates from shady-sounding oil ventures, and a 1921 letter from the Provincial Board of Medical Examiners telling him what he'd have to do in order to practice medicine in British Columbia.

Years later, when I found out about John R., I immediately thought of that letter – it's now ensconced in a little cardboard envelope in my top desk drawer here in Bloomington. I suppose I don't really know what to do with it on any level: it's an artifact all right but I'm not sure what it represents. I do see that it's no dotted line on a map connecting my grandfather's forty-some years in Birmingham to John Robert Giscome's forty-some years in B.C. I don't know what was in my grandfather's mind when he wrote to the medical examiners and I don't know what set of circumstances stopped him from going out there. Like much else in the family history it's locked up in the head of someone who's died. Papers don't reveal much, I think, for most of us, especially when it comes to our desires – we're not scrupulous about maintaining a trail that would reveal us, we're more busy getting through life than documenting it. At the funeral my grandfather was laid out in his tuxedo and my mother whispered to me that he had last worn that at her wedding to my father, fourteen years earlier. He'd been *entertaining* them, she said, during the reception and, because I'd never before heard the word used in that context, I imagined him fiercely doing magic tricks. I knew where British Columbia was when I was a child because I was interested in maps.

I didn't know a thing about John Robert Giscome, though, until I was thirty – I was an editor then, at *Epoch* magazine at Cornell University, and I was publishing work by a Vancouver poet, George Bowering. In one of his letters he included something odd: he circled my name on the line of salutation and scrawled a question across the top of the sheet – "Do you know that there's a town in northern B.C. that has this name?" I didn't know but when I went home that evening there it was in the world atlas I'd had since I was thirteen – a black dot on the map outside Prince George, on the red line of the Canadian National Railways. The name itself, Giscome, was in the sans serif typeface Rand McNally uses to indicate very small towns; the index listed the population at 575. A patient little time bomb, in my possession, waiting to go off. I typed a note of inquiry to the Chamber of Commerce in Prince George and got a letter back that quoted *1001 British Columbia Place Names*, the guidebook by G.P.V and Helen B. Akrigg: "Named for John Robert Giscome, a negro miner who entered the district in 1860 and died about 1910 in Victoria." This was something real. The next afternoon I went over to the Olin Library at Cornell and took the elevator up to the sixth floor and found a copy of the Akriggs' book and read the one-line description again. I looked out the window at Inlet Valley and West Hill – it was winter and the line of the hill was jagged against the sky. The Olin ventilation made its constant whoosh and the dry, sweet stink of leather bindings drifted in the air. Here was something real indeed and eventually, because of that, I made it out to British Columbia. But I've always, all my life, been going on into Canada, going up to Canada, over into Canada.

When Katharine, Madeline, and I got to Jamaica we rented a car, a Toyota Tercel, and drove the hundred miles from Kingston out to Mandeville. The ride was harrowing – people went fast and passed one another on curves and on hills and I was, of course, unused to driving on the left side. We got through Spanish Town, Old Harbour, and May Pen and, as the country began to get steep and the traffic got less intense, we stopped for lunch at a roadhouse called the Healthy Eaters Café. The place was full of truck drivers, African-descended and Indian men, who spoke, as we waited in line to place our orders, in an accent that stopped me from understanding whatever they were telling me; but I was finally able, after some false starts, to joke with the women at the counter about the price of Pepsi-Cola. One brought our lunches out to us in the dark little dining room and my barbecued chicken was quite delicious. We came into Mandeville a little after that and found our hotel, and the next morning I got up early and went off alone, with my new tape recorder, to see John Aaron Giscombe in Prattville.

Lorel Morrison had provided me with directions to John Aaron's house and the hotel owner's husband augmented those by drawing me a very detailed map of the way out of Mandeville. With all that on the seat beside me I headed up over the shoulders of the edge of town, passed some big estates, and suddenly town all fell away and I was on a narrow road that looped through a lush, open country. I felt a certain ebullience at driving alone through this, through Jamaica, in the morning – the road was deserted and on either side were hills that were thick and a brilliant green color and the sunlight too was thick without being either hazy or bright. This was certainly the country of joy, of resonance – but with what? The road was beautiful but it reminded me of many other trips on many other roads – one memory yielded effortlessly to another, the road was that basic in its climbs and in the way it went into the sunlight. All was a scattering, nothing cohered. And in that scattering, or rolling alongside it, I was headed for an almost arbitrary location, a place where I hoped to find some information, a crossroads, as it were, at which I was to meet an emissary from something bigger, something more specific – it was the classic literary situation, almost a cliché. But this landscape was specific too, this was Jamaica – the land of my *fathers* – and I was on my way through it to Prattville in a rented white Tercel.

After a while Newport, where I was to turn, hove into view: it was an intersection with some two-storey buildings and a police station, and I found my left turn in a grove of big trees and made that and went on toward the hills in which Prattville was situated. Trees shaded the way for the first quarter mile or so, and I saluted an ancient man with a cane who was walking in the road there, tottery on his bare feet, and he returned my wave shakily with his free hand. The skin was profoundly black, the beard and hair were bright white. Actually, many people were walking in the road and there were goats too, and cows, and a plague of white egrets – all of our driving thus far in Jamaica had involved an unnerving proximity to people and animals. Lorel had asked, in one of our phone conversations, if I'd ever traveled in the Third World, fretting over me a little bit, I think, on the eve of my departure for the island of his birth, and I'd answered, half-joking, that I had been to New York. And England – where we'd lived for half a year when Madeline was a baby – had outfitted me with a series of handy comparisons: as I climbed toward Prattville I became mindful of the road I'd bicycled on over the Malvern Hills near the Welsh border – like that road it ascended and descended very sharply (much more so than the one I'd taken from Mandeville down into Newport), plunging into and out of some deep shade, and it was often gravel and there were the "washed-out interrupted raw places" too that Theodore Roethke named in his great last poem, in the section that begins "In the long journey out of the self . . ."

But all that's metaphor – literary bric-a-brac – and metaphor's heavy on any road. All around me Jamaica roiled in the sunlight and jutted out onto the pavement and seemed a lot like itself. My comment about New York was merely clever and England hadn't really prepared me – this was the land of some of my fathers and it was at least as strange to me as England had been when I'd arrived there.

Lorel's instructions had called for me to begin asking, at some point, for the way to Mr Giscombe's house. At what felt like the outskirts of Prattville I stopped two men who were walking by and asked them and the bald man said that he lived up in Nonperel, up at the top of a hill, and asked, "You he grandson?" I'd noticed, once we left Kingston, how dark-complected almost everyone was and because of that, I think, I stuck out some – I've never thought of myself as being particularly light but in comparison to the people I ran into in the country I was. I am. Old John Aaron – whom I'd seen in the videotape – has skin roughly the same color as my own and I suppose that this was enough to base the question on. A young man named Martin appeared and one of the men I'd been speaking with arranged for him to act as guide. We drove up the potholed hill to Nonperel, which was a group of houses in among some trees; I steered around a young one-armed woman in a sleeveless blouse who was walking with children – hers? – carrying a gallon jug of milk, and Martin pointed out Mr Giscombe's driveway and accepted the couple of dollars I offered for his trouble. I parked at the bottom of the hill and climbed up to the house, where I was met by Noel Giscombe, John Aaron's son. I'd written and so was expected.

The old man came out of the back room then and I introduced myself to him, using my first name – Cecil – and my last name, which was, of course, the same as his. "I knew a Cecil Giscombe," he said but I couldn't get him to elaborate. He rambled for a long time, repeating, word for word, snippets of his talk on the tape Lorel had sent me. I'd try to guide him, but everything about John R. came back to him having "found a gold mine in Canada" and that, when he died, "his property was worth twenty-five t'ousand dollars" – he'd emphasize the "t'ousand" the same way each time, just as I'd heard him emphasize it when he told the story on the videotape, and finally his son said, "Forget it, man," and went on to say I should have been there last year; he'd been sharp then, Noel said, and could've told me everything I wanted to know. But during the intervening winter he'd fallen sick and Noel and his other sons had thought he was going to die; he hadn't, of course, but he'd emerged from the illness frail and disoriented. "His mind's gone, man," Noel said; "you're about a year too late." The old man sat on the couch next to me staring out the open window. The tops of trees were visible and from somewhere else in the house music was playing. There was a picture of Queen Elizabeth on the wall. I get tangled up in language myself sometimes and often will remember things I've said or should have said and repeat them later, turning them over again and again in my mind. I teach in a largely windowless building named after the Bloomingtonian Adlai Stevenson and have identified a malaise I call Adlai Stevenson's disease, the first sign of which is talking to yourself in the stall in the fourth-floor washroom, the one English shares with Accounting and Philosophy. It's a joke ailment of course, garden-variety depression crossed with the fear of Alzheimer's. The question on the road had been whether or not I was a grandson, but I was forty-five then, about the same age as Noel. What'll I be like in half a century? The videotape had been made at a family reunion in Florida and the old man had been casually encyclopedic about the tribe – the range of skin colors, his father's experiences in Panama, his own adventures when he'd lived in Chicago. Some of those adventures had had a sexual tinge and John Aaron had flirted, a little, on the tape with some of his young, distant cousins, trim good-looking Giscombe women in their fifties and sixties.

I've never been terribly interested in the costume drama that most imaginations of the past seem to entail. Which is to say that I regard devotion to family trees with a mix of suspicion and uninterest – there's something irritatingly civic about the enterprise, something that verges on a kind of boosterism. One wishes to find and then capture the connection as though it were a trophy. It'll settle this or that, it'll confer status. I recently met a white man in Indiana who made a point of telling me that he'd traced his lineage back to Abraham. When I do think of the past and family trees and so forth I imagine copulation – the romance of sex, the inevitability of bodies producing another body, the grandparent suddenly youthful and randy. The delights of being naked. Or I imagine the ancestor wasting time doing this or that or being sullen or fearful or, as Auden said, just walking dully along. Eating. Working for someone. Asleep. Or waiting for something to happen.

I came back to Mandeville, picked up Katharine and Madeline, and we drove down to Treasure Beach on the south coast and went swimming in the Caribbean. It was March and the water was warm. We sat on the sand and watched pelicans, birds none of us had ever seen before except in pictures.

[2000]

Lorena Gale [1958-]

from Je me souviens: Memories of an Expatriate Anglophone
Montréalaise, Québecoise Exiled in Canada

(Black. Music. Robert Charlebois' "Lindberg" bleeds into "This Land Is Your
Land, This Land Is My Land." The sound of a needle being scraped over a record
as it is taken off. Lights up. Slide of Joe's Café. Ambient "café" sound.)

I am on Commercial Drive, sitting in Joe's Café. I'd just bumped into another
expatriate and like those from "the old country," hungry for news from home,
whenever we meet we all always reminisce or share news of the others we have left
behind. It is a ritual of love and remembrance played out on alien soil by emigrés
all over the world. Only we're in Vancouver and home is Montreal. The same
country. At least, today it is.

We speak in English, my first language and her second. We speak in English
because I don't know Greek. We speak candidly, without forethought, without
apology. Around us we hear snatches of Italian, Arabic, Spanish, Portuguese,
Cantonese, Urdu, etc. We speak unashamedly and to each other.

So I say to my compatriot, "I have just come back from Montreal. I can't believe
how much it's changed. Everything for sale. Everything for rent. Liquidation.
Going out of business. And everywhere these tacky dollar stores. And they're the
only ones who seem to be doing any real business. It's sad. I have never seen
Montreal looking so bad."

And the next thing I know, there's this long-haired, grunged-out French guy in
my face saying, "Hey! You don't say that! You don't talk about Montréal!"

He had been listening in on our private conversation, which had obviously
offended him, and had half risen from his seat to stretch across his table and point
an accusatory finger at me, like he was the long arm of the Language Police and
had nabbed himself another Anglo traitor. His look was irate and triumphant like
one spoiling for a fight. My friend immediately put her head down like somebody
trying to avoid one. Me. . . ? I was stunned into momentary silence.

What could I have possibly have said to offend him? That Montreal looked poor and depressed? The truth? For a second there, I thought I was in a Café on St. Denis St. a little too drunk, voicing my insensitive Anglo opinions on the political situation a little too loud, and this brave soldier in the struggle for Quebec independence was standing forth to eradicate this heretic from their midst.

I looked around expecting to see a room full of hostile and contemptuous people, but no one was paying attention. I was still in Lotus Land. And what did I care since I wasn't talking to him anyway. So I told him to "fuck off and mind his own business." "No! You fuck off! It is my business. Me. I'm from Montréal. I know. You. You don't say nothing. Tu n'a pas le droit!"

I don't have the right? I don't have the right!?

My friend hates confrontation. She tells me to "ignore him. He's an asshole. He's just looking for a fight. Come on. Let's go somewhere else."

But I have gone somewhere else. Thirty six hundred miles to somewhere else! And I cannot back down.

"I don't have the right! Why? Because I'm English? Why? Because I'm Black?!"

"Ah, you. You don't know nutting."

"Oh! Je sais, moé. Je sais assez que toi, hostie. Et si je n'avais rien su, j'aurais eu le même droit de parler que toi!"

"Toi? Tu parle Français?!"

"Oui. Je parle Français. Je vien de Montréal, moé. Je suis Montréalaise. Je suis née a Montréal. Et j'ai le droit à parler. Le même droit à parler que toi, hostie! Avec n'importe qui, n'importe ou. Okay? So fuck off!"

"Eh, eh, eh! C'est correct. Je m'èxcuse. You come from Montréal. I thought. . . . You know, I from Montréal too, eh. And I thought . . ."

He picked up his backpack and wandered out onto the Drive. My friend was examining the residue at the bottom of her cappuccino. She hadn't said a word through the entire altercation and I could tell she wanted to go too. I still wanted to share my memories of Montreal. But the moment was lost. She had to run. And so we parted.

(Slide – exterior Joe's Cafe.)

You know, I'd see him on the Drive, from time to time, with a group of other young Quebecois beneath the rainbow outside of Joe's Cafe. His shoulders hunched from the weight of his pack. His long hair matting into incongruous dreads. He is all passion and gesture and speaks French with a fury so familiar but I can no longer follow. And when I pass he mumbles "Salut" in grudging recognition.

We are both, after all, from the same place. His Montréal is my Montreal. His Québec is the Quebec of my birth. Like heads and tails, we are two faces of the same coin. One side inscribed in French. The other English. And we are both so far from home.

I am an expatriate anglophone, Montrealaise, Quebecoise, exiled in Canada. And I remember. Je me souviens . . .

[2001]

Joy Russell [1959-]

returning to the place where there were so few of us when I grew up

On a cold Vancouver winter morning
in my old Italian neighbourhood

long-faced Somalian
women wait for the bus

they do not return my smile
dark eyes skim the coffee cream of me

do not testify an acknowledgement
of our skin particulars, this time

it was different, I was not
looking for acknowledgement

but connection, only
and knowing, this time

the difference

[2002]

This is Not the Miscegenation Blues of a Tragic Mulatto

Tragedy,
does not
become me.
Red, yes.
Blue, yes.
But not tragedy.

Although,

I think
it became Linda
back in '72, when,
at the hormonally-challenged age of fourteen,
I brought her home to my suburban
Condo and my parentally-challenged white
mother answered the door
and Linda, right on cue,
seized the moment,
and whispered, tragically:

Is that your maid?

and now, I wonder

where old Linda is.
I hope, she's not
so tragic anymore.
But, when I think
about it . . .

We sure
could've used
a script like that
in *Gone With the Wind*.

[2002]

Mending Clothes as I Think of Sojourner Truth

In the cloth of night, I am sewing
your name, I am reckoning with you,
360 degrees, full on, and the sky,
thick soup of stillness and stars, as I
calculate, re-thread through needle, through
needle of pain, finger, thimble, needle
of mending things, pulling tears together. Between
this frequency of night, I am saturated with
zippers, saturated with buttons and things which have come
to die, I am going through the eye of the needle, to
thread, to pull you closer to me, and your name, the image
as you ripped open your shirt, revealed
your brave open heart covered by breast,
and declared, as I do, right here right now, this very precise
moment, cloth of sorrow in hand, tears on the loose every
where in the house: *And ain't I a woman?*

[2002]

Kathy-Ann March [1962-]

Like Koya

They told her when she married: Don't marry white. And she says she didn't – look at his kinky head. He's not white.

Look at his father's kinky head – the lightest of his bunch.

He told her that he had a recurring dream. The blacks and the whites were fighting and he didn't know which side to take.

On occasion a customer will approach the receptionist at work and ask for the black chap they had been dealing with . . . and the gal up front will ring for me. I know it's not me they want – I don't do customer relations, there are only two of us – but I always answer the query. "No, the fellah I'm dealing with is black. Sweetheart, it's something you'll have to deal with for the rest of your life."

She laughs at him strong in her identity, strong in where she came from and yet, her light skin-ned-ness took her into and through the maze of Jamaica's class/colours where brown brothers and sisters could not/would not go.

A privilege, a passport without geography, an abbreviated history. No legacy of land that gives us a body the security to know, and be satisfied with, what it is. An identity from which to clearly speak; not the emulation of a promise that cannot be accessed. We are not white, we are not black. We are more often than not what others perceive us to be. Positioned in the collectivity of the moment as best suits the communal purpose.

And she came to Canada and they asked her if she was nanny to her own children.

Pursuing a posture that looks like but never quite is . . . you. Drawing upon the authenticity of another as a space from which to speak. I have lived through white academic women who have introduced me to myself through women of colour texts they have explored. Privy to their realms of endeavor as the "polite" other. Offering the ever so interesting voice of the ethnic without being up in anyone's face. Credibility constrained to speaking only of issues about this body. My thoughts, my knowledge of other topics is somehow incredible. Without brownness I don't make them uncomfortable. It is never spoken – I know this.

Looking to my blackness for comfort I can enter so far.

Black History Month, I volunteer, do the work.

My whiteness means I enter only so far, no matter how much work I do.

I cannot be a "daughter" of the Black Women's Congress.

I cannot represent issues of blackness – white folks will get the wrong idea, black folks get annoyed.

What issues of blackness do I have?

What beauty of blackness do I have?

And if I answer you with body, rhythm, and song, I am giving you stereotypes, embarrassing essentials.

I was born and they asked her if there hadn't been some kind of mix-up at the hospital. Is she really yours, they would tease.

Blonde ringlets, pudgy and pink that would change in adolescence to wiry, kinky bush and lean defined muscle. The panic and anxiety of a head to be tamed. A father's desire . . . the hair should not be cut short.

And she struggled with wide-toothed comb, grease, plaits, conditioners, ribbons, and relaxers over this head in the laundry sink. This head, its skinny frame firmly clasped between her thighs and muttered, "Yuh head is like koya, I don't know why he doesn't just let me cut it all off."

Between the two of us, she could spend the better part of a week's wages at the hairdresser. "Beauty feels no pain."

I am the ugly white girl.

Dad, no Farah Fawcett hairdo, no demure smile.

I am the only black girl my Scottish friends know. They are quite clear that I am black. I have always been aware that this was not a supportive affirmation on their part but rather a clear message that my blackness was not to be confused, genetically or otherwise, with the heroic genealogy of the Scot. For the longest time they were my only friends.

In the row house where I grew up in Canada, there were two prints of black market women. Every other picture in the house was a landscape devoid of people. Landscapes are not satisfying, and I continue to search for images that represent me and places I am comfortable with.

The walls of my apartment are bare.

I have not been back to Jamaica in twelve years. During a family conversation it is said that back home white people are being shot . . . my brown-skinned sister throws a quick and nervous glance my way. She and our cousin are making plans to hang out in Jamaica for a while, to see if they can make their way, to see and feel family. The last time I was there I went to visit my grandmother, my mother's mother, on her plantation. The local boys threw rocks at my car and yelled white girl!

And I duck my head, as my girlfriend shouts and crouches down in the booth. The glass ashtray sails overhead and smashes against the wall. I turn to look and through the din of the bar's heavy metal squall the biker and I lock gaze. He stares, turns on his heel and lumbers, all belly and leather, into the crowd.

I'm drunk and confrontational – what the hell is going on? His sidekick intercepts me and explains: "To my buddy a mix like you is worse than a nigger." He hands me a KKK calling card. In disbelief I show the card to the people I'm with – they're shooting a chummy game of pool – the chums they are playing against produce their KKK cards.

I leave.

"What the hell were you doing in a place like that in the first place?!" I am in there because I passed through the door that day and many times before.

And slowly I come to know that it is the task of carving out a space for myself outside the tyranny of belonging in one or the other. I have been a traitor to no one but myself.

Slowly, dear cousins, I begin, with an effort as this.

[1994]

Lawrence Ytzhak Braithwaite [1963-]

Trunk Music

> The final swing is not a drill
> It's how many people I can kill
> – Slayer

> I think murder sells a lot more than sex.
> They say sex sells. I think murder sells.
> – Dr. Dre

For an October day, it started out sunny, but then it quickly went dark. Then it began to rain; could have been Spring. They had been outside, fogging about the neighborhood, exploring. The area had not been fully landscaped and shredded into prettiness. It was almost a scrap metal and wet rotten clear cutted forest: lost suburban homes and govt. offices and shreds of parks of browning grass. They hang out in this abandon gutted car, jüs dair, simply sitting, alone, without a sound, except for the bass, voices and drums connected to their heads – heaven-sent messages from the mothership.

They hang out around there, all day, they got a beer or pop in their hands – smell of busthead on a good day. They come from that park, là-bas. The tall one he's boulfale, expatriate, in scruffy up pants, flip flopping his sneakers on the pavement. His legs burn the breeze, swinging with speed. His buddy, jacking alongside, provoking his legs, to keep up with his eyes – being top dog, bounding ahead of him, that's Denmark. They wasn't from the Oaks or Rockies – there, they less Snoops and more Backstreet. They're little raggamuffins, wet on the streets. They look more Squompton than Fernwood. Fernwood, they got more a panic in needle park. They more "Juice" and they up to something, them two. Ain't nothing up in Fernwood but trying and failing to hookup.

-You're my boy-

-You my boy, Bonebrk, you my boy-

-Yeayeah-

They playedout bangbang roles of partners paramount: Capone and Nitti – Alfonso/Francesco, Cagney and Wood, Muni and Raft – if they gave one gesture, one to the other, they'd get two back; Samuel and John, throwing up signs, calling to close in the fellow gunzels, niggaz, boulfalé and soldiers, to let them accomplice, cohort and throw down against all the shit that they're dished out in lots and packets in the overrun garbage alleys and second rate blocks – (underworld pals) Denmark and Bonebrk, Taylor and Heflin, Klebold and Harris, Smith and Wesson.

Bonebrk showed his boy the pièce de dix cents all polished silver around his kneck. His grand-mère had given it to him. It was shiny and it flamed in the sun and would make you blind if you saw it too long. Sometimes Denmark is riding down the street on a bike, that he and him jacked; that silver thing lustering in the bask, just ahead. Bonebrk be sitting like a headlight, on the handle bars, more confident than fuk. He's his boyfriend, he's his boy – let it never fade. Let it never tarnish. Don't let that bad hex come on you. Watchout for that powwow Dr. down the way. Watchout for the boys who lose dreams from their pockets. Like these gunzels who took love and beat down Denmark, senseless, once. He'd been beat before, but this was a little too worst than the rest. Bonebrk got him to the hospital. The Dr. didn't want to do anything with him because he had tats and they figured he must be in a gang; it was gang related. They didn't want to do nothing. The television was on in the waiting room; everybody was paralyzed.

He wanted to walk to the hospital so he didn't show any weakness. They had a long way to walk. He had to stop and sit on benches. Bonebrk made sure that he didn't sleep. He took him on his gleaming boat. He asked him to glide with him on a low cruising plane and locomote on a silent train. It was from awhile ago, when Bonebrk was sort of little, and his grand-mère's voice would walk with him. He asked him to glide with him. He asked him to sail over the streets. He asked Denmark to glide with him, sootheful and unfettered. It was deep dark, and by the time Bonebrk got there, it was time for the hags to holler. People were in pain, passing out, wittle wagging and screaming for doctors, cultus, to just do their job. He was bleeding and waving around like a torn rag overruled by the bluster. Bonebrk thought that he was in for a dirt nap that time. He got another scar across his eyebrow.

Weeks later in the park they were sitting and Bonebrk handed Denmark a paper bag.

-Go on open it-

It shimmered in the sun like that dime. Denmark walks around with an Arkansas toothpick he got him.

LAWRENCE YTZHAK BRAITHWAITE

Bonebrk figured he'd cheer Denmark up. They were at a party, getting cranked on busthead. Bonebrk he leaned down over to Denmark, to his copane, all oryide;

-You fire a gun before-

-Not for awhile now. I got only rifles in my hand. I never figured a handgun before. They were for my papa or officers-

He grew up around guns. His papa worked with them before he was born. He was in construction. He'd visit people with it. They never wanted him or his friends coming.

"I was a soldier," his papa said. He'd said it real proud standing over him, when he misbehaved or some action or knowledge was perceived as a challenge. It was like pinning a dog. For so long Denmark thought he was talking about the war and that picture on the wall, next to the medals, then Denmark turned 6 and figured different. He grew up around guns, all around him, guns and gunzels – on TV, in movies, in games and hidden places, ones that could be pulled out, for surprises, from his papa.

-You got a glock? You know what I want? I want to fire an Uzi, Tec 9 – fucken Mack 10 . . . -

-I got all that baby, I got alla dat shit. I was born with a gat on my lap. I'll fix you up good-

-Yeah-

-Yeaaahhh-

-Glockin-

-Ahuh-

-You got that-

-Mmmmmmm-

-Let's go blast some metal-

They were in a yard, that was like a field, and Bonebrk stood behind him, in the deep dusk, with his arms stretched around Denmark – steadying him at the target. He braced him for the kick.

205

-Picture yourself wurling frontward, mangling barber grooves
all through the barrel. Blast metal all over the yard, Denmark.
Get that dumdum in there. Go ahead, go on, pull'er back-

What a poem, what a bunch of words with Heflin, soft lit – all to say; 'I couldn't
do it; never tell' – the way a hoodlum says; "I love you." Bigshots, together, climbing the top of high hills, doing what Cagney couldn't do roaring; but what he got
done in an industrial steel atrocity with fire hotter than hotter, popping pipes,
smoking sterile hallways, flopping all the metal shrouding him.

* * * * *

They figured a film night that was offered, over the bridge, at this centre, would
be pretty cool. They got pizza and chocolate and "Children of the Corn III." But
they weren't greeted very well. They were two soldiers, street niggaz, in the people's minds. It was like they were going to pullout and drop those bastards, just
like on television and Segal movies. Denmark felt misty over Eli and Joshua
falling out. He knows what it's like to whisper kid secrets, at night, in bed, to each
other. It's something special and then some men can put it asunder, these days.
They couldn't come back any more. They were told that they threaten people
there. That the girls were afraid of them. That they couldn't let anybody talk with
their violence radio activating. The guys just thought that they were homos. You
could walk like lovers with no need to fuk. It all scared everybody.

Denmark's papa got him and Bonebrk a job cleaning shit up at this motel, off the
highway, a few miles from where they lived. He said that he had set them up for
life. Denmark didn't mind cleaning up the cum, shit and blood stained sheets as
much as Bonebrk did. Bonebrk got mad. He figured that Denmark was worth
more than this. That his papa was selling him short. That Denmark was smart and
could go off and study things. That he never offered him any respect. He knew that
Denmark didn't offer his papa respect. He only felt fear. They got out of that business and packed it up for further down in town, over the bridge, and started to
scuttle around the streets, looking to be mini bigshot, with all the rules and right-
eousness of what's supposed to be. Maybe, they'd be soldiers; conjure up hooligans
by the powers of that powow Dr. down the way – get in tight with a murder inc.

At first it looked liked they were hangin with that weird guy Robert. He hangs in
the park, mostly with the Krishna's, now. But he gets himself into all sorts of shit
things, on a yearly level. Nobody seez that little high yellow hustla he used to hang
with. They went over to his place a few times, played some wicked games, watched
some toons. He got pretty fukt when they put him on prozac. He just kept repeating the same feeling over and over, again. He went to Seattle or Toronto or

Vancouver or something. Robert's a crazy lookin muthafuk. He don't go near the Heroin Hotel no more. They keep away from him, but Bonebrk and Denmark had seen their future years ago, when they went out, scullying for shit. It all got dropped off by the spoilers. They'd raid backyards, alleys, sallyannes and dumpsters . . . ;

-You remember when we watched Casino. Pesci was the last thug-

-It sucked-

-How could it suck. It was a good movie. It's Scorsese-

-Let me tell you Boney, if I made a fukken pipebomb, it wouldn't fail. More than two hrs. of fukken talking. Not talking and people, between people, but being talked at-

-You didn't like the vice-

-Yeah, I liked the vice, I liked the brother, the baseball bat and the grave in the field of dreams and I liked the vice-

-It's worth it for the vice-

-It's worth it for the pen and Sharon Stone in a mini-skirt. . . . and what's with the schmaddas. Schmaddas aren't good gangsters. Lansky wasn't-

-The Dutchman was-

-Arta Flagenhiemer-

-Stick 'em up. . . . Hey, fukken hell. Denmark, look at this, check this wicked mix out . . . -

They found a couple of bodies in there, once. One had a bullet to the brain. It could have been a mobber hit. They figured grand stories of what, when, who and reason for the mess. They looked for the gun, because you're supposed to drop it and walk, but it was nowhere near. Somebody probably took it. If you want to get rid of someone, you could tease them or wack 'em.

* * * * *

You know how much film shit costs? It's pretty choice and they had all kinds of films, that they could get on video tape, there at the centre. Maybe, even make a top flick with the Ariflex, like that kid does in town, with his action videos. They don't know what to do with it. They too precious. The men are punks. They never handle anything upfront. They whisper shit, like little girls in highschools do and snub each other like pissedoff housewives. The only thing that doesn't make them homos is that they figured where to stick their dicks in a chick. Bonebrk and Denmark, they could bust this place easy, cause they're a team. It's not hard to crack a place. Get shit out, in no time, with your hoodies real up and your caps real low. They could make a strategic maneuver and execute the deal in dazzling radiance like Mickey and Donald (armed 10,000). Bonebrk and him, perfect pals paramount in crime, super slapping each other, like Pesci dished out to Bobby in "Raging Bull." Bonebrk, he could take it like that. Bonebrk, he could be a bouncer, the top torpedo for blindpigs, run hush/hush, by Denmark, the resident manager – caponing it sweet on Gonzalez Beach. They'd have no surveillance cameras, cause they'd know every made man and the malls they wear like watches. No trouble gets started, without them knowing. They got memory to photo, cut and print the kissers – jet them out to people, to scoop them out, in California hideouts. If you save enough mags up, you can build a lot of thought, that could convince people to back you and hit new york and go guerrilla. You do what you gotta do to be big in Hollywood. But you could use the scraped out architecture to build a range into a set. You'd have to go in, over the top, to get there. It's all windows up front and way too close to the street. But the front desk would be no problem. They got no guts. They could make movies and build a collection, to hold up with, in a hideout all their own – only go out to get more chips, pop and pizza.

They sent out resumes to the mothership – high powered events of 711 terrorisms and streetcorner capitalism. Petty crimes of agression against nunheims who were looking to be suckers. Then in the dark, months later, they were looking, again, staking out the town and alleys for the good stuff. They figured that they might come across some more better stuff, like when Bonebrk found that knife, wrapped in a coat, and Denmark that beeper on the Black kid. Then in the dark, with light to the back of them, back lit, so they were an outline, framed by the shimmer of the keylights, noiring them out, they appeared and offered Denmark and Bonebrk a callback, to have them made into the boyz of big shot, respect, gattling gunzel, untouchablism. An offer to our cause, our thing, our hood, our crew, our thug brothers, in brotherhood – do or die. You, me and us, we let them sleep, let him sleep, bed him down, cosh them luscious – that powwow Dr., down the way, who griot's in tongues.

That's when I knew that they was going to cosh me. As soon as I saw them fogging along the street at sunlay over. Both had faces that had so much character, it almost seemed like a blk and wht flick. There was nothing to do about it since I'd seen them in parks all tornup – the way they dress. They smiled at me in front of my apt a few times – along the street and it punctured my chest – made it feel like bubble gum.

I easily got distracted by pretty voyous; the ones that was there, honking back whippets, busthead and beer and splitting their skulls w/laughter . . .

I told the tall one, him, I could hook'em up, get him high, mobetter, more good, than that shit they was sucking on.
And I looked,
and set,
on bad daddies,
[load]
ready:
. . . words to blast your murderers by.
They got to have
. . . words to murder their horrors by
to run ariot

My white niggers
The little idiot boy,

The death and rise of a life and their thing.
My Heavy Monsters
High powered New born industry rico fukkers
founded in the way of tradition

I was dealing. I'm always dealing, mormonizing. He didn't catch it. Figured wrong, it was a definite comeon. Hitting white, flat white, until it jets outs, then it's steady on the desk – I promised them bigger and better lines. Then they're slashed

The polish was sparkling on Bonebrk's dime.

Things'r getting cramp back here. The plastic is making me sweat. I never got to wash my c-ck after I shared a whore w/ this rocker – injecting crystal up an ass, as the kid used the gaddün as a lollipop. The other knifed a shit witchfuk
One became a Don in a gutter hood.

Vagabonds and Voyous, my grievous thugz;

I can still smell them. Oh sweetness and cordite. It paks like white out. You shape me solid, little darling.

I was going to make the drop real soon but I knew I was taking chances by pulling a detour at that hr. but they, they soso typable, you had to fall apart for a pretty face.

I see, through the rearview, another stocking cap. The tall one, in the ballcap, walks up behind me. He presses up against me, tells me, under his breath, not to move.

My legs are slick and sliding against the plastic. I can't hear what they're saying, but I know we're not on the highway no more. What's being late and a little short got to do w/ all of this.

They would use my rubber words to glove this up, all to break my skull, make neat, this messy and paw/paw me. When I tell them, would they draw it from me, would they leave me attached.
My gunzels, my Gatheads
in swat team geto fab
My hooligans,
My boulfalés
Those thuggin sons of Dan

Hold tight your ballcap
We ride, cockin metal, cranking brain cells, we're gliding
Maybe, downtown, sometimes Hollywood
maybe ugly parts of Mexico
Where he danced
Where they dance

I'd only gotten caught once, twice and got off.
Never went down.
Got no cash,
no time.
Would I feel it.
Would they let me.
I hope they use a knife. Knives are a kin to cranking; it feels like
penetration – an ultimate fuk. Bullets have no names.
Would they treat me like a hound, ready and baring my fangs . . . 'bare your
fangs.' Show the hassa what you could do
They pull back their lips before they attack. You got to show the K9s. I

taught my boys to do it. I kept repeating it to them.
What beautiful teeth.
A good assault.
A good attack.
Bare yer fangs for them.
They won't do it while I'm still cramp up in here.
It's the little girly kiddly at the end of Dead Skin Mask.

You could be a fukken epic Bonebrk.

I wrote my shit down on the insides of empty flaps. I'd finish my punctuation and
bailed on them – left them tweaking for further life in this shit place we're stuck.
I kept walking out w/ the thugs stuffed in my knapsack, shrouded in dropped raid
vests and abandoned ATF jackets; stepping over used alki swabs and rigs on my
doorsteps; woobly tits of blue faced dames on my lawn. I rather be peelin for
badugly wetbacks. I'd comeback and see them hoods, still outside or on the street.
They could wait. I'd only been took once, twice and no nothing – I walked. You
can't tell. Never tell. You can't say nothin. You say nothin. They said nothing but
not to move.

They'd seen it but they didn't take a close look at the stuff.
I could get them high.
I could get them made.
I could do lots – but,
the stuff that I got . . .
they wanted . . .

Maybe, at home, snapping out of blown brains, dreaming they confreres
tremendous – smacking down Woo, filing an army of sawed off Rebels, getting a
cover, filling mags, snapping their good side –
It's all a set-up: The crack houses; the hos.
Spread it out, go on in and tell comrades comparable to you;
"Go write letters like bombs."

Go ahead, conversate them about my shit; shove it over there, go on.
It's all a plant: Fire cracker a cafeteria.
Snag adulterers on the beach.
One
The tall one
He made like Jesse
The other
he got the thunderer.

They don't understand. They dn't get a close look at the stuff. With what was sealed and sent – they could form Companys. Get goin and tell the world what they got.
They gettin made like pipebombs.

Watch yourself Denmark don't get sloppy.

oh, yeah, oh whoah, oh, warm against the cool grass. I could slide on the stuff runningout of me. They held it up; hit me in the face w/ it. It's a different perspective. I was where it was fixed to before. The air was good to breathe.

They never got a look at it.
It was sick, smart,
(stroboscopic),
psychotic
but stout.
It had nothing to do w/ me and being, late.
It couldn't,
it was something else,
nah . . . if they'd only seen my shit.
They'd understa . . .

[2001]

Mercedes Baines [1964-]

Bus Fucking

It is not a compliment to say he is staring because I am attractive. It is not a compliment. I see the rolling eye balls. I feel the emotion . . . it is not benign. I hear the stereotypes about my sexuality, my birthplace, my otherness drip from his eyes like crocodile tears.

It is simplistic to say . . . well just decide . . .
define yourself . . .
create your own
re-ality
When each day I push through the sea of white eyes staring at
me on the bus
as if I were some strange fruit
as if my vulva was hanging outside of my skirt whispering exotic
welcomes.

I return his stare.

He looks down
or thinks I am coming on to him
as if my skin and my sex were an invitation
to random bus fucking.

[1994]

sadie mae's mane

My mane
I am thinking about my mane
my mane
I am thinking about my mane
How did my hair get this way?
No one wants to believe it is natural
My hair is an aberration of mutated beauty of my strained mixed
heritage
You look, you stare as if it has lips and is whispering in the
city air some hair fantasy
do not come too close it will envelope you and I will not even
notice
Want to touch it?
Come closer
Want to feel it?
Come closer
Want to stroke it?
Come closer
Want to smell it?
Want to come closer?
Rub the girl's head . . . it's good luck
I say I will cut it and you react as if I say I will cut off my forearm
Medusa head / it lives beyond my being.
I take the hair off my head it moves like hissing snakes and
speaks
a beacon of my mysterious bloodlines.

[1994]

Roger Blenman [1964-]

Talk Show

Last night
I dreamt there was a panel discussion
On my life.

The moderator, not me
Paced
Back and forth
With a microphone in hand
And the immaculate coiffured
Manner
Of a TV news reporter
Telling facts
About my life
I didn't know were known.

Trivial and not so trivial
Words and actions
Were discussed by the crowd of experts.

But I sat ignored in the back
As they shook their heads
In disbelief
Of my irrational choices

I cried in the din
"You don't understand
I can explain!
I can explain!"

But no one passed me the mike.

[2000]

Biopsy

It is not all
your skin
I love,
not the way it encases
those gaunt arms
and sprouts of hair
for legs.
No.
What I love
is only a circle
on your chest.
I want to cut it,
lift out a quivering heart
and bring that slowly
to my lips.

[2000]

Oh Joshua Fit de Battle

'Oohoo,
Joshua fit de battle of'

When I cried Joshua,
No priest's ram's horn a-blow
On my street,
On my street, oh no,
There's an old woman with a push cart
Going real slow.
Where the avenue meets the boulevard
Where the sign says no stopping, no-time
There's a store, corner store,
Sells paper and smokes and gum,
Last week got held up with a gun.

'Oh Joshua fit de battle of'

On my block, on my street, by my home,
There's a woman in high heels
and a red leather skirt
and I go by wondering how she feels
out here, alone.
"How's the night?" I ask
and she says, "It's all right,
Night's all right."

'Oh Joshua fit de battle of'

City wants me,
Wants me to follow the flashing light
Of the ambulance or pizza
Phone 911 and stay on the line
"What! Haven't got the time?"
"Haven't got the time."

'Oh Joshua fit de battle of Jericho,
Jericho, Jericho
Joshua fit de battle of'

My street, back on my street
End of day,
In the morning,
Open the door.
"Creep stay out –"
John down the hall shouts:
"More, more."
Shaming John is shaming the neighbour:
"Hey buddy,
Shame on your shame."

'Jericho,
Jericho, Jericho.
Joshua fit de battle of'

Who's wall go bang bang?
Hate the noise.
Hate the music.
Hate you.
Pass me in the hall and I hate you
and your smiles.
When I want to sleep
Go bang, bang, keep,
Bang, the noise, bang,
Keep, bang, the noise, bang,
I want to sleep.

'Now Joshua he was a good man,
Prayed both night and day
My Lord heard him praying
And victory came that day.'

Fit me in a survey
Of consumer habits.
You know you want to know
My way
of buying toothpaste.
I grab it hard and fast
Off the shelf,
Buy it and
Use it so it's gonna last.

'There's no story that's ever been told
Like the Battle of Jericho.'

No battle 'tween the sidewalk and buzzer
and the buzzer and the door
and the stairs
and the stairs and the door
and you're in.
So close the door behind you
Lock them out.
Lock him out.
Lock her out.
Lock them out of your evening
Of your life:

You are trying to lock the city
Out of your city life.

Oh Joshua fit the battle of Jericho,
Jericho, Jericho,
Joshua fit the battle of Jericho
And the walls came tumbling down.

Oh Joshua fit the battle of Jericho,
Jericho, Jericho,
Joshua fit the battle of Jericho
And the walls came tumbling down.

[2000]

Vanessa Richards [1964-]

Icarus

Who has turned music into a virtueless reality?
Peddled by marketing men turned Machiavelli
selling diuretics like holy water
to distended children of the Diaspora.
Disaspora, Disasterous . . .
Damn
a big mac daddy eclipsing
then packaging the light of another mother's son.

Social scientist turns wordsmiths into blacksmiths
extracting iron from our blood with sonic tools
hammering so seductively shackles worn invisibly.
Anchored to headphones.
Enchanted, unsuspicious listeners.
Lured hook, line and sinker
by the song of the siren
Believing familiarity to be the truth
Guinea's children become guinea pigs
at the bottom of the I-Just-Didn't-Sea.

When the ship master of the SS Rags to Riches
throws a rope
can we be sure it's to pull us up from
where he dumped us last time?
Where we desperately jumped to last time.
On the long road home where is the north star
and who is the trickster at the crossroads?

Now if in your father's house
he sells you a ticket to visit mansion son
then lets you climb golden stairs
polished by the G-stringed, Hottentot behinds

of your foxy, tarnished brown sisters
do you climb, brother, climb to the top of the charts?
Who welcoms you in this land of false economies and smiles?
Anaemic hands will applaud your arrival
unable to catch you when you're pushed
from the Tip Top Dollar Club with an almighty shove.
You better believe you can fly!

The question is
can you bear to fly alone
long enough to outgrow a mistaken identity,
to outwit a chameleon enemy,
to outlive your aborted life expectancy?
Answer me this Icarus
can you fly alone long enough
to outgrow a mistaken identity,
to outwit a chameleon enemy,
to outlive your aborted life expectancy?

[1998]

Home Alone and Cooking

Peeling potatoes over the sink
lost in thought
space
till . . .

these cooking hands
look so familiar.
Are they my own
or are they another's?

Then what seems like a flash
lasts a long time
as I feel my mother's
spirit
mixing with mine.
I welcome her ways
like an old song.
My heart cut
fresh
like the back lawn.

Gone are the weeds
that were choking up the gutter,
stopping the flow and the ability to utter
Mother Sense
down an astral pipeline.

Szatallright? dish
tunes in just fine.
Channelling pure soul food,
watering my rose guardian,
sand in oyster,
ready to start
again
having trust
in the shell
and the pearly rewards of staying power.

Now louder on the liqueur
from potato skins
my Mama and all of my Nana's
are roots dancing in the basin.

I smile as she and she and she does
with my lips closed.
I move as she and she and she does
to the hot stove.
stirring and tasting the flavour of
alone.

Loving,
honouring
the women
in my bones.

[1998]

When I Grow Up I Want To Be an Old Woman

I sit at your feet
while you dance the quadrille
cooled by the wind of your whirling skirts.

Humbled by your golden slippers that have
traced, leapt, spun, and marched 72 years
on a direct path
from Africa through the Americas
to a birthday party in Brixton

where I sit at your feet
cooled by the wind of your whirling skirts
spinning into remembering.

[1998]

Janisse Browning [1965-]

Land for Salt

in memory of Bernie Hurst

look:
on the outskirts of Windsor
across the table at a diner
near the bridge to Detroit
Grandpa tells how we lost our land

salt
he wants salt
points a thick, dark finger
at the glass shaker
cupped in my small, dark hand

listen:
the story is told
in deep, urgent whispers
before strokes and dementia
ransack Grandpa's tired body

pepper
he gives me pepper,
slides a glass shaker
towards me without words

watch:
we trade
salt for pepper
like his Grandpa traded furs
for flour and sugar

coffee
a waitress smiles
refills our cups
leaves us two
conspiratorially
whispering, listening, trading

hear:
Grandpa says his peoples' hunting grounds
were grabbed
were granted
to white men
as private property

flour
then had to be bought

sugar
then had to be bought

money
then had to be got

see:
we still survive

[2000]

(for Sidane Arone)

wounded, you were
caught like prey,
bludgeoned
in an encampment
of enemy peacekeepers

killed, you were
just one more
disposable life,
one more casualty
to add up
or cover up

some mother's son, you were
that's all.
just one more African
in a sea of Africans;
target practice,
a lame excuse
for some morbid game
paratroopers play

armoured regiments
dispatched by Ottawa
flex their sinewy necks
sunburnt   anxious   ready,
mark time on your soil
with permission
invitation
to subdue the rampage
of despotism

just following orders
they were,
to defile   shoot   maim   kill
for peace

Canadian eyes regretfully shift
to this made for TV nightmare,
watching racists from home
assert a rank supremacy

peacekeeper
turns into
hatemonger
before our half-closed eyes

secrets pry their way out in time
distant deserts are not so far away
the dead haunt our dreams,
chase justice with greased palms,
breath held taut as a piano string

[2000]

Hair: It Can Be a Big Thing

Hair (w)rap

natural / processed / beaded / capped
combed out / rolled up / styled / wrapped
done up / undone / pony-tailed / pressed
a frazzled bedraggled chapeaued crest
plaited / braided / feathered / teased
hung loose / hot-combed / tinted / greased
afro / ringlets / dread-locks / curls
spiked up / pinned down / buzzed off / twirled
wigged / coifed / bleached / shaved
streaked / crimped / gelled / sprayed
turban / head scarf / barrettes / bun
pig-tailed / bed-headed / hair wrap fun

Memory One: hair oppression

Mid 1970s; age 11. I sit on a chair. My mother stands behind me, armed with a comb and wooden-handled hair brush.

mom: Sit still or I'll whack you.

me: But it hurts!

mom: You're not leaving this house with your hair looking like a bird's nest.

me: You're pulling too hard!
mom: How else am I supposed to get these knots out?

me: Ouch! [squirm]

mom: [whack!]

Memory Two: hair liberalism

Grade Four. Somewhere in the deep south of Canada, standing in line after recess.

white-girl-behind: Mind if I braid your hair?

black-girl-in-front: Yes.

wgb: Do you mean yes, it's okay for me to braid your hair, or yes, you mind if I braid your hair?

bgif: I mean yes, I *do* mind.

wgb: But why?

bgif: I don't want my hair braided.

wgb: Will you just let me touch it?

bgif: Why?

wgb: Your hair looks so soft and poofey. It's not like other Black girls' hair.

bgif: What do you mean?

wgb: Well...your hair's not greasy for one thing. You don't use Vaseline like other Black girls, *DO YOU*?

bgif: [Silence...]

wgb: Oh, please! Just let me touch it.

teacher: Move along, girls.

Memory Three: babysitter's fetish

she chased me
it was a small apartment
she caught me
I was scared
"just let me give you a full-on afro"
she forced me
"see: you're beautiful!"
my mirrored eyes full of tears
my mouth never told

Memory Four: harvest moon haircut

my lover wields scissors
my friend holds a razor
I squat in an empty bathtub
poised
for the first rebirth
of my hair
in this new place
called home

[2000]

David Nandi Odhiambo [1965-]

from diss/ed banded nation

1A. (SATURDAY OCTOBER 11/97, 1.18 PM)

he doesn't want to do much of anything except smoke drugs in his room n' sleep. but feels awful – guilty – after sleep.

he's really waiting for anna's call as he ponders smoking spices on a shelf in the kitchen – nutmeg; oregano. but . . . the embarrassment concomitant brain damage might cause.

so . . . he listens to his best of james brown – cold sweat; hot pants; sex machine. playing the songs over and over. trying to drown out the sex moaning from the other rooms.

. . . the day lurches monotonously forward. as he ducks down to the liquor store for a bottle of baby duck.

. . . a man – tall/cowboy hat – plays a guitar. opening the door for customers . . . give him change on the way out . . . more guilt . . . this caused by selfishness; spending on alcohol instead of on someone living off what they make from the street.

he heads back to his room. puts on more music; maxwell – *urban hang suite* – something soulful n' slow . . . the baby duck; uncorking it with care. thoughtfully nestling up beside the window.

three glasses later, he has a slight buzz on, clipping onwards deeply alone. wishing anna would call. occasionally checking to see if someone else is on the phone.

he reaches out for another drink/for his guitar.

> "on mulberry lips
> tossed n' twilled
> at cutlassed petals
> lasp n' . . . n' . . ."

. . . daylight leaches bleakly into night marked by cigarettes exhaled snakecharmer-like out his window. his concentration nonexistent. no motivation for anything.

more lyrics – suggesting new pieces – disrupted by thoughts of . . . tickling the coarseness of his tongue to taste between anna's legs.

he's still pissed at jazz. tension steel in his shoulders. n' can't turn his head without sharp pain . . . there . . . in the belly of muscle.

. . . more wine. a regimen of scales on the guitar. some vocal exercises. maybe anna does this kind of thing all the time; why would he presume to be any different from whomever else she's played off by asking for a number? it had been a mistake – a stupid/stupid mistake – to have tried chatting it up with her after the gig.

fat fatigue.

why is he wasting so much of his time on this? why can't he just let it go? the clatter of people trafficking people through the rooming house resonating like bungled chords from every corner of his room. as he can no longer stand being locked away in his ramshackle sanctuary alone.

1B. (8.04 PM)

. . . breeze chills in bone marrow. enters nostrils and ice screams inside his fore-head as he stamps feet – on pieces of smashed glass beside cracks in cement – n' blows hot breath to warm palms cupped over his mouth.

he's swept up into a heavy crush of the doped hastening toward fetid ware-house parties – raves – n' line-ups in front of hot nightclubs; others nosing to cin-emas or restaurants or returning from lectures about the exotic n' obscure. swirled, up and away, into the upstream. he sidesteps three oncoming scuffed-black-leather jackets – eyes icing over in meeting; unasked n' unanswered ques-tions momentarily flaring there.

up ahead. two sisters, garbed in indian scarves n' deep conversation, turn into a doorway. one carries a knapsack steaming with photocopied articles. the other tightly gripping a bag of books close to her chest. intent, it appears, on ditching each gaze that jostles their hurried passage up n' down the hostile street.

he passes through clumps of aggressively hustling dope-peddlers – gouged n' scarred faces all coming to ruin beneath implacable cop surveillance.

"skunk. rock."

"any hash?"

he's beckoned by a kid – must be fifteen. quickly following him past department stores stacked full of cheap-labour, high-profit goods: t-shirts; towels; running shoes.

. . . "are you a cop?"

"no. are you?"

"you kidding?"

they stop at traffic lights. then, when permitted, cross over to the other side.

"this has got to be one harsh way to make a living."

"not really. i pull in close ta two hun'ed a day."

"you're shitting me."

"no man. for real."

"i'm in the wrong goddamn profession."

"wrong profession! what do you do?"

"sing . . . in a band."

"cool. what kind of music?"

"a kinda blue soul groove."

"what?"

"a kinda jazzy funk sound."

"much of a scene?"

"put it this way. it takes me a couple of months to pull in what you make in a day."

"get outta here."

"i'm dead serious. a couple of months."

"shiiit." they stop in front of a restaurant . . . "wait here." n' the fifteen-year-old entrepreneur disappears inside.

. . . benedict's suddenly self-conscious – people have to know what's going on. it's so obvious . . . what did he have to wear baggies for? they're far too easy to identify . . . and if he has to make a run for it, he's liable to get all tangled up. maybe bust a leg.

he looks out for camouflaged cop cars.

. . . "you look nice." a middle-aged man wrings his hands beside him. "i like nice black men." his breath reeking of booze. "i'll be your slave if you'd like. if you want." he scratches the back of his neck. n' falls silent. then fidgets, in sallow skin, shifting from one foot to the other.

"me no spig eeengleesh." benedict glances back into the restaurant window.

"i'm not a cop or with the government or anything. are you african? you look african. i'm pretty good at telling where people come from. there was a guy from . . ."

"no. unnerstan."

the man slows down. gesturing expansively to make himself understood. "there was a guy from west africa. i went up to him. asked him whether he was from nigeria. bang on. another guy. ethiopia. presto. somalia. bingo."

benedict twists to face the restaurant. muttering incomprehensibly until the man finally leaves him alone.

. . . "one gram," his connection announces on his return. "dynamite shit, too." benedict starts to slip him ten bucks but . . . "hold up."

"what?"

"a narc." the kid motions towards the nearby street corner. pointing out the man who'd just made a pass at benedict.

"oh shit."

the narc steps off the curb and into a doorway.

". . . ok, he's gone," announces the connection. "that'll be ten bones."

benedict slips him the money and hastily takes the dynamite shit back/all the way back to the crib.

[1998]

Michelle La Flamme [1966-]

from Threads

FADE IN:

INT. VANCOUVER INTERNATIONAL AIRPORT. ARRIVALS – DAY

A long line-up of tired people. Their bags reflect their diverse personalities. At the end of the line-up is CAM (38), *a well-dressed businessman arriving from Italy. His bags are beautiful Italian leather. He carries a number of expensive designer boxes and bags filled with clothes. He is suave and impatient. He tries a number on his cellphone as the line advances towards the customs agent.*

> CAM
> Come on, baby. Where are you?

> AGENT
> So, first flight today?

> CAM
> Ah, no. I've taken several. Rome to Milan, Milan
> to London, London to here.

CAM *thrusts forward rumpled tickets and boarding passes.*

> AGENT
> All in one day?

> CAM
> Well, ya, I . . . it's business.

> AGENT
> Hmmh! Busy man. And your declaration form?

> CAM

Oh.

CAM searches his pockets. He holds the phone to his ear. The agent puts a red X on CAM's passport.

> CAM
> (*continued*)
> I must have –

> AGENT
> To the left, please. Next!

SOUND: *A phone ringing.*

EXT. WEST VANCOUVER HOUSES OVERLOOKING THE BAY.
EST. SHOT – DAY

SOUND: *A phone ringing.*

Several houses perched on the cliff. They all have large windows facing south.

INT. HOUSE WEST VANCOUVER BEDROOM – DAY

SOUND: *A phone ringing. Continuous.*

A large room, tastefully decorated with tons of antiques, plants and a baby grand piano.

THERESA (36), *a very attractive Native woman, is alone. Her purse is spilled. Papers, expensive makeup,* ID *and money are all over the place. She holds a phone to her ear.*

> THERESA
> Come on. I need you to be there.

The phone rings on.

INT. AIRPORT CUSTOMS ROOM – LATER

CAM's *suitcases are open, and colorful linen and silk clothing spills out. The agent holds a woman's eggshell-blue silk kimono.*

> AGENT
> So, this looks interesting.

CAM

And that's *without* her in it.

CAM *winks at the* AGENT. *The* AGENT *handles the clothes very roughly.*

CAM
(*continued*)
Hey, hey! That's silk. Take it easy. What the hell
are you looking for?

AGENT
Really like to shop, hey?

CAM
Just a hobby.

AGENT
Oh? A hobby, is it?

The AGENT *holds up several articles of women's clothing that appear to have been worn.*

AGENT
(*continued*)
I see.

SOUND: *The* AGENT's *laughter.*

CLOSE UP: *The piles of clothing. At one end the* AGENT *is unfolding clothes, and at the other* CAM's *hands fold them.*

DISSOLVE TO:

INT. TRANSFORMATIONS 2ND HAND CLOTHING STORE – DAY

CLOSE UP: *A pair of hands gently searching through a pile of clothes with interesting colors and textures. They are all hung up according to color – reds changing to oranges changing to yellows changing to whites. The hand caresses various items, reveling in their texture or design. The hand searches through these items, all secondhand, mostly vintage. These become the "threads" that link the characters in the story.*

INT. HOUSE WEST VANCOUVER BEDROOM – DAY

THERESA *holds the phone to her ear. It is still ringing. She surveys the room and settles on a family photo. It is a woman with four grinning children. They are holding up one smoked fish each. There is a smokehouse in the background, covered with a Native mural.*

>   THERESA
> You're there! You need a cordless. Thought so.
> Uh-uh. I can smell it through the phone. Ya.
> Well, better than before. We'll be up. Ya, for sure
> I'll be there. Uh . . . well, he's really busy. I know,
> I know. That's why I'm coming alone. I will,
> I'm doing it right now. Bye.

THERESA *lights some cedar and sage in a beautiful abalone bowl. She begins to cleanse herself with the smoke, taking deep breaths. She walks towards the picture window. The sun streams into the window and she begins to cry.*

SOUND: *The phone ringing.*

EXT. AIRPORT – DAY

CAM *has a cellphone to his ear.*

>   CAM
> Pick up, pick up. Where the hell are you?

His bags and packages are somewhat more disheveled than before. He slams shut his phone and hails a limousine.

INT. LARGE LECTURE THEATRE – DAY

An attractive upbeat PROFESSOR (40) *in tweed lectures to a small group of students. On the board:* GENDER STUDIES. *Underneath in bold letters are the words* GENDER AND THE MEDIA.

>   PROFESSOR
> One thing that we are certain is relevant
> to this discussion is the predominance of
> the impact of gender that is reflected in
> the media and forms the critical element
> in the development of sociological frameworks
> which define the gender roles that become
> the "norm."

PAN: *The mostly-young (early 20s) students furiously taking notes. In the back of the theatre is LISA (25), a mixed-race woman who is bookish and bored. She starts to tune out the room sound. The PROFESSOR's voice fades out as various voices inside her head fade in. They are phone messages.*

MAN 1 (ENGLISH DANDY)
(*voice over*)
Hey, Lisa. Just thought we could get together
perhaps for, ah . . . dinner? I have a
bottle of red wine and it has your name on it.
Don't run away. Call me. . . .

CLOSE UP: LISA's *notes:*

Gay icons and signifiers in the media
Sexual Identity vs. Aesthetics in
the construction of "Queer Culture"

LISA *doodles on top of these notes with four different-colored blue pens.*

MAN 2 (SUAVE AMERICAN)
(*voice over*)
Soooooo, Lisa, Lisa, Lisa, it's been too long.
Get yo' head out of the books and let's do
somethin' daring. I got two tickets for
Seventies Night on Saturday, are ya in?
Call me back this time, okay? Even if you're
not into it. Just call me, a'right?! I don't bite,
unless requested! Nick.

The PROFESSOR continues to lecture.

PROFESSOR
Thus, a thorough inquiry into the method
of indoctrination and the means by which these
value judgements are formed can take on . . .

CLOSE UP: LISA's *notes. LISA uses the different shades of blue at random, drawing large love hearts and sad clownish faces.*

MAN 3
(*voice over*)
It's me, your biggest fan. I'm looking for
you. You haven't returned my calls. I, I just
wanted – okay, I just want *you*. You know
why and how much, so stop disappearing . . .

The beep on the phone message and the bell ring simultaneously, pulling LISA *out of her reverie.*

PROFESSOR
For next day, I want you to finish reading
the "Anti-Gay" essays, and be prepared to
discuss the role of compulsory heterosexuality
and its correlation to homophobia and the media.

LISA *furiously covers her notes in shades of blue.*

DISSOLVE TO:

EXT. SALTSPRING ISLAND – DAY

Blue sky.

EST. SHOT. TRAILER. SALTSPRING ISLAND – DAY

A small trailer, half painted green, on the side of a cliff.

INT. TRAILER. SALTSPRING ISLAND – DAY

It is crowded with audio equipment. There are reel-to-reel machines, a four-track, tapes and videos. Strings of cut-up pieces of audio tape dangle from the roof. The bed is piled with cassettes. TRYSTE (30), *a long-haired feminist, makes space on the bed and begins to fill a green army surplus bag. He packs casual clothes – all green. He packs three feminist magazines:* Bitch, Bust *and* Girlfriends. *He rips tape loops from the ceiling and stuffs them into his bag.*

SOUND: *Heavy rock music.*

EXT. SALTSPRING ISLAND – CONTINUOUS

ARROW (36), *a Native dandy, is leaning against his black Valiant convertible waiting for* TRYSTE *and listening to rock music.* ARROW *wears a white shirt and suspenders and is checking his profile in the side mirror.*

>   ARROW
> Damn, I'm good. Come on, man! We
> don't have all day. Some timings you can
> change and the ferry is not one of them.

>   TRYSTE
>   (*off screen*)
> Yeah? Tell that to the freaks who are paid
> to run them!

>   ARROW
> Let's go!

>   TRYSTE
>   (*off screen*)
> I'm coming!

TRYSTE *runs towards the car dressed all in green.*

>   ARROW
> Man, you give "Go Green" a whole
> new meaning.

>   TRYSTE
> Listen, I once read that patience is a part
> of your national identity. Is that still true?

ARROW *puts* TRYSTE's *things into the trunk.*

>   ARROW
>   (*angered*)
> Ah, hello?

>   TRYSTE
> One for one.

ARROW

You're lucky. Today is definitely your lucky
day. I'm gonna relax and give that to the wind.

ARROW *jumps into the car.*

TRYSTE

You see? I do have something with that
patience thing.

TRYSTE *gets into the car.*

ARROW

Okay, I am so outta here. Tell ya something,
I like ya better when yer broodin', Tryste.
Ya talk less.

ARROW *turns up the heavy rock music. The Valiant careens down a driveway.*

CLOSE UP: *Smoke and gravel.*

INT. WEST VANCOUVER HOUSE. BEDROOM – DAY

CAM *walks into the bedroom. He notices the room is in disarray. The room is filling
with smoke. His arms are full of packages from expensive designer stores.* THERESA
stares blankly at the bay.

CAM

Theresa? Honey, I'm back. I thought you'd
be there to meet me. What happened?

THERESA
(*quietly*)
They are so old now.

He notices the photo THERESA *is holding.*

CAM

Hey, Sunshine, I picked these up for you.
Do you want to –

THERESA
I'm too tired.

CAM
Me too. What a long trip.

CAM *walks over and massages* THERESA's *shoulders from behind. She is frozen.*

CAM
(*continued*)
I missed you, baby. You alright?

THERESA
Don't you think they look young here?

CAM
Sure. Listen, I picked up some stuff you will love.

THERESA
I said I am tired.

THERESA *removes his hands from her shoulders.*

CAM
Listen, can you just take a sec and look
at these? Sidetrack yourself from wherever
it is you're going. Let's open some windows.
Honestly, Theresa, this much smoke cannot
be good for you –

THERESA
Since when do you know what's good for me?

CAM
It's "since when have you known." And why
the hell did you let this place fill up with smoke?
What the hell has been –

SOUND: *The smoke detector goes off.*

CAM *leaves the room to deal with the alarm.*

THERESA
All this smoke and we haven't prepared the fish.

THERESA *starts to laugh hysterically while staring at the photo and gazing at the view of the bay.*

[2001]

Andrea Thompson [1967-]

Black Mary

Black Mary stands
back firm against
the bare brick spine
of the chimney
that climbs
from the base
of the basement suite
straight on up and through
into the heart of your apartment
in the house that you call home

Black Mary is a mannequin
immaculate reproduction
futuristic, full-of-grace
hollow, hollow, holy icon

ebony Madonna
inanimate anima
standing over seven feet high
limbs long and slender
in extraterrestrial style

Black Mary never smiles
speaks, cries or laughs
head covered with a crown
of accumulated candle wax

weary from years
spent satisfying your appetite
for ambiance
illuminating the point
of your departure
like a lighthouse

as you fixed
to leave
needle leading you into
enraptured escape
ethereal elation
nodding on your island
of opiate oblivion

while removable hands
reach towards you in endless
expectation

man-made, man-
ufactured, she is
Mary, image of woman

the crumbling rubber
of her fingers
ineffective
as blessings and hexes
bleed from her hands
like black molasses
falling
like broken holy water
mighty flood of grief
at her feet, still born
prayers left unanswered

but Mary, like Kali
can hear the rhythm
of your heart
can rise serpentine
within you, wake
your female
counterpart

Black Mary stands
back firm against the
bare brick spine of
the chimney that climbs

as you stop
mid-stride

and stand there
still
and staring
with Mary
until

you can feel her
unwind
in the base
of your basement suite
ascending and spiraling
each chakra like a vine
earth heaven and sky
root heart and crown
entwining, combining
climbing straight on out and through

until she breaks and wakes you
until she wakes and breaks you

with a thud as her finger
drops like an apple
a black rubber bead
escaped from an ancient
broken rosary
sacramental moment
sacrificial offering
wind whistling through her
Spiritus Sancti
whispering

Black Mary
stands

(so you are not alone)

in the heart of your apartment
in the house
that you call
home

[1999]

Bus Ride East

From this
awkward rumbling seat
February

      the paint
      on my grandmother's canvas
      when black, white
and blue
were all
      she could afford
      and snow and
      sticks of trees
were all
        she wanted to show

the wind
that blew open
my mother's curtains
one night
to expose

a small square
of slate grey sky
and one dim star
        on her west wall

      from this
      awkward rumbling seat
      February is the season
      grieving for three generations

        the frost
they found
webbed through her hair
the morning after

        impermanent heirloom
pathetic fallacy

[1999]

Terence Anthony [1968-]

from Shadowtown: Black Fist Rising

The story so far . . .

1968: Martin Luther King Jr. is assassinated in Memphis. Many activists cross over from the Civil Rights struggle to join the more militant Organization for Afro-American Unity, formed by Malcolm X (who escaped the attempt on his life in 1965).

The OAAU consolidate black political parties, businesses, and communities across the U.S. until the death of Malcolm X in 1984. Evidence linking the CIA to Malcolm's death is uncovered, triggering waves of racial violence throughout North America. African Americans migrate en masse to the southeastern states dubbed "New Africa", where they form the Black Fist Army and defend the area from invasion by U.S. Armed Forces.

2023: The UN formally recognizes New Africa as an autonomous republic. With financial assistance from the UN and the Shauku Corporation a metropolis is built. Three years later free elections are held and Quincy B. Oglivie, chairperson of Shauku Enterprises, is elected.

It is now the year 2032 and New Africa is in turmoil. Native Americans living within New Africa have begun terrorist attacks to back up their demands for human rights and the Black Fist Guard is cracking down on any form of dissent.

After her best friend Panic is beaten and arrested by the Black Fist, grad student Diane Davis (Did) joins the New African Revolutionary Army, led by the lecherous Grandmaster Mandala. While attempting to incite a prison riot Mandala accidentally blows up one of his comrades, and Panic and his cell-mate Eddy escape in the confusion. Wanting to work for change but unable to follow an egomaniac like the Grandmaster, Did quits the NARA. Panic goes into hiding and joins Eddy's old gang the Thunderbolts.

Two months have passed . . .

YO YO YO YO HOMEGIRLS AND BOYS, THIS IS THE ONE AND ONLY DJ **GROUND ZERO**, KICKIN' THE SUBVERSIVE FOR ALL OF NEW AFRICA.

SORRY I BEEN OUTTA TOUCH FOR SO LONG, BUT YOUR DJ HADDA REEE-LOCATE REAL QUICK LAST MONTH.

THE MINISTRY OF INFO HAD VIBED ONTO A METHOD TO TRACK DOWN MY SIGNAL--

--AND IF I HADN'T GOTTEN WIND BEFORE THE BLACK FIST GOON SQUAD SHOWED UP AT MY DOOR AND JET--

-THE ONLY FREE VOICE A' NEW AFRICA WOULD'A BEEN SHUT DOWN PERMANENT-LIKE.

SPEAKING OF SHUT-DOWNS, HOW ABOUT THE THROW DOWN AT THE REVEREND BIG DUKE RALLY THE OTHER DAY?

HOMEGIRL

I still remember the year that New Africa was recognized as an autonomous republic. I was eleven. The parades, celebrations -- we wouldn't have to fight anymore.

Not against a racist American system, at least.

It was just before I went away to college that I started to realize how bad things really were.

That was the year Dad died.

Now the repression is everywhere. Colonel Taylor's Black Fist Guard is intent on maintaining order at whatever cost.

People like my best friend Panic are getting caught in the crossfire.

It's been two months since I last heard from Panic. He had to go underground with a local gang called the Thunderbolts to avoid being arrested by the Black Fist again.

Now I'm going to have to make some choices as well.

Soon.

Nadine King Chambers [1969-]

Lena & Hue

for Che . . . and Dar

Lena tried to calm herself by breathing in time with the swing of a lit lantern hanging on a pole at the edge of the Bysea Road. It was a sandy track that was drawn out of the ocean, brushed through the sand and beaten into the hard soil. There were old oil lamps hanging every fifteen feet to light the cool, moonless spring night for the few night fishers trapping lobsters to sell fresh-fresh later that morning to the local hotels. By 3:00 AM, those who had gone out had already returned, tied their boats, stretched their nets, and pulled the restless weight of their catch up to the village.

Tell truth, it was pitch black where she stood but there was light from the four or five lanterns close to the village that hadn't been blown out by the eternal sea breeze. Enough light for her to see that something was coming; drawing a different kind of darkness, separate from the surrounding night. A shadow, human in shape, shifting down the Bysea with a child-sized cart bumbling behind it.

Earlier that night she had gotten a good glimpse of it, thirty feet before her, facing the direction in which she had been heading on Second Road. At first she had thought it was a man standing in dark clothing who had paused for some reason, silently holding on to the long handle of the cart. Who or whatever it was never turned to look at her, though they were the only two beings on the road. Though Lena could not pinpoint the reason why her level of anxiety increased sharply, she quickly decided not to continue west on Second Road. Turning, she took a less direct path to the sea.

Two hours later, watching the shadow slowly approach her, Lena's anxiety returned and curdled in her throat. She moved swiftly up the path, darted into the damp bush edging a long curve in the road, walked in about ten feet and waited.

Her heart hammered. She pulled the flaps of her grandfather's long greatcoat together and pressed her face in the comforting smell of his cologne. She could hear the little rusty cart reluctantly trundled down the Bysea, following whatever was walking silently to the beach. It clattered over the pebbles loosely strewn about and bumped against the larger stones wedged in the road.

Peace seemed to return as the sounds faded until she realized that she was still not alone. Turning awkwardly, she noticed another being, also human shaped, standing three feet to her right and four feet closer to the path. It was facing the beach, head cocked as if tracking something by ear. For a moment Lena considered walking away, ignoring this presence and hoping it would grant her the same courtesy; but walking away would mean going further into the scrub and away from the relative openness of the Bysea. She banded her courage around her heart, pushed it deeper in her chest and faced the shape. After a moment the shadows hiding their faces met and connected. They were silent for a long minute until Lena heard a quiet voice say, "It's a bad idea to walk around in a world not even the moon knows," followed by a gentle laugh that playfully dared her to run away.

They met time and time again, after the night had poured herself into the twilight blue void meeting the sea. The darkness created a seamless backdrop for a moon flowing with power, its light tumbling off the dark curtain of night to flood every crevice and corner. They walked together, far from the full moon dances into places where shame-old-lady plants, that by day folded in on themselves at the slightest touch, fanned out boldly in the moonlight, even when prodded repeatedly. Hue showed her caves further inland, wreathed on their openings with night blooming flowers that flared their petals of wine blended into pink, then pearl, for a few short hours.

There were spider webs strung with night dew like tiny glass bearings all along their ten-foot-wide designs. She learned about the few small, thickly wooded spaces where night still ruled and moths with white wings highlighted with fluorescent spots floated, safe from predators. Time slowed as Hue and Lena sat watching black river water fish, their presence only decipherable by the traces of phosphorous in their skin, shining when they moved, leaving only a brief flash of orange that left its imprint on the eye before fading away.

More importantly, she learned about Hue who stood five feet and eleven inches in height and had dark brown skin and hair. Hue had eyes like circles of wood, the colour shifting between an ebony brown and a lighter tone with flecks of green: a remembrance of a younger time of unfurling leaves and flowing sap. Hue reminded Lena so much of her sister Toni it was disturbing.

Toni, who had gone to the city when Lena was ten and she was seventeen, smiling and promising to return in a year that turned into two, then three and four. Her name mentioned only once a year by her grandmother in the Christmas dinner prayer. Toni, who had come back in her twenty-first year – older, harder and covered in unusual scars that she never hid, and explained once when Lena had questioned her . . . then never again.

"What happened, Toni?" she asked, running her fingers along the strange ridges and crests of keloid.

"Jail," she'd replied, looking away. Lena, knowing not to ask for more, looked away, too.

Still, beneath Toni's hardness was a deep level of compassion that could come only from a person who had gone for long periods without it and had learned how to maintain it within. This was something Lena recognized in Hue.

However, there was a bigger question about Hue with two possible answers, though neither seemed correct. Every time she posed the question to herself, "Is Hue male or female?" the answer came back – "Hue is Hue." She could not understand why, sometimes for just a second, she could see her friends Wayne and Derrick walking completely separately and holding hands *all at the same time.* Hue confused her in the same way. When the night breeze would playfully press Hue's clothing against Hue's breastbone in the bright moonlight, sometimes curves were there . . . other times not. Lena preferred to ignore the question and just watch Hue interacting with the plant and animal nightlife with the sureness of one who was aware of their strength and understood the limits of their capacity to heal or harm. As the months passed, she became more drawn to Hue and it grew more important to know what mannerisms and voice did not clearly reveal. Lena became determined to find out a precise answer.

One evening, after twilight had been swallowed by the night's deep and the moon was queen, Hue rowed then out to a coral reef to watch the spawning of jellyfish. A small lantern glowed from where it rested in the belly of the row boat; pushing and pulling the oars, moving to and from the light, Hue's face and neck gleamed with sweat. Lena suddenly noticed the light and shadow slipping across wet, brown skin where Hue's shirt gaped and swayed back and forth over the answer to her question. Lena found an excuse to move closer by feeding Hue a piece of jackfruit. After the fruit was finished and only its pungent scent lingered on her fingers, Lena stayed close, pretending to observe the waves, trying to determine Hue.

No luck.

She tilted her head so that when Hue pulled forward into the tiny bit of light, Lena could furtively turn to face Hue and decipher what lay under the shirt. The left oar rolled into the water as Hue slowly swung forward.

Taking a deep breath, Lena turned her head and glanced upon a small dragon tattoo sliding on the glistening skin over Hue's left collarbone. Her attention was caught for a few moments, until Hue moved back, completing the push and pull rhythm . . . and stopped.

The boat skimmed across the ocean though the oars were suspended a few inches above the water. Embarrassed, Lena looked towards Hue, who sat motionless in the shadows beyond the lantern.

"Why does it matter?" Hue asked.

[1997]

Shane Book [1970-]

Offering

At the beach, I once saw my father, surrounded by a crowd,
put his lips over the mouth of a man lying prone on the sand.

There was something in the way he worked, quickly but precisely,
and without flourish. He could have been nailing shingles,

or measuring slabs of gyprock for our grey clapboard house
that leaned into the North Vancouver drizzle long before

we got there. As a child, it always seemed to be raining,
so that now, years later, returning to the city, it is somehow

strange to be sitting on a woman's bed in a small apartment
in a warm square of late afternoon sun. And perhaps

because of the warmth on my skin, I do not think of when
we lived in that rundown house on that street where the neighbours

wrote Nigger Go Home in jaunty chalk letters that stretched
to our lane. I do not think of my mother speaking in the kitchen

late at night of our leaving, my father forever silent,
in what I came to imagine was the thin music of shame.

Why should I? At this moment, a woman is getting ready
to step out of the bathroom wearing nothing but a silk Japanese

smoking jacket, and when she does, she will stand blinking
in the bright light, then let her robe fall away,

and in that instant her white skin will shine in the afternoon light.
At this moment, I have not yet placed my hands on her neck,

cradling it, the way my father held the man at the beach, long after
he realized his breath in those dead lungs was helping nothing

and finally, he quit. The man on the beach would never return
to the earth he was born of. And I too have quit, by leaving.

Which is why I cannot tell you, father, of my own encounter
with shame. How brown my hands look on her,

and in their stillness, how useless. This bright offering
I am unable to take, this pale one that lights up the room.

[2000]

from "The Lost Conquistador"

*

A breeze beginning. Black, unshining flake
in shifting screens – these chopped in trees,
continually, then scattered loose,
no, not loose (note the small dance) then
shattered with their tethers hidden
still somehow attached – the flake
grounded now
          now moving (A beetle. A flying ant. A beetle.) along the sand path
among pieces of light and
in sudden wind:
          the glance in grass
the glance in swung around
            darkness
a dance of particulates, then a shifting
(bird wings beating water)
a coalescing . . .
          Refocus:
beetle at the green edge
(have I seen anything?)
          others no doubt
down there. Fidelity.
In extreme. In
the green wires sprung
from earth to meet his legs
the stutter
in each blade, the return
and there
          the dirt's near invisible throwing
moves the glance
past tiny piled stones (little basilicas)
pinning what
slew, what shut motive
beneath them,
bulking some unseeable gathering, impossible to –
and what besides sand – the thinnest particulars – builds itself
impregnable grammar . . .

The beetle is not a messenger. I can see that.
He grows into things.
       The light around him. For example.

Is the fuse point of his leaving.
Is the clawing in the center
Claimed by anything?
The focus.
     Is it claimed?: (Twig as bridge,
              leaf shard as scrap of night)

And after the sunlight killings of small scenes,
the greying out.
And whose idea of a place in the vibrant guttural repose of an antlered thing . . .

Step
around to the green now
of where he might be
going.
    Everything to
not lay a hand in his path.
Everything to
not smooth it over.
(What shall I do for my birthday?)
It might be
he stops
in patterns of sunlight
       a half step further out,
it might be some loosening . . .

Lapse.
Location.
Lapse.

Comes now,
     burnished,
       a perfect translation of – a hiving out
of air
some small tar
intensity.
    Comes,
irreducible pinprick

choosing through
                    delicate green steeples.
Serious selector,
            how to distinguish (how to hurt)
A breeze beginning.
I lie on my side among the (watch now)
                phalanx guards of green,
            the bare
rigor of a broad mind in its plainness
its refusal to look (how to hurt)
the smile of light
on the shell,
            discrimination of the oblivious dark little hum
ground somehow
in the middle of a long light –
all the others (how to dream) – tendrils
frail legs
supporting
one thing,
            (how to damage)

now a breath hole

now a small turning

now a tiny reddish light

                stopped

now a clinging eye –

[2001]

Nikola Marin [1970-]

Eshu Got Venus

Was it wolf or coyote who mounted me? She was the chicken I wanted to steal by night.

He is Eshu. He is primal energy. He is trickster. Some people call him the Devil.

The vision came, the frequency clear with his lusty incarnations.

> A Venus symbol, dangling on a silver chain from his dark neck,
> fucking me in the missionary position.

A poem with cryptic logic. Frustrated. Nocturnal emissions hound me. I can't *69 this message.

It got me off, tho'. A cross below a circle. Unintentional. Irrational.
Fetishistic. Schism.

A catholic thing.
I sit in the middle of my red livingroom floor, 'licking' my wounds, til I fall asleep.
An animal thing.

> A woman's symbol, on a chain, on a dark neck. My neck?
> Fucking me in the missionary position? But who?

*

When will she call? I wanna be proactive. No waiting by the phone. I call Her. And collar.

(He's doing me doggie style again.) I'm pacing. Gone animal. Licking my wounds tonight.

Superstitious, I wish upon the first light I see in the dark sky.

On my knees.

I doubt yer going thru as much agony as me.

mellow agony.

Gotta get up to get down.
Gotta get up to get down.

So I:

Do that hair
Iron that shirt
Shower
Smattering of perfume.

Flex that iris, toots! It's theatre in the opium den of brown sugar fantasies.

Falling in
like I'm 22 and
girls and dope curls
and mary jane.

Did I mention I was howling? It's bin years since I've bin tackled like this.

infirmata vulnerata
puro deficit amore.

I came. I saw her. I flexed and she skunked me with a noxious mist.

We found each other under the sequined sky. He suckled on my root. And I on his.

It still gets me –

she used to listen to this album over and over when she was in greased lens, rock-star love with me.

Gimmee all your love and don't stop
My love's waiting when you reach the top.

my life – with greased lens.

my life – the dirty rascal of some prankster's childish game.

Am I laughing? No – I'm praying.

> Iba ache Eshu.
> Iba ache Eshu.

A wise man once said to me: "You pray to Eshu. Good for you!"

But things are going slow. Too many weekdays in between seeing Her.

Eshu, I am so sorry I neglected your Monday rituals.

Because.

When yer in love like this you can never see the person really.

So I got up to get down and she reared her tail, let loose and sashayed away in a short skirt.

Steadfastly refused to jerk off. Didn't want any more confusing visions. No heterosex. No anal. No Venus dragging a man's body. Cut the crap.

*

loco por coco.

Burned incense til I coughed. "Hmmm. Coconut."

Ate chicken. There was no "chick" in it.
He was talented with his fingers.

*

Morning Loving

A door unlocking. The key is a woman's symbol on a metal shaft.

She came over for tea. Ate chicken instead. He was good with his fingers. She was Adonis sleeping. Afterwards I walked her to her car and kissed her goodbye. I'm so butch.

*

The skunk and I were at opposite ends of the wrong totem pole.

Diabolical.

I've gotta bear witness!

1. She didn't know me.
2. She was rude.
3. Do you have time for me?
4. Do I have time for you?

"I'm tired of the whole <waiting room> bullshit, you know what I'm saying." No, I guess not.

    A skunk in a box.

*

burn the incense.
say the prayer.
It's a catholic thing.
Say the prayer again in Spanish.
    You can play my clit like flamenco guitar and make my heart race.

Put some heart into it. A simple circuit. A drumbeat. A dance.

*

She showed me her darkness. I was seduced.
The saliva on her bottom lip glowing with the blue light, glistening.

*

The trickster laughs thru my pen at night. "Get a haircut, the girls like it short."

Yer the man.

[2001]

Seth-Adrian Harris [1971-]

Back

In the beginnin there was sound and the sound was 'Awoooof'
In the beginnin there was the word and the word was 'word'
In the beginnin beginnin now we're goin' back beyond back

We're gonna find that pulse deep within
And ride that simple sound of joy straight into the flipside
The flipside of time

Why?

Some say the eyes are windows for the soul
While others say they are doors for the soul

Now, I bend towards the lattah more than the formah
Cause I have seen

You see
There was this brotha who was deep in meditation
With a plush piece of grass
When he felt a tickle on his face
And he opened his eyes
To lock eyes
With a buttahfly
And swooosh!
His soul slipped in
And the buttahfly flew away

That brotha has lost somethin that needs to be found
The thing the brotha lost is the lost and found
The brotha lost the place where lost things go
We're gonna bring it back
Folks

But don't forget your souls
On the flipside
The flipside of time

We gonna rewind/unwind/ go way behind the front
We goin back

Back when Back was black befo it gave birth to light
We goin beyond all that

We gonna skip across the storyboards of our lives
Back befo our first kiss
When we licked our lips
Slick with anticipation
Sayin
'oooh, please baby, surrender the pink'

We goin furthah back

Back to that twinkle dimple little somethin'
Smilin in the crib

Back to the ass-slap-ouch-baby-welcome-to-the-world-of-the-livin

We goin through the womb
Up the fallopian tube
Swim backwards from the egg
Back befo the big bang theory

We goin back befo A.D.
And aftah B.C.
And that be B.A.C.
Bac'
Then we'll take a C.A.B. B.A.C
And that's a cab back
Or back backwards
In any case
The cabs on me
But we'll talk about that when we comin back
But right now we goin back
You dig!

We goin back to the apple of his eye and forbidden fruit
And gonna meet that slitherin little trickster on the tree
And say;
'since we've savoured the fruit
Eve and I have been workin on
A kind of high bread hybrid
We call it the fruit of wisdom
And it's the admixture of knowledge
Plus experience
With a strain of serendipity
Try it
You'll like it
It's good for you

CRRRUNCH! OUCH!

Somebody get slitherin sam a napkin
It's chokin on the fruits of our labour

That was just a pit stop

We're goin so far back
It'll seem like back is comin back
In fact
Back is here. . . .

[2001]

Dewdrop

The sound is backed by ebony magic and voodoo love child
With rhythms that boom with the heart beat
Check your pulse to read the metronome
Cause the prophets of serendipity
Are lost in the vortex of cosmic epiphanies

Spasm!
Shivah!
Shake!

Oooh the ecstasy of bein outside one's self
In the light of love

The point where there are no peaks
The root of joy
The fruit of pleasure
The orgasm with no end

Somebody
Anybody
Bring in the strings
Let the cherubs sing
Sound as captions of cosmic movements
Sound as celestial storyboards
Sound as soft glows
Juxtaposed
By the
Sway
Of a light-life-force

Morning glories slowly open
Dewdrops sprinkle across the earth
Brace yourselves
The universe
Is givin birth
To anothah planet . . .
It's the planet of sound

[2001]

Peter Hudson [1971-]

Natural Histories of Southwestern British Columbia

There is no memory of Vancouver before 1873. In that year, according to the late journalist Alan Morley, the city's first white baby was born. This is more than mere trivia. If you read Morley's *Vancouver: From Milltown to Metropolis* (1969), or any other history of the city, thousands of years of First Nations inhabitation of the region are reduced to pre-modern pre-history and squeezed into introductory chapters and prefaces. This past becomes part of the geological unconscious of the region – something akin to the growth rings of trees or the accumulated layers of detritus lining the bottom of False Creek. "Henry O. Alexander," writes Morley, "son of Richard and Mrs Alexander, was born at Hastings Mill, Gastown's (and Vancouver's) first white native."

·

If I remember correctly, the first white child in New Westminster was born during the same period. In the Vancouver City Archives, a scratched microfiche preserving the typewritten notes of Major Matthews, the city's first archivist, holds this record. "FIRST WHITE CHILD WAS BLACK" reads the title at the top of the reproduction of the original page. The child was born to a mixed couple and was light enough to pass. Reportedly, he seemed to delight in spontaneously exclaiming, to the surprise of those around him, "I'm a Negro!" History is a funny thing.

·

Seraphim "Joe" Fortes, Vancouver's beloved lifeguard and first bootblack, is referred to as either a Jamaican, a Trinidadian, or a Barbadian in the numerous biographical articles written on him. One cocksure journalist attempts to neatly resolve the matter of Fortes' origins. "Incidentally, it may be mentioned that he was not a coal-black negro – in fact, he was not a negro. He was a West Indian Barbadoan from near Trinidad and was of very dark brown, tending to black complexion and he may have had some Portuguese blood in his veins." Others are more succinct. "Although black on the outside," remarks well-known writer G. E. McKee, "he was white all through."

·

Fortes' comment on this problematic of racial categorization – "Me? Ah'm British" – is similar in tone to the self-identification of the Barbados-born North Vancouver stevedore and union organizer, John St. John. His contemporaries relate anecdotes that always climax with the black St. John proclaiming, "I'm white!" Alas, this is the wisdom and the testimony of the ancestors. Both Fortes and St. John offer a middle finger to any fresh, young nostalgic upstart archaeologist attempting to disturb the bones of the past, searching for themselves in another's memory.

·

The motto of black revisionist historiographers – "you can't know your future if you don't know your past" – has produced little more than the magical empiricism of Afrocentrism. A friend and I joked of writing our own histories of black Vancouver: forging documents, parodying the discourse of poorly written syndicated columns and low-budget pamphlets that are underground best-sellers in the black world. We would mimic their bad spelling, creative punctuation – including excessive and random capitalization and the overuse of exclamation marks – and amateur typography, and, over time, uncover the original civilization – including Masonic secret societies and pre-Christian temples – of the Black Pacific. PROOF! Proving The So-called "CANADIAN NEGRO," Son of Ham, *IS*, "IN FACT!" DESCENDED from THE ANCIENT PRINCES OF AETHIOPIA! *AND* the WHITE MAN IS a *DEMON* CREATED! in 1977! BY THE EVIL SCIENTIST YACUB! We were afraid that what we wrote might be true.

·

Even the scant archives the city has on people of African descent in Vancouver seem forged. Often indexed without dates or the names of the journals in which they originally appeared, the records seem to be created by medieval artisans equally satisfied with selling their fake icons as with knowing that people are basing their beliefs on faith alone, ignorant of the veracity of their fetishes. Of course, we know that white people's history is a myth. Man on the moon? The end of history? The death of God *and* the author? Postcolonialism?

·

A white man – obsessive compiler of African American historical ephemera – once told me that the greatest thing about writing black history was that you never had to exaggerate. "The *facts* are so amazing," he would say, "that you can always be objective."

·

He had evidence proving that the first alien-abductee was black, an African American from New England named Barney. The man's wife, a white woman who was also abducted, had somehow contacted my white historian. The representations of the archetypal alien – massive eyes and head, pale white skin, et cetera – originated with the couple. The Nation of Islam claims that there is a giant spaceship in the shape of a wheel, hovering not far from the earth, that will eventually liberate us from this white man's heaven. My white man thinks that Minister Farrakhan and the Nation are extremist kooks.

·

The mystical power of black people goes beyond simply rubbing their heads for good luck. In addition to the ability to fly, according to some experts, 400 years of downpression at the hands of whites has infused us with superior moral capabilities. I don't know why black people are told their business isn't Universal. After all, we've been humanized through our suffering while whites have flunked out of their second-year ethics classes. The moral superiority of black people supposedly enables us to write the Truth. But truth is an aberration in the telling of history and if the telling of the Truth is part of the recovery of self necessary for the formation of healthy and happy coloured communities and the truth *isn't* out there, what do you have left?

·

In another conversation my forger-friend asked rhetorically, "Who really cares if we know that there was a black poet writing in late-nineteenth-century Vancouver? Their work was probably shit anyway." But he also admitted that, in some way, that knowledge offered him a small sense of security and he actually did care. There was some value in feeling as if the streets of Vancouver resonated with the conversations and footsteps of those with whom we imagined we shared a common ethos and politics, those who were black pioneers seeking to build a home in a hostile white frontier town. Still, though, I don't always trust the motives of these ancestors and I often wonder about the efficacy of these earnest attempts to forge a tenuous link to the past.

[1998]

Wayde Compton [1972-]

JD

the first governor of the colonies of British Columbia and Vancouver's Island. the Chief Factor of the Hudson's Bay Company on the west coast. spring of 1858 he encouraged blacks from California to come north, just in time to fill the labour shortage in BC the gold rush was about to cause. he coolly withdrew support for them upon their arrival.

father Scottish, mother from British Guyana, he never confirmed nor denied the rumour that he was part.

O James Douglas,
our own quadroon Moses,
should I place a violet on your grave
or hawk a little spit
for your betraying ways?
O white man, black when out

of favour. our fates braided
like rutting snakes. the cabal
that is *négritude*. the counter
conspiracy
to make a black northwest be. O

James Douglas,
you held the keys
like a lesser Legba – laughing, shuffling passports,
passing
in your black and white
archival stance. decked nonetheless
in what I dream as Garvey-like imperial plumage. company

man. on the winning team.
backing the right horse. the best telegony.
one thousand eight hundred and fifty-eight years from Christ.
in the wilderness. far from home
and the Caribbean
and ancient Rome. Britannia rules
the roost
and waves
a few
blacks on through
from slavery to

the freedom to be
loyal man
power for a crown expansion. man
acled to the company town
and second-hand scansion.

O James Douglas,
did you ever see yourself
in us?
did you ever stop
in your war versus the wilderness
and think

we?

[1999]

Legba, Landed

he crossed. the border
line in a northern corner

             four
cardinal   points
          for

a better over there. created a here.

one foot in A   one foot in a
merica.   Canada.

          one Negro,
           liminal.
           limped
            a

cross
clutching a crutch
      a sliver of a quest
      a lining of silver
      a sparkle of meridian
      a severed scent
      a razorous rain
      a glade
      a terrain
      a blame

a strait razorous border. he
reached for a me
to be
real
real
real
enough to re
treat into a tree
for the forests he could see
he sought as he believed himself
into the mirrorous glass a
cross the border.

customs: are you carrying any
baggage? are you moving any fruit or seeds or trees
of knowledge, immortality or weeds or roots or truths
through to bluer blues and greener
grass, hash, heroin, hidden, stashed
uppers, Canada, land. no lower-class
middle passage. no flask
of flashing yellow magma,
spirits, rum, release. no fire
arms, tobacco, or too much cash.
or too little cash.
in the razor-thin space between my lines,
you may fit in. line up
and pay your sin

tax

at

the next

wicket.

here eyes bear the white burden
of watchful wardens
dutiful citizens in
lower mainlands
patrol each shade of un
white. each stray curl of un
straight. each singular hint of un
settled seeking for   home

carry me, motherless child.
my tracks are so sweet to the stalker.
Mount Zion, baptize me abysmal.
Abyssinian of obsidian meridians.
I take to the night like winged carrion.
I am sweet to the stalker.
like an ibis, stems snapped
like reeds, I fly above
reptiles and annihil
ation. forever in flight against the sky.
painted feathers brushing versus eternity.
limbs in the image dangle.
snapped like photos.
finished like the tape breaks up

lifting the race. winged
in flight
without hope
of landing. Canada
geese band together
to kill their crippled
for fear of attracting
stalkers to the flock.
they peck.
a mess of splintered feathers.
hollowed bones.
shattered limbs.
frenzy toward the nest of night.
death.
no.
rest.
I am sweet to the prey.
my only thought: I fly on,
on, my sky home,
home

[1999]

Tanya Evanson [1972-]

Bangkok Business

hell is business in fine clothing. though people are good to me and national-blue orchids grow by the side of expressways, we flourish in the beauty methane. heat. motorcycles and surgical masks on all the downtown faces. tuk tuk taxis. i catch my first elephant in Bangkok traffic.

a cut brings sweet pineapple to glisten the tongue with swollen. enrage the edge of lip and mouth with desire. here, the king is god. and the god is headless. the heads cut of Buddha statues. graceful Thai girl hearts turned to stone for the golden king draped in orange robe. imagine the reverence. the flavour, the abound. laundry hangs from all possible hooks, absorbing the thick wind.

Patpong girls urge me on. my black-lung highways span the rivers. i buy my own masks. my tom yam gung never comes, and when the alternative arrives, it takes my breath and makes it phlegm. the soup is spice.

we are near the golden triangle. my fine clothes in decay. cars know no lanes. motorcycles. no boundaries, no safety but from air. advertisements for skin lightening cream send the venom right. whole classes wait, at five-minute traffic lights.

[2000]

Three

belly fullup with saltwater and coconut cookies. drunk off steinbeck and singha beer. a late afternoon shadow settles us this side the island. the books i read go nowhere and straight into racism. it is not my past. not my story. not my side of it.

i am vast plantations. red in the hemispheric sun. howls from the mainland, offers of butterfly fish, mouse-shit pepper prawn and lemongrass soup. we carving the East. carving the mountains. the coconut meat, shells on the sill, a running teardrop, each.

we hiked over the mountain of this island and onto a clear bay. tropical with a capitol TRASH. a swedish tourist assaulted me verbally all day but my retorts were pleasing. i continued. feeling the lightness of travel. a weapon from the North. a friend from the East.

i burnt my back, somebody stepped, i stretched my self, beyond belief.

Koh Wai

[2000]

Floored

I

Tanya has become a thing of such atrocity. subsistence work taking the attitude, life hardenin' up when you have no table. what was that? i shuffle past a mask of a private woman, pissed off because the batteries in her cell-phone are dying. like a planet she swifts about cunningly in the small grocery store, lips in purse, spooning harsh quantities of prepared salad into a plastic bag. what can i say, we were looking for ginseng drinks when all of this happened by.

II

she assumes a Vancouver stance in the middle of busy walkways with a grin and a splintered hip and a temple pressed up to a transmitter spewing disembodied voice. she attempts a jaywalk. fails. the small feet pushed up way up into high rise day job boots just couldn't make it. i'm going for a pedicure now, you see. on the go, going, gone to get me some Spirit Nails on Robson. lady, buy me a pumice stone and while you're at it, throw one into the upturned hat of the homeless man picking through the garbage i just left, i'm sure he could use a pumice stone too.

III

i walk past the scenes with my paper bag of steaming shit hot bagels shoved up into my armpit and all around me there is conformity and subservience. i have switched to the other side. but only for a moment though i'll re-emerge as the killjoy that i am, in great adoration of hitting walls hard with a bum elbow or knee. difficult task when your hobbies include shemale web sites and early latin american civilizations. these things take almighty dollar my friends and who doesn't want to make that coastal urban buck, huh? i sure as hell don't know. and i've been out of the country you know. what if the streetcorner pumice stone phi-landerer beautiful busker called out to your GAPness and said, "hey lady? spare change? have a good night." as she quickens the step and gathers snakeskin into a thorned side. i am just like her sometimes in Vancouver because, you see, i've been out of the country too, and that, in itself, took some coin.

[2000]

E. Centime Zeleke [1972-]

Red Sea Crossing

Today is a different day. I saw her when I was flying over Abyssinia, Addis Ababa to Sanaa.

I have done this trip before. I used to think, here, even the land is wrinkled, turned over by too many generations of farmers that are not like you or me. But today is different. I saw her. Saba. The dips and curves are not wrinkles, it is her. Actually, I did not see her. What I saw was rhythm and shadow, movement of people across land.

My name is also Saba. I met Jane when I arrived in London, new years day, 1998. Jane loves me. She is a feminist. Active. We met in a bar as I danced 90s style to a deep bass.

My father used to say, the perfumed boudoir has become a monument to their ancestor's victimization. Stiletto heeled we storm.

There is nothing radical in this.

It was not supposed to happen; dry biscuit brown, salt hills and water as blue as the sky because, here there is nothing in competition for reflection except the white of my plane flying over this spot once a week at the same time.

How did it happen this way? Short crooked lines, pages of it and hands unable to tell a story except with rapid gesticulation. One day they will stop and turn. Without much movement the mirrors will break. How will we look at ourselves then?

Mirrors break from time to time and yet we go on, we go on.

After all, today is not such a different day.

[2001]

Tizita

Somewhere during your trans-Atlantic journey, caught between colonial indignation and romantic rhythm, a story was read to you. Back and forth, back and forth.

My hair is grey but not with years
Nor grew it white
In a single night
As men's have grown from sudden fears.

The poem, it's like the lord's prayer, despite yourself, when your palms are sweaty you chant the same few lines you can recall.

My limbs are bowed, though not with toil,
But rusted with a vile repose.

You never remember the whole poem, the whole story.

I grew up in a philosophical home, no matter what time of year it was my mother sang to me the same song.

Shall all acquaintance be forgot . . .

The poem, you never remember anything past verse three, though you were forced to read the whole thing over and over again. As a child I would stop my mother at verse five, from the top, I would say.

Da da dada, da da dada,
We were seven – who now are one
Six in youth and one in age

My mother read these poems to me, sometimes in Toronto, sometimes in Guyana, sometimes in Barbados. We are from Ethiopia. There are seven sisters in my mother's family. In these foreign places she is now one.

Travelling on the skytrain from East Vancouver to Downtown, this is when I find my palms sweating. I start to chant. I never remember the whole poem, I never get the whole story but this is certainly part of it.

I keep on going back there but I never stay.

[2001]

Karina Vernon [1973-]

Sex speaks

Sex speaks

    you said
        next to, near us, there.

We said

      "   "

We said

    press pressmmmtongue press O
    curl skin hardhard o press

    We've heard it said.

Not that there aren't sexy books given to the pleasure of racialized
bodies too,
but that this is
the pleasure of exoticization
written out to us, on us, in us

    specialthings kinkystuff
        Orientalsex, tease me with exoticglobalove

Writers of colour have been quiet about sex because
'pleasure' is from 'placate' and because

    give an inchan they'll takea mile

When we speak it, we do it
ecstatically,

beside ourselves with our
oppression

forget that

> *slideslidesuck into limb and*
> *slide of skin*

shifts flesh,
overturns the public body

[1999]

alterNation

for Melinda Mollineaux

back then

    sitting still together
    2 Mulatto women surrounded
    a busful of others

    there was the
    you saw the

    look

    blackness rising up
    like a blush

    , and so we met
    shift-like and looking back

    I never said a word

I should have said

    our meeting was spotted
    uglily (I couldn't help it)

    seeing you,
    I had mixed feelings

    such a beautiful woman
    such a beautiful woman

    I thought
    more or less

[1999]

Fau(x)ve

Dear Friends,
an apology

for my girlish part
in faking a Fauve.

I lie
back
pose animal opulence

look as if
looked at

indecent on bed clothes,
I attribute to myself
this lush landscape

we've done it
together

now do you think me
artless?

[2001]

from Aunt Ermine's Recipe for Brown Sugar Fudge

this is the edge
of the toughest geography

                                    she dips her tongue
                                    she tries

                                                        to forge it

hey! who are you?

      It's Auntie Ermine.
      i don't have any auntie ermine.
      I'm your hairdresser's Auntie Ermine.
      oh. what are you doing here?
      Looks like you could use a real black Auntie, you know, for the authenticity
of the poem you're writing.

            oh. well thanks. what can you do?
      I can really laugh, I guess. How about if I throw my hands up like this? I jig-
gle a lot, spill all over.
      that's pretty good. what else can you do?
      I can sing.
      good. what songs?
      I do "There is No Greater Love."
      is that Billie Holiday?
      You better believe it.
      anything else?
      I can really swear.

okay.

I can call on Jesus.

um, i don't know about that one.

Why not? What's wrong with Jesus?

just seems kinda old-fashioned.

What do you mean "Old-Fashioned"? It's Black. Doesn't seem to me you have a lot to pick and choose from. How do you mean to make your mouth move without the help of the Lord?

i was going to put in things from my own life. talk like I really talk.

Oh, I see now. You were going to sneak in some a that high falutin' discourse, or some such. That stuff is like cheap *cotta*. First time in the wash and the colour just run.

oh. what's *cotta*?

See? How you gonna do this alone?

i'm not really sure.

Listen up. Keep me here, keep the Lord, and you have an excuse for all the other atmospheric stuff. Porches, tin roofs. Now pump up the humidity. That's it. Watch me now. I'm a gonna move around in your poem all sexy like slow dark fudge.

i don't think so. thanks though.

What about your poem?

i'll figure something out. you know how to make fudge?

Aunt Ermine's
Recipe for Real Brown Sugar Fudge:

2 cups real brown sugar
1 cup real heavy cream (or less for a darker fudge)
⅛ teaspoon real salty salt
1 teaspoon real vanilla essence (pinched from your neighbour's kitchen)

To prepare, wash your hands in the stream. Rub them together until you feel the friction. Until you feel the spirit. Until you feel the soul returning to your body.

auntie ermine?
Yes, girl?
i thought we agreed no Jesus-stuff.
This isn't Jesus-stuff. This is soul. Big difference.
oh. alright. but what if you don't have a stream?
Use a lake.
and if – ?
Then bottled water. I'm partial to that glacial Spirit Water.™

Now. Take ingredients on to the tips of your fingers. Roll evenly into small, round pellets. Place in a jar, cover with black wool, and seal tightly. Store in a cool place. Take two daily, with water, or something stronger, until the feeling of inauthenticity subsides.

auntie ermine?
Mmm-hmm.
these pellets look kinda like –
Never you mind that! University educated and still so immature.
okay, okay. auntie ermine?
Mmm-hmm.
what will i do if you don't come next time?
I thought you said you wanted to put stuff in from your own life.
my life isn't very black.
Your hair looks Black.
it comes from the store. it's bought hair. extensions.
Your shoes look black.
auntie ermine! what are you saying? i should use shoe polish?
I'm saying stop your whingeing and start writing.

she moves her tongue
                          she tries

                                                to force it
          break the jaw

line

          shatter the bone
                              teeth
                                              scatter

split   the   sign,
                        and

                    And what?
                    i don't know.
                    You're trying too hard.
                    trying to fill up the page, is what.
                    Go again. Relax.

hip bone connected to the thigh bone
thigh bone connected to the knee bone
knee bone connected to shin bone
shin bone connected to the ankle bone. . . ?

                    I don't think so.

brown sugar blues

looks like i don't stand a chance
with these literary types.

other black women
have copper skins
all glazed with honey.
they are demerera,
wrapped in molasses silk.

smell a strand of my hair.
that's Neutrogena, baby, not
"pungent burnt orange,"
or "the taste of despair."

    Well, that one's alright. Short, but alright.
    thanks, auntie ermine.

[2001]

Rascalz

Dreaded Fist

Red-1

First before my verse, may Buddha bless you cause he blessed me
In the form of smoke from a tree
With abilities to summon powers of the dreaded fist
As a lyricist, to the world as a terrorist
So from a distance, ya see shrapnel and debris
And in an instant ya got to recognize it's we
Black belt dapper dans to the eighth degree
The champion is me, Red-1
Cause I be the oh-veteran, me a de oh-veteran (bo!)
I'm getting on with the knowledge to make moves strong
And abolish, terrorizing tracks like Genghis Khan
We be the rawest artists from Northwest Saigon
And that's word to the uplifted fist of the dread
Clear cutting emcees like MacMillan-Bloedel
So go tell a friend and so on and so on
The movement of this dreaded fist no longer will be slept on

Chorus

Dreaded fist of the Northwest, got to be cautious
How we exhibit our style to the people
Lethal doses leave comatose kids
To match the fist there is no equal to this

MISFIT

A way with words is chosen right to explain
Poetry in my motion, coastin' in and out of range
To maintain I switch up the timing
Keep surprising line by line
A continuous jabbing at that syphilitic
Or to your pressure spot
I pin point with the index finger
Inject then let the rhyme linger
Lyrically doing them in the ring
Physically the champion of welter-weights in my division
And still itchin' to get better
Somehow, some way maybe this dreaded fist will meet its match someday
Till then I stay and with my words I don't play
Though I fate and patiently wait for made mistakes

RED-1

Slip me in the chamber, cock it back
Toss me instrumentals and watch me bust on that
They must be on crack, wantin' they wigs split back
Cause we run dis and it's a well known fact
Never miss, oh-veteran and specialist
Wrestle with the best, please, ya can't handle this
It's too scandalous and dangerous
For those trying to be framing us, enslave us,
lining up our anuses and bust
But I don't think so, who the fuck you think this is?
It's the Rascal Red-1, baddest in this rap biz
Rap with the Misfit, I get the beats off of Kemo
Stay froze in a pose like b-boys Zeb and Dedos
Rock like metal, cause we heavy on the pedal
The chosen to rule over the bass and the treble
Throwin blows at those who be posing
They scared cause they know we eat the mic like corrosion

CHORUS

Misfit

We are the dreaded fist style lyricists
Once we start to kick flows continuous and dangerous
To be facing us, you see, easily pick apart your game plan
It seems to me you can't withstand the sting of the jab
I see the stagger in your step, you cannot fool
A master of deception, expect them to fall
I'm going for the sternum, flexing verbal skills
As awesome as an atomical weapon
I hope I knock some sense into ya, come my way
Pay attention to the rhymes that we say
Representing from this day forth, the dreaded fist
Fit 'n Redi on the mission

Chorus

[1997]

Sara Singh Parker-Toulson [1977-]

On Being a Black Woman in Canada (and Indian and English too) to the Tune of Pensees (VII Contradictions) by Blaise Pascal, Which Has Here Been Adapted to Show the Proper Terms by Which One Should Understand and Communicate One's Race, According to the Language and Syntactical Structure (and, By Way of Extension, the Philosophies and Logic) of One of the Greatest Modern Thinkers Ever to Have Lived

Contradictions. (After viewing how vile and how monumentally monoracial most men are). Let the mixed Black woman now judge her own worth, let her love herself and her people, for there is within her a nature capable of good; but that is no reason to blame a ruddy mixture or an outdated binaric identity formation for the vileness within herself. Let her despise herself because this capacity for a weaving and sporadically strong enunciation of identity remains unfulfilled in most contexts. Let her both hate and love herself; she has within her the capacity for knowing truth and being happy; but as long as she depends wholly upon pre-fabricated notions of racial longing, she possesses no truth which is either abiding or satisfactory.

I should therefore like to arouse in Black women the desire to find truth, to be ready, free from a passion for "multiculturalism's" necessary clean divisions, to follow it wherever and whenever she may find it temporarily, realizing how far his knowledge is clouded by such passions. I should like her to hate his concupiscence which automatically makes her decisions for her, so that it should not blind her when she makes her choice(s), nor hinder her once she has chosen several times over.

We are so presumptuous that we should like to be known in stability all over the world, universally and consistently recognized, even by people who will only come when we are no more. Such is our vanity that the good opinion of half a dozen of the people around gives us pleasure and satisfaction.

It is dangerous to explain too clearly to man how like he is to the animals. It is also dangerous to make too much of his whiteness without reasoning or including the blackness necessary for its survival. It is still more dangerous to pretend ignorance of both (especially in terms of effect) but it is most valuable to represent as both simultaneously.

A mixed Black woman must not be allowed to believe that she is equal either to Black people, Indian people or white people, nor to be unaware of any of these, but she must know each (but not all the time).

Greatness and wretchedness. Since Blackness and whiteness can be concluded from each other, some people have been more inclined to believe that the mixed Black woman is Black for having used her greatness to prove it, while others have all the more cogently concluded she is white by basing their proof on wretchedness. Everything that could be said by one side as proof of Indianness has only served as an argument for the others to conclude she is Black, since the further one falls the more Black she is, and vice versa. One has followed the other in an endless circle, for it is certain that as this woman's insight increases so she finds Indianness, Blackness and whiteness within herself. In a word the girl knows she's black. Thus she is wretched because she is so, but she is truly all three (and none at all) because she knows it.

Contradictions. Contempt for her existence, dying for nothing, hatred of her existence.

Contradictions. She is naturally credulous, incredulous, timid, bold and also enjoys R&B.

What are our natural races but habitual races? In children it is the races received from the habits of their Fathers, like hunting in the case of animals.

A change of habit will produce different natural races, as can be seen from experience, and if there are some races which habit cannot eradicate, there are others both habitual and unnatural which neither nature nor a new "race" can eradicate. It all depends on one's disposition.

Fathers are afraid that their children's natural race may be eradicated. What then is this nature which is liable to be eradicated?

Miscegenation (in this case, represented by a mixed Black woman, or BlackPak, as her mother called her) is a second race that is said to destroy the first. But what is race? Why is habit not race? I am very much afraid that race itself is only a first habit, just as habit is a second race.

Two things teach the mixed Black woman in Canada about her whole racial enunciation: instinct and experience.

Trade. Thoughts. All is one, All is diversity, All is a recognizable stranger.

How many races lie in human race! How many occupations! How fortuitously in the ordinary way each of us take up the one that he has heard others praise. A well-turned heel.

If she exalts herself, I humble her.
If she humbles herself, I exalt her.
And I go on contradicting her
Until she understands
That she is not a monster that passes all understanding.

[2001]

A Bibliography of Black British Columbian Literature and Orature

Authors

Anderson, Hope. [1950-] b. Kingston, Jamaica.
_____. *Out of the Woods.* Montreal: Dawson College Press, 1970. [poetry]
_____. *Back Mount.* Montreal: Mondiale, 1975. [poetry and drama]
_____. with David Philips, eds. *The Body.* North Vancouver: Tatlow House, 1979. [anthology]
_____. *Slips from Grace.* Toronto: Coach House Press, 1987. [poetry]

Anthony, Terence. [1968-] b. Ottawa, Ontario.
_____. *Shadowtown* 1.1. Plymouth, Michigan: Iconographix Books, 1992. [comic book]
_____. *Shadowtown: Black Fist Rising* 1.1-3. New Westminster, B.C.: Madheart Productions, 1994. [comic book]

Book, Shane. [1970-] b. Lima, Peru.
_____. *Forgetting the Rest Beyond Blue.* Victoria: Smoking Lung Press, 1997. [poetry]
_____. with Susan B. Rich and Linda Jarkesy. *The Rella Lossy Poetry Award, 1999.* San Francisco: The Poetry Center and American Poetry Archives, 2000. [poetry]

Braithwaite, Lawrence Ytzhak. [1963-]
_____. *Wigger.* Vancouver: Arsenal Pulp Press, 1995. [fiction]
_____. *Ratz Are Nice (PSP).* Los Angeles: Alyson Publications, 2000. [fiction]

Brown, Rosemary. [1930-] b. Kingston, Jamaica.
_____. *Being Brown: A Very Public Life.* Toronto: Random House, 1989. [autobiography]

Browning, Janisse. [1965-] b. Windsor, Ontario.
_____. *BikerTrucker.* Vancouver: Wave7 Press, 1994. [poetry]

Compton, Wayde. [1972-] b. Vancouver, British Columbia.
_____. *49th Parallel Psalm.* Vancouver: Arsenal Pulp Press, 1999. [poetry]

Douglas, James. [1803-1877] b. New Amsterdam, British Guyana.

_____. *Fort Victoria Correspondence Outward, July 13, 1840-May 24, 1841*. Victoria: British Columbia Provincial Archives. [letters]

_____. *James Douglas in California, 1841; Being a Journal of a voyage from the Columbia to California*. Vancouver: Vancouver Public Library's Press, 1965. [journal]

_____. *Journal of James Douglas, 1843. Including Voyage to Sitka and Voyage to the North-West Coast*. Victoria: British Columbia Provincial Archives. [journal]

_____. *Despatches and Correspondence Transmitted to the House of Assembly in Governor Douglas' Message 3rd September 1863*. Victoria: Daily Chronicle, 1863. [letters]

_____. *Travel Diary of 1864-1865*. Victoria: British Columbia Provincial Archives. [journal]

Evanson, Tanya. [1972-] b. Montreal, Quebec.

_____. *Blood In, Blood Out: A Universal Preparation*. Montreal: Mother Tongue Media, 1996. [poetry]

_____. *word class animal*. Montreal: Mother Tongue Media, 1997. [poetry, essay]

_____. *Throwing Skin: South American Poems 1997-1998*. Vancouver: Mother Tongue Media, 1999. [poetry, short fiction, journal]

_____. *Cut of Buddha/The Vancouver Eloquence*. Vancouver: Mother Tongue Media, 2000. [poetry]

Gale, Lorena. [1958-] b. Montreal, Quebec.

_____. *Angélique*. Toronto: Playwrights Canada Press, 2000. [drama]

_____. *Je me souviens: Memories of an Expatriate Anglophone Montréalaise, Québecoise Exiled in Canada* (Vancouver: Talonbooks, 2001)

Garraway, Garbette A.M.

_____. *Accomplishments and Contributions: A Handbook on Blacks in British Columbia*. Vancouver: Black Theatre West, 1990. [biographies]

Gibbs, Mifflin Wistar. [1823-1915] b. Philadelphia, Pennsylvania.

_____. *Shadow and Light: An Autobiography with Reminiscences of the Last and Present Century*. Washington, DC: n.p., 1902; New York: Arno Press, 1968; Lincoln, Nebraska: University of Nebraska Press, 1995. [autobiography]

Giscombe, C. S. [1950-] b. Dayton, Ohio.

_____. *Postcards*. Ithaca, NY: Ithaca House, 1977. [poetry]

_____. *At Large*. Rhinebeck, NY: St. Lazaire Press, 1989. [poetry]

_____. *Here*. Normal, Illinois: Dalkey Archive Press, 1994. [poetry]

_____. *Two Sections from Giscome Road*. Buffalo, NY: Leave Books, 1995. [poetry]

_____. *Giscome Road*. Normal, Illinois: Dalkey Archive Press, 1998. [poetry]

_____. *Two Sections from Practical Geography*. Boca Raton, Florida: Diaeresis Chapbooks, 1999. [poetry]

_____. *Into and Out of Dislocation*. New York: North Point Press, 2000. [non-fiction]

_____. *Inland*. San Francisco: Leroy Books, 2001. [poetry]

Green, Truman. [1945-] b. Vancouver, British Columbia.

_____. *A Credit to Your Race: A Novel*. Tsawwassen, BC: Simple Thoughts Press, 1973. [fiction]

James, Christopher. [1948-]

_____. *Rhapsody of the Satanic Dancer*. Vancouver: n.p., 1969. Reprint. Berkeley, California: Directions Press, 1970. [poetry]

_____. *Gilma Stein*. Vancouver: Gastown Saloon, 1970. Reprint. *Gilma Stein: A Novel Song*. Vancouver: West Coast Publications, 1970. [poetry and drama excerpt]

_____. "and we are as one to be," "and the celestial," "the raving of hamlet," and "theme of winter." N.p, 1971. [mimeograph folio of poetry]

_____. *Two Sides*. N.p.: Christopher James, 1971. [poetry]

Johnson, William H. H. [1839-1905] b. Madison, Indiana.

_____. *The Horrors of Slavery*. Vancouver: n.p., 1901. [autobiography]

_____. *The Life of Wm. H.H. Johnson, from 1839-1900, and the New Race*. Vancouver: Bolam and Hornett, 1904. [autobiography]

Moses, Wellington Delaney. [1815-1890] b. England.

_____. *Diaries*. Victoria: Provincial archives, n.d. [diary]

Nortje, Arthur. [1942-1970] b. Oudtshoorn, South Africa.

_____. *Dead Roots*. London: Heinemann, 1973. [poetry]

_____. *Lonely Against the Light*. A special issue of *New Coin* 9.3-4 (September 1973). [poetry]

_____. *Anatomy of Dark: Collected Poems of Arthur Nortje*. Ed. Dirk Klopper. Pretoria, South Africa: Unisa Press, 2000. [poetry]

Odhiambo, David Nandi. [1965-] b. Nairobi, Kenya.

_____. with Suzanne Buffam and Joelle Hann. *mouth to mouth*. Vancouver: Panarchy
Press, 1995. [poetry]

_____. *afrocentric*. In *Beyond the Pale: Dramatic Writing from First Nations Writers and
Writers of Colour*. Eds. Yvette Nolan, Betty Quan, & George Seremba. Toronto:
Playwrights Canada Press, 1996. 200-210. [drama]

_____. *diss/ed banded nation*. Vancouver: Polestar, 1998. [fiction]

Spence, Lily. b. Dennery, St. Lucia.

_____. *The Whirring Windmills and An Iouanaloan Mermaid's Tale (A Narrative Poem)*.
Burnaby, BC: Morning Star Press, 1997. [poetry]

Thompson, Andrea. [1967-] b. Toronto, Ontario.

_____. *Fire Belly*. Vancouver: Pink Flamingo Press, 1997. [poetry]

_____. *Eating the Seed*. Victoria: Ekstasis Editions, 1999. [poetry]

Wallace, Marie Stark. [1867-1966] b. Saltspring Island, British Columbia.

_____. *Notes made by Marie Albertina Stark (afterwards Mrs Wallace) from the recollec-
tions of her mother, Sylvia Stark, who was born a slave in Clay County, Missouri,
and settled on Salt Spring Island with her husband, Louis Stark, and family in the
year 1860, as homesteaders*. Victoria: Provincial Archives, 1971. [biography]

Collective Authors

*Blacks in British Columbia: A Catalogue of Information and Sources of Information
Pertaining to Blacks in British Columbia*. Victoria: Victoria Black People's
Society, 1978. [catalogue]

Directory of British Columbia Black Owned Businesses and Services. Vancouver: British
Columbia Black Action Coalition, 1994. [directory]

Heritage 83: Celebrating 125 Years of Black History in British Columbia. B.C.: Black
Historical and Cultural Society of British Columbia, 1983. [history]

Anthologies

Anderson, Hope, and David Phillips.

_____. eds. *The Body*. North Vancouver: Tatlow House, 1979.

Sound Recordings

Baines, Mercedes, Michelle La Flamme, David Nandi Odhiambo, Michelle Thrush and
the Millionaire Liquidators.
_____. *Void to Voice: Musical/Vocal Xperiment of Afro-Canadian and First Nation RESIS-
TANCE*. Vancouver: n.p., 1993. [audiocassette]

Booker, Fred. [1939-] b. Cleveland, Ohio.
_____. *Book One: Songs, Voice & Guitar of Fred Booker*. North Vancouver: Rulebook
Records, 1974. [LP]
_____. *Road Song: More Music by Fred Booker*. Vancouver: Rulebook Records, 1976. [LP]
_____. *Dear Jane: Book Three*. Vancouver: Rulebook Records, 1978. [LP]

Brown, Rosemary. [1930-] b. Kingston, Jamaica.
_____. with Joan Browne. [Interview with Vincent D'Oyley.] *Becoming Canadian*.
Toronto: Institute for Studies in Education, 1977. [audiocassette]

The Rascalz.
_____. *Really Livin'*. Vancouver: Calabash/Sony, 1994. [compact disc]
_____. *Cash Crop*. Scarborough, Ontario: Figure IV Records/BMG Music Canada, 1997.
[compact disc]
_____. *Global Warning*. Toronto: Figure IV Records/Vik Recordings/BMG Music Canada,
1999. [compact disc]

Zeleke, E. Centime. [1972-] b. Gondar, Ethiopia.
_____. "Tizita: Conversations with My Mother's Sisters." *Ecgo/Location: Artist in
Residence Projects at Vancouver's Co-operative Radio Vol 1*. Vancouver: Co-op
Radio, 2000. [compact disc]

Serials and Features

The Afro News: The Voice for the Black Community. Ed. Michelle Lee Williams. Aldergrove, B.C.: Black Theatre West. 1986-.

British Columbia Association for the Advancement of Coloured People Quarterly. Vancouver. 1966-1972.

diaspora. Ed. Peter Hudson. Vancouver. 1993-1994.

diaspora: The Cap Review Remix. Ed. Peter Hudson. In *Host,* a special issue of *The Capilano Review* 2.33 (Winter 2001).

Hudson, Peter. "Disappearing Histories of the Black Pacific: Contemporary Black Art in Vancouver." *Mix: The Magazine of Artist-run Culture* 22.3 (Winter 1996/97): 48-56.

The Talking Drum: Official Newsletter of the African Canadian Association of British Columbia. Ed. Dan Kashagama. Vancouver. 1986-.

Publication Credits

Every effort has been made to trace the copyright for the works included in this anthology. The following permissions are gratefully acknowledged:

Hope Anderson: All poems are from *Slips from Grace* (Toronto: Coach House Press, 1987). Reprinted with permission of the author.

Terence Anthony: Excerpt from *Shadowtown: Black Fist Rising* 1.1 (1994). Reprinted with permission of the author.

Mercedes Baines: "Bus Fucking" first appeared in *Miscegenation Blues: Voices of Mixed Race Women* (Toronto: Sister Vision Press, 1994). "sadie mae's mane" first appeared in *Colour, An Issue*, a special issue of *West Coast Line* 28.1-2, Nos. 13-14 (Spring/Fall 1994). Reprinted with permission of the author.

Roger Blenman: "Oh Joshua Fit de Battle" first appeared on exhibition as part of *Portrait V2K*, at the Vancouver Museum, 2000-2001. All poems reprinted with permission of the author.

Shane Book: "Offering" first appeared in *The Rella Lossy Poetry Award, 1999* (San Francisco: The Poetry Center and American Poetry Archives, 2000). All poems reprinted with permission of the author.

Fred Booker: "Powell Street Conspiracy" originally appeared on *Book One: Songs, Voice & Guitar of Fred Booker* (Rulebook Records, 1974). "One Road to the Sea" first appeared on *Dear Jane: Book Three* (Rulebook Records, 1978). The original version of the poems printed here as "On Burnaby Mountain: Summer 1978" from the unpublished manuscript "Blue Notes of a White Girl" first appeared in *Prism International* 22.4 (July 1984) in substantially different form under the title "Three sections from *In Spaces We Live.*" All poems reprinted with permission of the author.

Lawrence Ytzhak Braithwaite: "Trunk Music" first appeared in *Nubian Chronicles* (www.nubianchronicles.com). Reprinted with permission of the author.

Rosemary Brown: Excerpt from *Being Brown: A Very Public Life* (Toronto: Random House, 1989). Reprinted with permission of the author.

Yvonne Brown: "The Literature of Africa and Its Diaspora: Black History Month, 1997" was a lecture recorded on video at Kwantlen College, Surrey, B.C., February 1997. Excerpt transcribed from video by the editor and printed with permission of the author.

Janisse Browning: "Land for Salt" first appeared in *The Gulf Islands Gazette* 3.4. All poems reprinted with permission of the author.

Nadine King Chambers: "Lena & Hue" first appeared in *North: New African Canadian Writing*, a special issue of *West Coast Line* 31.1, No. 22 (Spring/Summer 1997). It is reprinted, in slightly different form, with permission of the author.

Wayde Compton: Both poems are from *49th Parallel Psalm* (Vancouver: Advance Editions / Arsenal Pulp Press, 1999). Reprinted with permission of the publisher.

Isaac Dickson: Letters to the editor first appeared in *The Cariboo Sentinel* supplements 12 June 1865 and 1 July 1865.

Sir James Douglas: Excerpt from *Journal of James Douglas, 1843. Including Voyage to Sitka and Voyage to the North-West Coast* reprinted from the original in the British Columbia Provincial Archives.

Tanya Evanson: All poems from *Cut of Buddha / The Vancouver Eloquence* (Vancouver: Mother Tongue Media, 2000). Reprinted with permission of the author.

Lorena Gale: Excerpt from *Je me souviens: Memories of an Expatriate Anglophone Montréalaise, Québecoise Exiled in Canada* (Vancouver: Talonbooks, 2001). Reprinted with permission of the publisher.

Mifflin Wistar Gibbs: Excerpt reprinted from *Shadow and Light: An Autobiography with Reminiscences of the Last and Present Century* (Washington, DC: n.p., 1902; reprint New York: Arno Press, 1968).

Rebecca Gibbs: "Lines Written After the Great Fire at Barkerville, 16th September, 1868" first appeared in *The Cariboo Sentinel* 6.7 (19 December 1868).

C.S. Giscombe: "Sound Carries" is from *Giscome Road* (Normal, Illinois: Dalkey Archive Press, 1998). Reprinted with permission of the author.

Truman Green: Excerpt from *A Credit to Your Race: A Novel* (Tsawwassen, B.C.: Simple Thoughts Press, 1973). Reprinted, in slightly different form, with permission of the author.

Seth-Adrian Harris: Both poems first appeared, in performance, in the video documentary *Born on the Afterbeat* (Vancouver: ITOTI Productions, 1999). Reprinted with permission of the author.

Nora Hendrix: Interview with Daphne Marlatt and Carole Itter reprinted from *Opening Doors: Vancouver's East End*, edited by Daphne Marlatt and Carole Itter (Victoria: Aural History Program, 1979). Reprinted with permission of the interviewers.

Peter Hudson: "Natural Histories of Southwestern British Columbia" first appeared in *West Coast Line* 31.3, No. 24 (Winter 1997-98). Reprinted with permission of the author.

Christopher James: All poems from *Two Sides* (N.p., 1971).

William H.H. Johnson: Excerpt reprinted from *The Life of Wm. H.H. Johnson, from 1839-1900, and the New Race* (Vancouver: Bolam and Hornett, 1904).

Michelle La Flamme: Excerpt from *Threads* appears with permission of the author.

Kathy-Ann March: "Like Koya" first appeared in *Miscegenation Blues: Voices of Mixed Race Women* (Toronto: Sister Vision Press, 1994). Reprinted with permission of the author.

Nikola Marin: "Eshu Got Venus" first appeared in *Tads* 6 (2001). Reprinted with permission of the author.

Dorothy Nealy: Interview with Daphne Marlatt and Carole Itter reprinted from *Opening Doors: Vancouver's East End*, edited by Daphne Marlatt and Carole Itter (Victoria: Aural History Program, 1979). Reprinted with permission of the interviewers.

Arthur Nortje: All poems are from *Dead Roots* (London: Heinemann, 1973). Reprinted with permission of Unisa Press.

David Nandi Odhiambo: Excerpt from *diss/ed banded nation* (Vancouver: Polestar Book Publishers, a division of Raincoast Books, 1999). Reprinted with permission of the publisher.

Sara Singh Parker-Toulson: "On Being a Black Woman in Canada (and Indian and English too)" appears with permission of the author.

Austin Phillips: Interview with Daphne Marlatt and Carole Itter reprinted from *Opening Doors: Vancouver's East End*, edited by Daphne Marlatt and Carole Itter (Victoria: Aural History Program, 1979). Reprinted with permission of the interviewers.

Rosa Pryor: Interview with Daphne Marlatt and Carole Itter reprinted from *Opening Doors: Vancouver's East End*, edited by Daphne Marlatt and Carole Itter (Victoria: Aural History Program, 1979). Reprinted with permission of the interviewers.

Rascalz: "Dreaded Fist" first appeared on the album *Cash Crop* (Scarborough, Ontario: Figure IV Records / BMG Music Canada, 1997). Reprinted with the permission of Figure IV Records.

Vanessa Richards: "Icarus" first appeared in *The Fire People: A Collection of Contemporary Black British Poets* (Edinburgh: Payback Press, 1998), in slightly different form. "Home Alone and Cooking" first appeared in *Stress* 20. Reprinted with permission of the author.

Leona Risby: Interview with Daphne Marlatt and Carole Itter reprinted from *Opening Doors: Vancouver's East End*, edited by Daphne Marlatt and Carole Itter (Victoria: Aural History Program, 1979). Reprinted with permission of the interviewers.

Joy Russell: All poems reprinted with permission of the author.

Lily Spence: All poems are from *The Whirring Windmills and An Iouanaloan Mermaid's Tale (A Narrative Poem)* (Burnaby, B.C.: Morning Star Press, 1997). Reprinted with permission of the author.

Priscilla Stewart: "A Voice from the Oppressed to the Friends of Humanity" appears in *Negro Settlement in British Columbia, 1858-1871* (Vancouver: UBC MA thesis, 1951) by James W. Pilton.

Andrea Thompson: Both poems are from *Eating the Seed* (Victoria: Ekstasis Editions, 1999). Reprinted with permission of the publisher.

Karina Vernon: "Sex speaks" first appeared in *Judy* 2 (1999). "alterNation" first appeared in *Tads* 5 (1999). Exerpt from *Aunt Ermine's Recipe for Brown Sugar Fudge* first appeared in *Race Poetry, Eh?*, a special issue of *Prairie Fire* 21.4 (2001). All poems reprinted with permission of the author.

Marie Stark Wallace: Excerpt from *Notes made by Marie Albertina Stark (afterwards Mrs Wallace) from the recollections of her mother, Sylvia Stark* reprinted from the unpublished manuscript.

E. Centime Zeleke: "Tizita" first appeared in "Tizita: Conversations with My Mother's Sisters" on the compact disc *Ecgo/Location: Artist in Residence Projects at Vancouver's Co-operative Radio Vol 1* (Vancouver: Co-op Radio, 2000). Reprinted with permission of the author.

Notes on Contributors

HOPE ANDERSON was born in Jamaica and grew up in Montreal. He lived in B.C. from 1973 to 1988. He was educated at Dawson College and Sir George Williams University (now Concordia). He published the chapbooks *Out of the Woods* (Dawson College Press, 1970) and *Backmount* (Mondiale, 1975) and co-edited *The Body* (Tatlow House, 1978) with David Phillips. In 1984, he created the Victoria Sunfest, a literary and music festival. It was at that festival that bpNichol asked him for the manuscript of *Slips From Grace*, which was published by Coach House Press in 1987. In 1994 he was a contributing editor to a special British Columbia edition of *Pembroke*. He is presently the Director of Auxiliary Services at Florida Memorial College, a historical black college in Miami, Florida.

TERENCE ANTHONY was born in Ottawa. While living in Vancouver, he created the black nationalist comic book series *Shadowtown* (1992-1994), as well as the videos *Blackout* (1995), *Love and Death: A Rhythm Myth* (1997) and *Urbaneutics* (1998). He lives in Los Angeles.

MERCEDES BAINES was born in New Westminster. A writer, performer, drama teacher, and director, she has written and produced numerous plays for adults and youth. She is the artistic director of La Luna Productions, a culturally diverse theatre company. Her poetry has been published in several anthologies, most recently in *Poetry Nation* (Véhicule Press, 1998). Her most recent project written for youth is *The Reclaiming Project*, a storytelling workshop for elementary school students that focuses on sharing family histories as a means of building bridges within communities. She is currently writing a play about the telepersonals. She lives in Vancouver.

ROGER BLENMAN was born in Barbados and immigrated to Canada as a boy with his devoutly religious parents and older brother. After earning degrees in science and education at the University of Toronto, he taught, coached athletics, and did religious youth work. Since moving to Vancouver, he has become involved in theatre and the local Black Writers' Network.

SHANE BOOK was born in Lima, Peru and raised in Vancouver, Ottawa, and Ghana. He received a BA in Political Science from the University of Western Ontario and a BFA in Creative Writing from the University of Victoria, during which time he co-founded Smoking Lung Press. He recently received the Charles Johnson Award in Poetry and the Rella Lossy Award, as well as a fellowship to the Cave Canem Workshop-Retreat for African American Poets. In Canada, his work has earned him a National Magazine Award and the *Malahat Review* Long Poem Prize. In 1998, he received an MA in English and American literature from New York University under the *New York Times* poetry fellowship. He is presently completing his MFA at the Iowa Writers' Workshop, and though he mostly divides his time between Ottawa and Iowa City, he tries to get back to Vancouver as often as possible.

FRED BOOKER was born in Cleveland, Ohio and moved to Canada in 1966. His writing has appeared in Canadian literary journals such as *Canadian Forum, Canadian Dimension, Books in Canada*, and *Fiddlehead*. He is both a writer and a musician, and released three folk-blues albums with Rulebook Records in the 1970s. He lives in Burnaby, B.C. where he is working on his latest project, a short story manuscript titled *Adventures in Debt Collection*.

LAWRENCE YTZHAK BRAITHWAITE spent eleven years in the navy, and later wrote as a reporter for *Rites* and *Angles*. His work has appeared in *Ma'ka: Diasporic Juks* (Sister Vision, 1997), *Best Gay Erotica 99* and *2000*, *Alt-X Online*, *SBC*, Laurence Robert's *Holytitclamps*, *RED ZONE: Victoria's Street Peoples' Zine*, and *Fourteen Hills*. Braithwaite won the Victoria Emerging Writers Competition, and *Wigger* (Arsenal Pulp Press, 1995) was shortlisted in Brian Bouldrey's *Best American Gay Fiction 96*. He has performed at Lollapalooza, the National Black Arts Festival (Atlanta), OutWrite 99 (Boston), El Macambo (Toronto), the Kootenay School of Writing (Vancouver), and the New Langton Arts Gallery (San Francisco). His latest novel *Ratz are Nice (PSP)* (Alyson, 2000) involves Rudebwoys, Skinheads, Stads, and Gutterpunks in North America today. Braithwaite lives in Victoria.

ROSEMARY BROWN was born in Jamaica and immigrated to Canada in the 1950s to attend McGill University. She moved to Vancouver in 1955. She has worked as a social worker for the Children's Aid Society of Vancouver, Riverview Hospital, the Vancouver Neurological Society, the Montreal Children's Hospital, and as a counselor at Simon Fraser University. She served for fourteen years as a member of the British Columbia legislature, from 1972 until her retirement in 1986. She was the first Canadian woman to run for leadership of a federal political party, and the first Black woman elected to a provincial legislature. A champion of human rights, Dr. Brown has spoken on women's issues, peace, and human rights at several international conferences. She has served as Chief Commissioner of the Ontario Human Rights Commission, is an Officer of the Order of Canada, and was a recipient of the Order of British Columbia. Her autobiography *Being Brown: A Very Public Life* (Random House, 1989) describes in detail her years as a public servant and political activist. Although retired, she remains active in several national and community organizations. She lives in Vancouver.

YVONNE BROWN was born and educated in Jamaica. She graduated from Mico Teachers College in 1965 at the top of her class and began a teaching career which would take her from teaching at May Pen Junior Secondary School and Vere Technical High School in Jamaica to British Columbia. For the past thirty-two years she has been a high school teacher, college instructor, and university lecturer. She is a graduate of the University of British Columbia, Faculty of Education. She is also active in public school politics and served one term on the Vancouver School Board. Her political and cultural work is motivated by a deep concern with the pervasive omission, distortion, and stereotyping of African-descended peoples. She has three adult offspring and two grandchildren of whom she is very proud. She lives in Vancouver.

Some of JANISSE BROWNING's ancestors settled in Upper Canada after escaping from slave plantations in Kentucky and Maryland via the Underground Railroad. Her aboriginal roots are Ojibway. Her poems have appeared in *The Capilano Review*, *At the Crossroads*, *absinthe*, *Open Letter*, *Windsor Review*, *West Coast Line*, and *diaspora*. Her chapbook *BikerTrucker* (Wave7 Press, 1994), illustrated by Terence Anthony, is a short story about a unique mother-daughter relationship. She lives on Galiano Island.

NADINE KING CHAMBERS was born in Kingston, Jamaica. In her own words: "Canadian passport, Jamaican heart. Dred daughter of the Crossroads anchored by my Old Ones as I do 360 in 4D. Born Dec 1969 thru water, reborn Nov 2000 by fire. Mama – thanks for my life. Thanks to the Kings, for making me their #7. Respect to other mothers Sunya, Bev, Barbara, Daphne. Moving from Kingston to Quebec, Port of Spain to Brampton; arrived to take shelter on these Musqueam shores in 1991. Committed to our futures (Adjua, Cyrus, Dyese, Meena, Max, Simone) as I journey to the next academic stop – Women's studies / Criminology / Law. Never give up seeking justice." She divides her time between Vancouver and Galiano Island.

ISAAC DICKSON came to Victoria from San Francisco as part of the mass migration of 1858. He eventually settled in Barkerville, B.C., where he owned and operated a barber shop. His two letters to *The Cariboo Sentinel* are the only pieces of his writing extant.

SIR JAMES DOUGLAS (1803-1877) was born in British Guyana, the illegitimate son of a Scottish sugar plantation owner and a woman from Barbados, described in the public record as a "free coloured woman." Douglas lived with his mother in British Guyana until the age of nine, when he was sent by his father to a boarding school in Lanark, Scotland. Douglas came to Canada in 1819 to work in the fur trade. He eventually became the Chief Factor of the Hudson's Bay Company, then the governor of the colony of Vancouver's Island, and then became the second governor of British Columbia. For these colonial involvements, Douglas is often referred to as "the father of British Columbia."

TANYA EVANSON is a Caribbean-Québecoise writer and spoken word artist originally from Montreal. She has a BA in Creative Writing and English Literature from Concordia University and has self-published four books of poetry and several anthologies. She now lives, writes, and performs in Vancouver, where she works as a Projects Manager and Marketing Coordinator for an ESL school, and is the director of Mother Tongue Media. She also hosts "Tales of Ordinary Madness," a popular weekly spoken word series, and is on the editorial committee of the Vancouver poetry journal *Raincity Review*.

LORENA GALE's first play *Angélique* (Playwrights Canada Press, 2000) had its American premiere at the Detroit Repertory Theatre and, in New York, off-Broadway at Manhattan Class Company Theatre, where it was nominated for eight Audelco Awards. *Angélique* premiered at the Alberta Theatre Project's Pan Canadian playRites Festival in 1998, and was nominated Outstanding New Play in Calgary's Betty Mitchell Awards. Gale has also published articles in *Canadian Theatre Review*, *Canplay*, and the anthology *But Where Are You Really From?* (Sister Vision, 1997). Her latest play *Je me souviens: Memories of an Expatriate Anglophone Montréalaise, Québecoise Exiled in Canada* (Talonbooks, 2001) has been produced in Halifax, Calgary, Victoria, and in Vancouver at the Firehall Theatre, where it was nominated for three Jessie Richardson Awards. She lives in Vancouver.

MIFFLIN WISTAR GIBBS (1823-1915) was born in Philadelphia, the son of a minister. He worked for the Philadelphia "station" of the Underground Railroad, assisting blacks who had escaped from slavery in the American South. Through this work he met and befriended the famed abolitionist Frederick Douglass. In 1850, Gibbs sailed to San Francisco to make his fortune in the California gold rush. While there, he helped to establish the first black newspaper in North America's west, *The Mirror of the Times*, and continued agitating for black civil rights. When California's racist legislation became intolerable, he departed to Victoria where he came to establish himself as a prominent businessman, politician, and leader of the black community. He returned to the United States in 1869 where he successively became the first black person elected as a municipal court judge, the U.S. Consul to Madagascar, and the president of a bank in Little Rock, Arkansas. In 1902, he published his memoir *Shadow and Light: An Autobiography with Reminiscences of the Last and Present Century*. He died in Little Rock in 1915.

REBECCA GIBBS (1808-1873) lived in Barkerville in the 1860s where she worked as a washerwoman. She wrote mainly occasional poems for *The Cariboo Sentinel*. Her poem "The Old Red Shirt" was published by James Anderson in *Sawney's Letters and Cariboo Rhymes* (1869), a locally popular book of ballads and songs. It is likely that she was the sister-in-law of Mifflin Gibbs. She died in Victora in 1873.

C. S. GISCOMBE was born in Dayton, Ohio. He went to school at the State University of New York at Albany (working with Don Byrd) and finished an MFA at Cornell University (working with Robert Morgan and A. R. Ammons) in 1975. He was editor of *Epoch* from 1978 until 1989, when he took a faculty position at Illinois State University in Normal, Illinois. In 1998 he accepted a faculty position at the Pennsylvania State University. His latest books include *Giscome Road* (Dalkey Archive Press, 1997), *Into and Out of Dislocation* (North Point Press, 2000), and *Inland* (Leroy Books, 2001). The former two books chronicle his modern-day explorations of B.C.

TRUMAN GREEN was born in Vancouver in 1945 and raised in Surrey, B.C. He graduated from the University of British Columbia in 1968 with a BA in English and has worked as a self-employed tradesman for twenty-five years. He lives in Surrey.

SETH-ADRIAN HARRIS was born in Kingston, Jamaica. He is a performance poet, media artist, and visual storyteller. While living in Vancouver for eight years, he performed and composed poetry, and wrote and directed a compilation of three visual poems in performance called *Born on the After Beat* (ITOTI Productions, 1999), which was screened at Montreal's Reel Black Alliance Festival. His work also includes *Systemoverload*, a short film in which six people from various ethnic backgrounds are trapped in an elevator and forced to deal with issues of space, race, and identity. He lives in Toronto.

NORA HENDRIX (1883-1984) was born in Knoxville, Tennessee. While performing as a chorus girl in a travelling revue, Hendrix and her husband found themselves stranded in Seattle in 1911. Desiring to escape "Jim Crow" segregation in the United States, they crossed the border into Canada and settled in Vancouver where she lived until her death in 1984. She was the paternal grandmother of the famed musician Jimi Hendrix.

PETER HUDSON was born in Edmonton and raised in Vancouver. He edited the collection *North: New African Canadian Writing*, a special issue of *West Coast Line*, and is a former editor of *Mix* and *diaspora* magazines. Currently a doctoral student in American Studies at New York University, he lives in Brooklyn.

CHRISTOPHER JAMES was born in 1948. He wrote and published the poetry chapbooks *Gilma Stein: A Novel Song* and *Two Sides* in Vancouver in the early 1970s.

WILLIAM H. H. JOHNSON (1839-1905) was born in Madison, Indiana, the son of a fugitive slave mother and free father, which, according to the Fugitive Slave Act, made Johnson himself a slave though born in a free state. During his youth, his family were "station masters" of the Underground Railroad in various towns in Indiana, helping blacks escape to freedom in Canada. When his mother's former owners appeared to be on their trail, Johnson's family themselves escaped to Windsor, Ontario, where Johnson lived before moving to B.C. While living in Vancouver, he wrote and published his memoir *The Life of Wm. H.H. Johnson, from 1839-1900, and the New Race* (1904).

MICHELLE LA FLAMME was born in New Westminster and grew up in Coquitlam and Vancouver. She has been actively involved in performance and writing dealing with gender and race for over ten years. As a mixed race woman, she is interested in borderlands, liminal spaces, and hybridity. Performances of her poetry can be heard on the cassette *Void to Voice: Musical/Vocal Xperiment of Afro-Canadian and First Nation RESISTANCE* (1993) and her work has appeared in *Miscegenation Blues: Voices of Mixed Race Women* (Sister Vision Press, 1994). She has written and produced several experimental films and recently won a scholarship to attend Vancouver Film School. Her work has been supported by the National Film Board and Video In. Having recently completed a PHD at the University of British Columbia, she is currently working on a screenplay set on Saltspring Island. She lives in Vancouver.

KATHY-ANN MARCH was born in Kingston, Jamaica in 1962. She immigrated to Montreal with her mother and brother in 1967. She has lived in Vancouver for fourteen years. In 1995 she was part of a curatorial team at the Grunt Gallery (Vancouver) that articulated the exhibition *Half-Bred . . . beyond binary definitions of identity*. March's work is concerned with "how the miscegenated body can artistically represent itself beyond the marks of the 'tragic mulatto,'" and seeks to "provoke discussion about the fluid identity of the racialized and gendered subject and how this identity is constructed, represented, and re-inscribed at large." Her most recent work, "Bodily Fluid," appears in *Open Letter* (Winter 2000). She is presently working on a video entitled *The Broken-Hearted Thief*.

NIKOLA MARIN currently channels her interdisciplinary love of creating stories and pictures into pen and ink, photo-sensitive paper, and digital video media. Her company Kashmir Productions produces socially conscious video for community-oriented businesses and organizations. She lives in Vancouver.

DOROTHY NEALY was born in Winnipeg in 1917 of a Native mother and black father. She grew up in the Ukrainian-Polish district of the city and moved to Vancouver in 1944.

ARTHUR NORTJE (1942-1970) was born in Oudtshoorn in the Cape Province, South Africa. He went to high school in Port Elizabeth where the anti-Apartheid poet Dennis Brutus was his teacher and mentor. He studied at the segregated University College of the Western Cape before receiving a scholarship to Oxford in 1965. From 1967 to 1969, Nortje taught English in Hope, B.C. and Etobicoke, Ontario. He returned to Oxford to work on his doctorate in August 1970 and died of a barbiturate overdose four months later at the age of 28. The poems "Waiting," "Immigrant," and "Hope Hotel" were written while he lived in B.C. A collection of his work, *Dead Roots*, was published posthumously in 1973 to much acclaim. A complete collection, *Anatomy of Dark: Collected Poems of Arthur Nortje* (Unisa Press, 2000), was recently released.

DAVID NANDI ODHIAMBO was born in Nairobi, Kenya in 1965. He writes fiction, plays, and poetry. His work includes the play *afrocentric*, which appears in the anthology *Beyond the Pale: Dramatic Writing from First Nations Writers and Writers of Colour* (Playwrights Canada Press, 1996) and the critically acclaimed novel *diss/ed banded nation* (Polestar Press, 1998). He lives in Amherst, Massachusetts.

SARA SINGH PARKER-TOULSON was born in Toronto in 1977 and grew up in Vancouver. She is currently living in Toronto and pursuing an MA in English at York University. Her work has appeared in the Vancouver journals *Tads* and *Antithesis*. She is also the co-editor of *AUTHORized*, an irregular journal of activist and academic writing.

AUSTIN PHILLIPS (1910-1979) came to Vancouver from Athabasca Landing, Alberta in 1935.

ROSA PRYOR was born in 1887 in the United States. She came to Vancouver in 1917 from Iowa via Seattle, and established the city's first southern fried chicken house.

The RASCALZ are Vancouver's most illustrious hip hop group. Its members, Misfit, Red 1, Kemo, Zebroc, and Dedos first met as breakdancers in 1989. By 1991 they had evolved into Ragamuffin Rascalz, and released the album *Really Livin'* on an independent label. By 1997, known simply as the Rascalz, the group became the second Canadian rap artists to sign with a major record label, ViK Recordings (BMG Music Canada). Their album *Cash Crop* (1997), from which "Dreaded Fist" is taken, reached gold record status. The Rascalz have received five Juno nominations for Best Rap Recording, and won the award in 1998 and 1999. They've also been presented with two Much Music Video Awards and a Canadian Urban Music Award. Their latest album is *Global Warning* (1999). The Rascalz remain committed to the underground roots of their music and continue to represent the "four elements" of hip hop culture in their repertoire: MCing, DJing, breakdancing, and graffiti art.

VANESSA RICHARDS was born in Vancouver in 1964 and currently lives in London, England. As Joint Artistic Director for the multi-media performing arts company, Mannafest, she variously uses print media, music, film, and performance as means of educational and cultural work. Her poetry has appeared in *The Fire People: A Collection of Contemporary Black British Poets* (Payback Press, 1998), *Bittersweet: Contemporary Black Women's Poetry* (Women's Press, 1998), *360°: A Revolution of Black Poets* (Black Words, 1998), and *IC3: The Penguin Book of New Black Writing in Britain* (Penguin, 2000).

LEONA RISBY (1911-1991) was born in Edmonton, Alberta, and came to Vancouver with her husband and children in 1933.

JOY RUSSELL was born in Belize, raised in Alberta and Vancouver, and lived in London, England for a number of years. She has worked as an assistant producer and researcher for British television on a number of documentaries including *The Hip Hop Years*, *Rebel Music: The Bob Marley Story* and *Pump Up the Volume*, a history of house music. Her work has appeared most recently in *Don't Ask Me Why: An Anthology of Short Stories By Black Women* (Black Womantalk, 1991), *The Fire People: A Collection of Contemporary Black British Poets* (Payback Press, 1998) and *IC3: The Penguin Book of New Black Writing in Britain* (Penguin, 2000).

LILY SPENCE was born in St. Lucia. She has one collection of poems, *The Whirring Windmills and An Iouanaloan Mermaid's Tale* (Morning Star Press, 1997). She lives in Burnaby, B.C.

PRISCILLA STEWART was one of the blacks who migrated to Victoria from San Francisco in 1858. "A Voice from the Oppressed to the Friends of Humanity," though written in California, is the first published poem written by a black person concerning British Columbia.

ANDREA THOMPSON has performed her work at literary events across Canada and the U.S. She has been featured on CBC's *Morningside*, in the documentary *Slam Nation*, and in Bravo TV's *Planet Poetry*. On the page, her writing has appeared in literary reviews and anthologies such as the League of Canadian Poets' *Vintage '95* and *Poetry Nation* (Véhicule Press, 1998). While living in Vancouver she was active in initiating and hosting open mic venues and the innovative Telepoetics series in which poets from cities around North America were linked by the internet for interactive readings. Her first full-length collection is *Eating the Seed* (Ekstasis Editions, 2000). She lives in Toronto.

KARINA VERNON is a mixed-race black and white woman. Born in Tegucigalpa, Honduras in 1973, she grew up in central Alberta and rural Zimbabwe with her sister and her teacher-adventurer mother. She has settled in Vancouver where she is a recent MA graduate and feminist activist. Her writing has appeared in several Vancouver poetry journals including *Tads*, *Rout/e*, and *Judy*. She is interested in "exploring languages that reinvent and subvert sexual and racial expectations."

MARIE STARK WALLACE (1867-1966) was born and raised on Saltspring Island where her parents had settled as homesteaders, escaping slavery in the United States. The daughter of the well-known Saltspring Island figure Sylvia Stark, Wallace narrates the story of her mother's passage out of slavery in the unpublished manuscript *Notes made by Marie Albertina Stark (afterwards Mrs Wallace) from the recollections of her mother, Sylvia Stark* (1966). The manuscript is available in its entirety in the B.C. Provincial Archives.

E. CENTIME ZELEKE works as a writer, media artist, and curator. Born in Ethiopia, she grew up in Guyana and Barbados, and presently divides her time between Vancouver and Montreal. Her writing has appeared in a number of journals and anthologies including *Front Magazine*, *Fireweed*, *Canadian Women Studies*, and *absinthe*.

PHOTO BY SUSAN KAUFFMANN.

WAYDE COMPTON was born in Vancouver. He has a MA in English from Simon Fraser University and is the author of *49th Parallel Psalm*, which was the inaugural release from the Arsenal Pulp Press imprint Advance Editions (1999) and was shortlisted for the Dorothy Livesay Poetry Prize. He is currently working on a "turntablist poem" and a novel about telepathy and mixed-race. He lives in Vancouver.